CRITICISM IN ANTIQUITY

CRITICISM
IN
ANTIQUITY

D. A. Russell

UNIVERSITY OF CALIFORNIA PRESS
BERKELEY AND LOS ANGELES

University of California Press
Berkeley and Los Angeles

© 1981 by D. A. Russell

Printed in Great Britain

Library of Congress Cataloging in Publication Data

Russell, D. A. (Donald Andrew)
    Criticism in antiquity
    Bibliography: p.
    Includes index.
    1. Classical literature—History and criticism.
2. Criticism. I. Title.
PA3013.R82   801′.95′0938   81-3348
ISBN 0-520-04466-5   AACR2

Contents

Preface

I HAVE tried to combine a personal impression of the complex phenomenon of Greco-Roman 'literary criticism' with a measure of detailed information sufficient to guide the reader towards further inquiry. I have had in mind the needs of literary students whose Greek and Latin is perhaps vestigial, though I am well aware that they are faced with special difficulties in approaching a subject which is mainly about words. Wherever possible, I have referred to the collection of translations published by Dr M. Winterbottom and myself in 1972 (*Ancient Literary Criticism*, Oxford University Press); an appendix to the present volume offers a supplement to this, in which I have tried to gather some texts which were not in the earlier collection but which I have felt the need to cite in the present discussion.

This kind of book necessarily rests on teaching; and I owe a great deal to the undergraduates who have from time to time patiently listened and produced comments and ideas. I should like also to record a special debt to Dr D. C. Innes, who identified and helped me to correct many weaknesses and obscurities.

D.A.R.

CHAPTER ONE

Prologue

I

THE surviving literary remains of classical antiquity include a great deal of comment on literature itself. Theory, scholarly interpretation and evaluative judgment are all to be found, and in some abundance. There is even a little literary history. The classical scholar approaches this material from his study of the ancient poets and prose-writers themselves; the modern literary critic turns to the ancients as precursors, in some sense, of his own art. Both have occasion to be bewildered, disconcerted, perhaps disappointed.

The scholars of course recognise in the literary theories of Platonists, Peripatetics or Stoics minor works of the great philosophical schools, shaped by their general metaphysical, logical or moral positions. It is the recorded critical judgments that are puzzling. We find them often inadequate and unsatisfactory, if we compare them with our own responses to the same texts. But at the same time we cannot help reasoning that the Greeks and Romans must after all know best, since the language and the culture were their own.

As for the modern critic, he too is likely to be divided in mind. On the one hand, he knows that there would have been nothing like the art he professes without the foundations laid by Aristotle, 'Longinus', Horace and the rest. On the other, he senses that it is all very different from what he is used to. There seems, for example, to be little or no attempt to delimit the critic's field, to fence it off against his three neighbours: the scholar, the moralist and the teacher of rhetoric. Indeed, these three between them, it may reasonably appear, occupy the whole area.

Not that it is difficult to assign historical reasons for this phenomenon.

Greek literature became 'classical' at an early period, because the earliest poetry to be recorded, the epic, set a standard never surpassed, and was never, in practice, rejected as the core of education. Many words in Homer were unintelligible, even to fifth-century speakers; yet everyone read him, many knew him by heart. Scholarly interpretation was thus a necessity from quite early times.

Again, philosophers and educators habitually attacked or defended literature on moral or social grounds, or sought to turn it to good account in their advocacy of virtue. This again is connected with the prestige of the epic.

And, finally, by the end of the fifth century, the practical teaching of rhetoric, the 'art of persuasion', had also become a dominant feature of education. This led to a fact which strikes everyone who studies this material, namely, that a very great deal of the detailed interpretation and criticism we possess has a clearly rhetorical purpose. It aims at drawing out isolable and imitable features which may be of service to the potential orator. 'Let us consider', says 'Longinus', typically, 'whether there is anything in our observations ... useful to public men.'[1]

2

Now the ethical bias of much of our material is something to which the modern reader may fairly easily become reconciled. There are, after all, many contemporary versions of the moralising sort of criticism, in which literary excellence is judged by its contribution to the 'good life', however that may be conceived. But he may find the dominant rhetorical element harder to bear. Yet this is of crucial importance. One essential feature of it is that the address is always to potential practitioners, not merely to readers or connoisseurs. This is so not only in

[1] *On sublimity* 1, 2. But by *politikois andrasin*, 'public men', the author seeks to define his audience not as public as opposed to private persons, but as orators who use their eloquence for practical purposes, as opposed to 'sophists' who merely teach and exhibit their skills.

overtly rhetorical works like *On sublimity*, but in the classical
works on poetry also. Horace's *Ars poetica* assumes—whether
as fact or as convenient fiction—that the two young Piso
brothers are about to sit down and write plays. Aristotle in the
Poetics works out the consequences of his definition of tragedy in
the form of statements of how one ought to manage plot,
character and language. Would-be orators were naturally an
important educational market both in the Greek cities and in
Rome, since political and private success and even safety could
well depend on skill in public speaking. Would-be poets on
the other hand are relatively few in any age, certainly fewer than
those who appreciate the art without wishing to practise it. It is
therefore natural to suppose that the prescriptive emphasis
which we find in works on poetry is due to the example of
rhetorical teaching.

There are in fact good reasons why rhetoric should have
seemed a relevant model. For one thing, poetry was believed to
have preceded prose as a vehicle of instruction and persuasion,[2]
and could thus be seen to have fulfilled many of the same functions. Again, the rhetorical analysis of the elements of discourse
into invention, arrangement and verbal choice was clearly appropriate also to poetry. In the fifth century, when teachers of
rhetoric began to develop their craft, they naturally made use
of the epic poetry which was part of their pupils' traditional
education. And so 'poetics', as formulated by Aristotle's
successors—though not, it is important to remember, by
Aristotle himself—turned into a specialised branch of rhetoric.
Poetry was thought of as an art aimed at producing certain
effects on the audience. True, these were not the same effects as
the orator's; they were pleasure and wonder, not conviction or
an emotional stimulus to action.[3] Both arts were clearly
'audience-oriented'. Theophrastus, in a famous formula,
grouped them together for just this reason.[4] He meant to

---

[2] Cf. Strabo 1.2.6 (*ALC* 302); Plu. *Mor.* 406c–f; Isidore *Etymologiae* 1.38
(from Varro); Lucian *De conscribenda historia* 46; and, in general, Norden
Antike Kunstprosa 32 ff.

[3] It was of course recognised that music, and so lyric poetry, might move
men to action: Horace *Ars* 401–3.

[4] Fr. 65 Wimmer (below, Appendix p. 203). See Lossau 47 f.; G. M. A.
Grube *TAPA* 83 (1952) 178.

contrast them with philosophy and mathematics, in which, as he thought, 'the facts' alone determined the manner of expression. In putting it like this, he also expressed in epigrammatic form something which Greek and Roman poets seem to have taken for granted: namely, that we always write for an audience, present or future. It would be to deny the essential conditions of the poet's craft, as antiquity saw it, if one were to write only for oneself, not caring if the work done were for ever hidden from the sight of man.

3

We shall look later in more detail at the nature of rhetorical teaching and its effect on the understanding of literature.[5] But it is so important and so central a matter that a little more should perhaps be said at the outset.

Rhetoric had two large consequences for the development of criticism. The first is this. An orator always faces a real and definite situation. What he asks of his technique is that it should show him how to deal with it: what to say and how to say it. A process of 'invention' precedes the process of expression, and there is thus a sharp distinction between content (*to legomenon*) and verbal form (*lexis*). With some hazy and uncertain exceptions, ancient writers on poetry also adhered firmly to this distinction. Secondly: we observed that the rhetor's pupil is assumed to be a potential composer. One consequence of this is that the teacher distances both himself and his pupil from the hearers or readers, conspires with the pupil against them, and so views them from above and perhaps with some disdain. Their moral attitudes, emotional susceptibilities, weaknesses, bad taste and gullibility are to be studied and used. We have to convince and please people whose faults we can see more clearly than we see our own, and whose characters we study in order to find out where they are most vulnerable. This disdain of the ordinary audience is known to Aristotle in the context not only of rhetoric[6] but of poetry: it is the 'inferiority

[5] Chapter VIII.

[6] *Rhetoric* II gives a detailed account of 'character' from this point of view.

of the spectators' which makes them prefer happy endings in tragedy, though the principles of the art make it clear that these are really signs of inferior workmanship.[7]

In short: the rhetorical critic is concerned with means to a predetermined end, and that end is the persuasion or entertainment of an audience whom he thinks of as inferior in intelligence and sensibility to himself and his pupil.

This may well seem a strange basis for adequate critical theory or practice. Yet it is just this pragmatic bias of so much ancient criticism that has strengthened a belief which most classical scholars—except those who have lain most completely under the influence of nineteenth-century Romanticism— have been inclined to hold in some form or other: namely, that this material provides a special insight into the attitudes and presuppositions of the creative writers of antiquity. We seem to glimpse the inside of the workshop. There is obviously something in this. The detailed illustrations of technique are there, in our texts, patiently and often intelligently discussed from the rhetor's standpoint. Moreover, there is no doubt that the principles underlying these discussions represent attitudes to the functions and excellences of literature which were generally held, indeed taken for granted, and which it is necessary for students of classical literature to understand. Nor is there any doubt that, at any rate in the Hellenistic and Roman periods, a rhetorical training of the kind implied by the works of Quintilian, Dionysius or 'Longinus', was part of the experience of everyone who tried to write; and that includes Virgil, as well as the countless adolescents of modest ability who 'gave advice to Sulla' in a *suasoria*,[8] or exhorted the Three Hundred to die bravely at Thermopylae.

But it is important not to exaggerate. It seems reasonable to ask whether the view of literature conveyed by 'Longinus', Quintilian or Hermogenes, with its delicate classifications of style and analyses of structure and expression, affords an adequate description of what one observes oneself. It is, after all, still possible to read Greek and Latin literature with sensitivity,

---

[7] *Poetics* 1453ᵃ. See now J. F. Moles, *CQ* 29 (1979) 77 ff.

[8] Juvenal 1.16. On *suasoriae*—fictitious deliberative speeches composed as practice—see Bonner, op. cit., in n. 19 below.

if one takes the trouble to learn the languages as well as one can. The limitations imposed by the remoteness and by the lack of speakers of the two languages are not so great that a modern reader need feel it impossible to form a valid impression of his own. For my own part, I am fairly certain that this ancient rhetorical 'criticism', though undoubtedly useful in suggesting principles of judgment and helping to elucidate authors' intentions, is fundamentally not equal to the task of appraising classical literature. If pressed to say why, I should be obliged to fall back on an impressionistic way of presenting the problem, and should base myself on the following consideration. The most distinctive feature in the pagan literature of Greece and Rome, taken as a whole, seems to me to be something only rarely hinted at in ancient critical texts: a creative tension between directness of thought and vision on the one hand, and sophisticated imagery and verbal formality on the other. This is something to be seen not only in Theocritus or Virgil, but in Homer, Aeschylus and Pindar too. Some such conflict, I might say, elevates tragedy and epic above the level of the sensational and the violent, and gives piquancy and elegance to satire and comedy. It is this tension that fashions for us a special world, in which emotion, amusement and understanding are combined in a way distinct from the ways in which such combinations are effected in other literatures, even those most closely modelled on the antique. This creative conflict, however, cannot be taken into account if we accept the common ancient doctrine that big words suit big things and little words little things, with the corollary that there are two mutually exclusive types of literature, the serious or idealistic and the realistic or comic. No doubt the resonances and ironies that I cherish could not arise unless the two elements of the conflict were apprehended separately; but to erect this separate apprehension into a principle of the classification of literature is to surrender judgment to insensitive dogma. Yet this often happens. It is typical of the critical consensus of antiquity when Longinus complains of impropriety in an evidently piquant and highly coloured passage of Theopompus' history.[9] It is typical too when Servius tells us that the style of *Aeneid* IV is 'comic', be-

[9] *On sublimity* 43.

cause the subject is love, no normal epic theme.[10] And it is an exceptional recognition of one form of the tension I have tried to define when Demetrius commends Xenophon for writing lightly of a grim and fearsome character, and sagely comments on the effect achieved by saying that 'one may be cooled by warmth and warmed by cold'.[11]

It is perhaps worth remembering, however, that the first evidence we have for this 'consensus dichotomy' of types of writing is in a context which does not encourage us to take it too seriously: the debate between Euripides and Aeschylus in Aristophanes' *Frogs*. It is reasonable to believe that sensitive readers in antiquity, had they chosen to make their responses articulate, would have seemed wiser and more sophisticated than their teachers and theorists.

4

When we speak of a 'critic', we do of course use a Greek word. The *kritikos* is the man who is capable of judging (*krinein*). What sorts of 'judgment' of literature were envisaged by the Greeks themselves?

Some Hellenistic literary scholars actually used the name. According to Crates of Mallus,[12] a *kritikos* was a superior *grammatikos*, who needed to have a complete grasp of all knowledge concerned with *logos*, not merely lexicography and metre. He was concerned primarily with the interpretation and authenticity of older books, especially the Homeric epics. His main rôle was thus to decide historical questions, not to make value-judgments; but he might well use internal criteria of style and content, or even moral considerations, in the course of his work. In Horace,[13] however, we find *critici* classing Ennius as a 'second Homer', and this seems to be a judgment on his importance and value. The grouping, ordering and labelling

---

[10] See Appendix, p. 203.

[11] Demetrius *On style* 135 (*ALC* 198), on Xen. *Cyropaedia* 2.2.15.

[12] Sex. Emp. *Adv. math.* 1.79; see, in general, R. Pfeiffer, *History of Classical Scholarship* i, 157 ff. Fragments of Crates are collected by H. J. Mette, *Parateresis*, 1952.

[13] *Epistles* 2.1.150 (*ALC* p. 273).

of authors read in school was indeed a common activity of the grammarian or *kritikos*, and sometimes of the teacher of rhetoric also.[14] It falls short of anything we could call criticism or reasoned judgment.

A more hopeful approach to the question is suggested by a remark of 'Longinus':

> The question we must put to ourselves for discussion is how to avoid the faults which are so closely bound up with sublimity. The answer, my friend, is this: by first of all achieving a genuine understanding and appreciation of true sublimity. This is difficult: literary judgment (*logōn krisis*) comes only as the final product (*teleutaion epigennēma*) of long experience.[15]

This prompts two reflections. (i) The function of *krisis* in this passage is to distinguish the good quality, 'sublimity', from errors which superficially resemble it and are incurred in the search for it. Now this is an idea which is also familiar in ethics. Aristotle's theory of virtue envisages similar risks of error. Demetrius actually makes the parallel between morals and styles explicit:

> Just as certain bad qualities are adjacent to certain good ones—as audacity to confidence, or shame to modesty—so, adjacent to our types of style, there are certain mistaken types . . .[16]

But 'Longinus' goes further than Demetrius. His desired quality of sublimity is not simply analogous to the moral quality of a noble mind, it is an expression of this, and the judgment to be made about it rests therefore on a moral as well as an aesthetic sensibility. (ii) The power to make such a decision comes not from the application of rules but as a kind of bonus (*epigennēma*) of long experience. This is a common point. It was generally understood in antiquity that rules (*praecepta, parangelmata*) had their limitations. The notion of an irrational criterion (*alogos aisthēsis*, 'non-rational sensibility') is common enough in Greek

---

[14] Most notably in treatises on 'imitation'; see esp. Quintilian 10.1, and below, Chapter VII 9.

[15] 6.1.

[16] *On style* 114 (*ALC* 194).

criticism of literature and the arts. Dionysius[17] seems to have
believed that the 'pleasantness' or 'unpleasantness' of a piece
of literature is judged by such irrational sensibility, but its
'beauty' and 'excellence' as a specimen of the craft by rational
principles. 'Longinus' once again goes further. For him, the
essential faculty of judgment is both moral, as we have seen, and
at the same time dependent on experience rather than on
precept. He thus represents a point of view distinct from that
of Dionysius. Presumably it differs also from that of his nominal
opponent, Caecilius of Caleacte, who was, it seems, a friend of
Dionysius. For the complaint levelled against Caecilius at the
beginning of the book is precisely that he struggled to define
'sublimity' at inordinate length—in other words, to give a
rational account of it—without explaining how it is to be
achieved. 'Longinus', we should infer, would disapprove of any
claim to teach *krisis*, 'judgment', by means of rules. Like most
Greek critics, he works largely by drawing attention to features
in particular examples.

To find a statement of rules which purport to make possible
a systematic evaluation of a work of literature we have to look
elsewhere, and at a lower level of writing altogether. Two short
treatises, attributed to Dionysius, and probably dating from the
second or third century A.D., provide something of what we
want. These treatises[18] deal ostensibly with the 'examination'
(*exetasis*) of declamation and with mistakes (*plēmmeloumena*)
commonly made in such exercises. Now declamations (*meletai*)
were forensic or deliberative speeches written for fictional or
historical occasions, intended to exercise the future orator in
the invention and selection of material and in stylistic ingenuity.
They were a natural part of rhetorical education, as it developed in Hellenistic times. On the one hand, they reflect the
desire of students for something less humdrum than strictly
vocational teaching; on the other, they show the tendency of
teachers to give their instruction a more liberal and imaginative

[17] *Thucydides* 27 (with notes in W. K. Pritchett, *Dionysius . . . 'On Thucydides'*,
108): D. M. Schenkeveld, 'Theories of evaluation . . .' (*Mus. Phil. Lond.* 1.
93–107).
[18] Extracts in Appendix, p. 183 ff; text in H. Usener–L. Radermacher,
Dionysii . . . Opuscula, 359–87; more detailed analysis in *Entretiens Hardt* 25
(1979), 113 ff.

look. They maintained their popularity down to the last age of
classical antiquity, and indeed throughout the Byzantine
period.[19] Their fictional content and the freedom of invention
which they demanded make them a bridge between practical
oratory and imaginative literature. When Quintilian[20] recom-
mends the study of the classical comic poet Menander as
valuable to the future orator, he qualifies his praise by adding
that he is perhaps most valuable to the declaimer, because the
declaimer has to adopt various personalities according to the
problem he has been set. Character (*ēthos*), important in all
oratory, is of special importance in this scholastic form.

It is thus natural that the scheme which 'Dionysius' pro-
pounds should give pride of place to *ēthos*. This is said to be of
two kinds: 'philosophical *ēthos*', which here means the overall
moral tendency of the speech, and 'rhetorical *ēthos*', namely the
appropriateness of what is said to speaker, audience and subject. Critical judgment has to concern itself with each of these
separately, and then with the relationship between them. The
'one great philosophical *ēthos*' determines the tone of the whole,
and should control other representations of character in the
same way that reason should control temper and desire in our
lives. The analogy here drawn between the unity within the
human mind (*psuchē*) and the unity of a speech is striking.
Though the concept of structural unity is common in antiquity,
attempts to clarify and illustrate it are not. This writer is unusual. And it is evidently not so much the unity of oratory that
he has in mind as that of the Platonic dialogue (a genre which
he cites) and of comedy. The practice of declamation has led
at least this one rhetor to ideas which have a wide literary
application.

Ethos is the most significant of the headings under which he
considers the function of judgment. The other three are thought
(*gnōmē*), art (*technē*) and language (*lexis*). The critic is to ask,
first, whether the ideas are consistent, adequate to the case, and
economical; secondly, whether they are sugared with the right

[19] See, in general, S. F. Bonner, *Roman Declamation*; and, for the Greek side,
G. A. Kennedy in *Approaches to the Second Sophistic*, ed. G. W. Bowersock
(1974), 17 ff.
[20] 10.1.69 (*ALC* 390).

embellishments of rhetorical skill; and finally whether the language is clear, pure and elegantly diversified.

This pedagogic synthesis reaches no great depth of insight. It would be foolish to make much of it. But it does—and in this it seems to be unique in ancient criticism—attempt to state a comprehensive set of rules for critical judgment, uniting both rhetorical and moral standpoints.

Its presuppositions, however, are by no means unique. They are typical of the consensus achieved in the imperial period by classicising critics and readers whose primary interest lay in the old Attic literature and the ways in which it could still be imitated and reproduced. Taken with what we have seen of Dionysius and 'Longinus', it enables us to form some view of what literary judgment (*krisis logōn*) was supposed to entail, at any rate in the fairly stable cultural conditions of the first three centuries of the Roman Empire. The *kritikos* in this sense, the man good at making such judgments, would need at least three qualities. He would have to have a keen sense—a trained sensibility rather than articulate principles—of linguistic and stylistic form, an awareness of the moral aspects of literature, and a realisation that the writer is a member of a community of letters which stretches back into the past and includes the great classics themselves. Would he also need scholarship? Only, it seems, as an aid to moral and rhetorical discrimination. Plutarch may help us here. It is scholarly (*philologon*), he tells us,[21] to understand the hard words in the old poets. What is absolutely essential, however, is something different—an understanding of 'how the poets use the names of the gods and of good and bad, and what they mean by Fortune and Fate'. For Plutarch, the old poetry is a means of moral education, and its study can be defended for this reason. Scholarly knowledge is thus sought not for its own sake but in so far as it subserves the moral purpose by preventing misinterpretations which might lead to dangerous misconceptions about matters of ethics and religion. A similar attitude prevailed about historical knowledge. What is called *historia* in the Greek of this period covers not only history in the modern sense, but many kinds of scholarly and scientific facts. All this too is ancillary—if not to

[21] *Moralia* 22c (*ALC* 520 f.)

moral education, then to rhetoric. A certain knowledge of the
historical background of Demosthenes' speeches is clearly
necessary to understand the text and appreciate the rhetorical
techniques. But that knowledge falls far short of a proper
narrative history of the period. For all the effort that the ancient
schools put into the study of the classical orators, no true
historical commentary on their works was ever put together.
The consequences of this for modern understanding of fourth-
century Greece have been serious. The Romans perhaps did
rather better: Asconius' commentaries on Cicero go somewhat
deeper than their Greek equivalents.

5

'Longinus' spoke of *krisis logōn*, 'Dionysius' of *exetasis logōn*. We
have seen something of what this 'judging' or 'examining' involved. But what about the object of the process? What is
meant by *logoi*? Though 'Dionysius' is writing about declamation, we have seen that what he says is not limited to that kind
of composition; indeed his doctrine of *ēthos* seems actually more
appropriate to dialogue and drama than to speeches. And in
the passage of 'Longinus', the word is an embarrassment to the
translator. No one English word suffices: 'words', 'speeches',
'discourse', 'literature', all mislead.

Behind the verbal question lies one of substance. What kinds
of discourse does 'Longinus' believe to be the appropriate subject of the *krisis* which he envisages? His own practice, and that
of the other 'critics', make the range fairly clear. It includes
poetry of all kinds, oratory, history and the philosophical dialogue. Treatises and letters of a certain formality could safely
be added. But it does seem as though evidence of conscious art
was required; no one in antiquity ever propounded the view
that every use of language, however ephemeral or casual,
could be subjected to formal or moral examination of this kind.

Yet there is no general term, either in Greek or in Latin, for
the whole body of 'critic-worthy' literature. It is usually described by means of an enumeration: 'poets, orators and prose-
writers' or the like. Cicero in his *Orator*[22] uses five categories:

---

[22] *Orator* 61–5. See below, Chapter X 6.

orator, sophist, philosopher, historian and poet.

The only thinker who tried to establish a classification of the formal uses of language which was not based merely on the superficial difference between verse and prose or on habitual descriptions of genres which actually existed, was Aristotle. In this excursion into literary theory he was unique. Nothing written after him equalled the precision and suggestiveness of the opening chapters of the *Poetics*, where the scope and classification of poetry are considered.[23] According to the view set forth here, *poiētikē*, which covered in common usage the composition of epic, drama, elegy and lyric, belonged to a genus of 'mimetic' arts employing speech, rhythm and harmony —any or all of them—in the representation of human character, emotion (or 'suffering')[24] and action. It differed from in- strumental music and dancing in being unable to do without speech. But it was not unable to do without metre; Aristotle reckons as *poiētikē* the composition of such prose works as Socratic dialogues, because they imitate people doing some- thing, while at the same time excluding verse written for the purposes of scientific exposition, such as the philosophical poems of Empedocles. It follows that had Aristotle known any developed form of the novel, he would have reckoned it as *poiēsis*. Indeed, in much later times, when Greek novels had come into being, become respectable and finally achieved the status of classics, Byzantine scholars used Aristotelian termin- ology and ideas to define their characteristics.[25] On the other hand, if Aristotle had known the very human and emotionally evocative didactic poetry of Lucretius and Virgil, he could not consistently have included it, though there would have been nothing to prevent his admiring its language, technique and imaginative use of metaphor.[26] So Aristotle's *poiētikē* remains a

[23] See below, Chapter X.
[24] A disputed passage (1447^a 28), see Lucas *ad loc.*
[25] Examples of Byzantine novel-criticism may be found in M. Psellus' critiques on Achilles Tatius (*Achilles Tatius*, ed. E. Vilborg, 166 f.) and Heliodorus (*Heliodori Aethiopica*, ed. A. Colonna, 364 f.).
[26] Aristotle (fr. 70 Rose) did in fact admire certain poems of Empedocles; but those mentioned here are not the philosophical ones (which he alluded to in *Poetics* 1) but one on the war with Xerxes, a 'prooemium' to Apollo, and 'tragedies'.

narrower concept than what we usually mean by 'poetry'; *a fortiori* it is narrower than the 'literature' we are seeking, if by that we mean the whole proper subject of moral and formal criticism.

This must of course include oratory. And this is one thing that Aristotle strictly excluded. In his view 'rhetoric' was a wholly distinct art from 'poetic', and was not 'mimetic' at all. The orator uses language primarily for persuasion, and he uses it as a part of his real activity in life, not in play or pretence. This difference is fundamental. It was however not felt in early times: in Hesiod,[27] the Muses help the king as well as the poet, the persuader as well as the charmer; and Solon and other early poets appear to have used both iambic and elegiac poetry for the practical ends of public policy. But Aristotle regarded the difference as vital. Plato, from a more moralistic standpoint, had stressed both common features[28] and (more seriously) differences. Both arts, in his view, were dangerous: rhetoric, because she deceives people into acting on false information and 'prefers the probable to the true'; poetry, because the practice of imitation corrupts the mind, and the corruption extends to real-life activities. The grounds of objection are different, because the things themselves are different.

Of course, any 'rhetorical' use of speech can be 'imitated', but the imitation—a work of *poiētikē*—possesses no direct power of persuasion, but only the capacity inherent in all poetry to induce habits of mind, good or bad, which may subsequently be shown in our own actions. Poetry thus contains much 'imitation' rhetoric, and this is especially true of Homer and the dramatists, on the observation of whose practice most Greek poetic theory in fact rested. Similarly, oratory might well involve *mimēsis* of words and actions which the speaker needs to describe in order to further his case. Again, an orator may pretend to doubts or attitudes he does not really feel; his studied speech then becomes an 'imitation' of reality.[29] Yet these overlaps are superficial. Essentially, Aristotle was surely

[27] *Theogony* 80 ff.; see M. L. West *ad loc.*
[28] *Gorgias* 502C ff.
[29] See the passage from Alexander's treatise 'on figures', Spengel 3.11 ff.; translated in Appendix, p. 176.

right: rhetoric and poetics are different, even opposed, arts, the one dealing in reality, however ignoble, the other in illusion, however splendid.

Yet the mutual influence and interdependence of these two branches of theory, and of oratory and poetry themselves, are very great. It is not hard to see why this should be so.

For one thing, there is the overlap of purpose which we have already observed. Both oratory and poetry aim to affect their hearers, though with different goals and in somewhat different ways. Both therefore need similar psychological techniques and understanding. Secondly, the skills of language are much the same for both. Aristotle's own discussion of *lexis* ('diction') in the third book of his *Rhetoric*[30] refers back to the *Poetics*. He sees the differences: poetic vocabulary must avoid the lower registers which are in place in prose. But the essential precepts are common. We have already touched on, and shall have occasion to discuss later,[31] the common ancient view that words are the outward dress of thought and that even in poetry the underlying 'thing said' can be distinguished from its clothing of words and, if need be, paraphrased in others. This is certainly part of the reason for the links between the discussions of style in rhetoric and in poetics. Moreover, Aristotle treated drama as the central poetic form, and the construction of a plot (*muthos*, 'story') as the poet's first task. The plot, like the orator's case, needed a clothing of words—the most appropriate, of course, and so wholly determined by the prior choice of content. The comic poet Menander, reproached with not having written his play for an imminent festival, is said to have replied that it was all finished really—the plot was made, he only had to write the lines.[32] This was to speak both as a good pupil of the Peripatos, and as a man with a rhetorical mind.

In view of these considerations, it is perhaps not surprising that the sharp Platonic and Aristotelian distinction between poetry as a 'mimetic' art and rhetoric as 'non-mimetic', should have had comparatively little influence on later classifications and evaluations of literature. Critical theory, as often, did not have much power over critical practice. In fact, the very

[30] 1404^a ff. (*ALC* 136 ff.). [31] Chapter IX.
[32] Plutarch. *Mor.* 347B (*ALC* 5).

classification which Aristotle regarded as the most superficial, that by metre, remained the most usual for all practical purposes; it is clearly seen, for example, in the lists of authors commended by Quintilian as useful reading for the budding orator.[33] Moreover, the qualities of style in poetry came increasingly to be regarded as different only in degree from those evident in prose,[34] and the elaborate systems of stylistic discriminations which were the pride of later rhetoric were based on observation of the poets as well as the orators, and were held to apply equally to both. It is easy to see historical reasons for this. One is the rise of a Greek classicising literature by the first century B.C., with standards of language and thought based on the whole corpus of approved older writing, poetry as well as prose. Another factor, closely related to this, is the retreat of rhetoric from public life to the classroom, with the consequent indulgence in fantasy and fun and divorce from the sterner needs of vocational training. All this tended to minimise the differences between the two arts. Indeed, metre apart, the essential difference (for practical purposes) came to be thought to be one of subject-matter, not of type of activity. Poetry had greater licence (*licentia, exousia*) both in language and in fantasy, whereas oratory had the closer links with reality and action. 'Longinus'[35] expresses this clearly in connection with what he calls *phantasia*, the imaginative visualisation of a scene or a mood:

The poetical examples . . . have a quality of exaggeration which belongs to fable and goes far beyond credibility. In an orator's visualisations, on the other hand, it is the element of fact and truth which makes for success.

Lucian makes a similar point:[36]

Poetry enjoys unqualified freedom. Its sole law is the poet's will. He is possessed and inspired by the Muses. If he wants to harness a team of winged horses, or make people run on water or over the top of the corn, nobody grumbles . . .

[33] Quintilian 10.1 (*ALC* 380 ff.).
[34] See below, Chapter X 6, on Proclus' account of these matters.
[35] 15.8. Cf. below, Chapter VII 7.
[36] *De conscribenda historia* 6 (*ALC* 537).

6

Let us, in conclusion, try to formulate some assumptions on which the 'critics' of the imperial age worked. I am thinking especially of 'Longinus'; a proper interpretation of *On sublimity* is at the heart of the whole subject. Four points come to mind:

(i) The 'critic' is concerned with all poetry and formal prose, which form a unified (though not very well defined) corpus of literature.

(ii) He feels bound to discuss it in both ethical and rhetorical terms, and to minimise the conflict between these two points of view.

(iii) On the rhetorical side, stylistic differentiation has become the single most important topic.

(iv) Poetry and prose differ in degree of realism, and the difference is a wide one; but the Aristotelian insight that imaginative literature uses discourse in a fundamentally different ('mimetic') way from oratory is either forgotten or set aside as not relevant to the business of reading, judging and reproducing the classical texts.

How did such a set of attitudes come into being? The story is long and complex; what follows is an attempt to outline its main features.

CHAPTER TWO

Narrative: from the Beginnings to Aristotle

I

THE earliest literature of Greece, the heroic epic, marks also the beginning of literary self-consciousness. The poet of the *Odyssey* has bards among his characters and praises their trade. A good poet, we are told, brings events vividly to life. He learns his ways of song from the Muse, and with her help becomes a valued and respected visitor in princely houses.[1] The epic poet is evidently expected to make pronouncements about his art—the bard is a part of the heroic society which he represents—and to display his profession as one of some consequence. The stories that Homer was a child of a servant of the schoolmaster Phemios, and that he became blind and begged his bread, are later romancing.[2] But there is no overt criticism in the epic, no suggestion that some tales are untrue or that some predecessors have gone wrong. There may of course have been suppression or expurgation, but that is unprovable.[3] Hesiod, it is true, intriguingly makes the Muses say that 'they know how to tell many lies that resemble the truth, and also, when they wish, to tell the truth itself'; but he makes no specific charge, and it is an uncertain conjecture that he is thinking of the myths in Homer.[4]

Nevertheless, criticism of the absurdity or moral offensive-

[1] *Odyssey* 1.366 ff., 8.477 ff., 22.342 ff.; *ALC* 1–2; Lanata 1–19.
[2] See the 'Life of Homer by Herodotus' (ed. T. W. Allen in O. C. T. Homer, vol. v), a work of the late Hellenistic or Roman period.
[3] The case was started by G. Murray, *The Rise of the Greek Epic*, 120–45.
[4] *Theogony* 26 ff. (*ALC* 2). See below, Chapter VI 4.

ness of the mythology enshrined in the traditional poems began, it seems, in the sixth century with the Ionian philosopher Xenophanes;[5] defence by allegory—i.e. the discovery of acceptable concealed meanings underneath the unacceptable surface—is said also to have begun about the same time, with Theagenes of Rhegium, 'the first man to write about Homer'.[6] Even at this early period, the epics, already obsolete and puzzling in language and content, were beginning to attract the interpretative activities which have never ceased since, and which contributed immensely to the development of articulate views about the nature and qualities of poetry.

2

Lyric poets—including the composers of choral lyric, who speak through the choruses they have trained—can come forward in their own persons much more easily than epic bards. The lyric poet is not primarily a narrator, though he may of course tell stories, as did Stesichorus and Pindar, and it is noticeable that both Plato and Aristotle emphasised this aspect of his work. It is thus not so violent a breach of continuity or of illusion if he steps forward with personal comment. In Pindar indeed this is common enough to look like an established convention. His own relation to the Muse as her prophet or spokesman, his rivals' plodding incompetence, Homer's seductive falsifications, the improprieties of myth, are all themes which he takes up, often touching briefly and allusively on them, as things expected and well understood.[7] It would appear also that it was the lyric poets who counter-attacked moral critics like Xenophanes. At any rate, when Plato[8] gives examples of what he calls the 'ancient quarrel between philosophy and poetry', it is from lyric that he quotes, though the provenance of the lines is unknown, sharp phrases like 'the bitch that barks at master',

[5] Lanata 113 ff. See also below, Chapter VI 5.
[6] Lanata 104 ff.
[7] Pindar fr. 150, *Ol.* 2.83–92, *Nem.* 7.12; *ALC* 3–4; Lanata 74–97; C. M. Bowra, *Pindar,* ch. 1; Maehler, ch. 6; M. R. Lefkowitz in *HSCP* 67 (1963) 177 f., and *CQ* 28 (1978) 461 f.
[8] *Rep.* 606c–d (*ALC* 74).

'mighty among the vain words of fools', 'the dainty thinkers starve', and so on. The later comic attacks on Socrates and the sophists perhaps only echoed and vulgarised this apparently earlier tradition of invective.

3

Drama and its attendant critical response are connected with somewhat different social and political conditions from epic and lyric. Plays were popular entertainments at great festivals, the dramatists competed normally under the auspices of the Athenian demos. The judges at the Dionysia, who had to rank the plays in order, were not a panel of theatre critics.[9] They were a jury chosen by lot, and they must have been expected to give decisions in tune with popular taste. No doubt their sphere was much limited by the fact that the archon had already selected the three competitors. No doubt topicality, sentiment and spectacle had weight. But we should surely believe that they looked also, and with some degree of connoisseurship, at the poetry and the plot-construction. The best evidence for this is the prevalence of parody and caricature in Attic comedy. The various Euripidean scenes of *Acharnians*, *Thesmophoriazusae* and *Peace*, not to speak of the brilliant lyrical pastiches and debates of the *Frogs*, are full of shrewd observations on tragic technique.

The function of Aristophanic parody is of course not strictly critical. Its primary object is not to show how something is good or bad—still less to teach technique or point a moral—but to exaggerate recognisable features so as to make them funny. Nevertheless, histories of criticism rightly give a prominent place to Aristophanes.[10] Many of the terms that constitute the standard vocabulary of later Greek criticism are first found so used in his plays. *Psuchros* is later the regular term for failures caused by misguided ingenuity or grandeur; *asteios* ('urbane')

[9] For the evidence relating to the judges, see A. Pickard-Cambridge, *Dramatic Festivals of Athens* (ed. 2, 1968), 95 ff.

[10] Sometimes an exaggerated one: see, e.g., the influential article of M. Pohlenz, 'Die Anfänge der griechischen Poetik' (*NGG* 1920; *Kleine Schriften* ii, 436–72).

is Aristotle's word for successful wit; *litos* and *leptos* are vague expressions for delicacy and daintiness in Alexandrian and Atticist writers.[11] Moreover, the general ideas expressed in the debate (*agōn*) between Aeschylus and Euripides in the *Frogs*, whether original or not, were clearly influential in shaping later stylistic theory. The essence of the *agōn* is the contrast: grandiloquence confronts wit, virility confronts decadence. The Greeks loved such antitheses; and the effect of Aristophanes' formulation of this one was to set a pattern for later stylistic descriptions. We shall see much more of this pattern; I have already suggested that it was unfortunate, but its influence and importance are beyond question.

The same debate also contains ideas about the moral and practical value of poetry which are of considerable significance. Aeschylus (1030 ff.) is made to enumerate the useful services of the early poets: Orpheus for religion, Musaeus for healing and oracles, Hesiod for farming, Homer for the art of war. The joke, which is aimed at a notorious 'bad soldier' called Pantocles, who tried to put on his helmet first and his plume afterwards, derives wholly from the reference to Homer. The rest of the passage makes no contribution to the humorous point, except in so far as it builds up expectation. Now Horace's *Ars poetica*[12] contains a very similar argument. The value of poetry is here demonstrated by reference to Orpheus, Amphion, the social functions of poetry in early times, and finally the martial inspiration of Homer and Tyrtaeus. Though Horace has elements which are not in Aristophanes—he allegorises the myths of Orpheus and Amphion—there is enough similarity to make some historical connection likely. Moreover, it may be inferred from Plato's *Protagoras* (316D) that some sophists claimed that *their* art was the great civiliser of mankind, and that Orpheus, Hesiod and Musaeus were, in their sense, 'sophists'. The historical possibilities are two. Either Aristophanes takes up a defence of poetry already current; or else he modifies what was originally a defence of *sophoi*, 'wise men', generally, for the particular purpose of his debate. In either case, it is interesting to speculate on what happened next. Is

[11] J. D. Denniston, *CQ* 21 (1927) 113–21.
[12] *Ars poetica* 391 ff. Cf. Brink 384 ff., Pohlenz, op. cit.

Horace's ultimate 'source' no other than Aristophanes? Or did some more serious sophistic apologia of poetry reach the Peripatetics and their Roman adapter independently of comedy? Rudolf Pfeiffer, in his classic account of the development of ancient scholarship,[13] reasonably suggests that Callimachus owed the expression of his literary ideal—the delicacy and *litotēs* of the Alexandrians—precisely to Aristophanes' formulation of the qualities of Euripides. If this is true, it is an instance of a habit we can detect even in Plato: the habit of taking Old Comedy too seriously, either as a historical source or as a quarry for ideas.

4

We are told by Plutarch[14] that the description of Aeschylus' *Seven against Thebes* as 'a drama full of the God of War' comes from the famous orator and teacher Gorgias of Leontini. It occurs in fact in Aristophanes, at *Frogs* 1021. Much has been built on this; it has been supposed that Aristophanes reproduces Gorgias' theory. But the building is shaky, for Plutarch may simply be mistaken. There can be no doubt, however, that, of all the sophists and teachers of rhetoric of his day, Gorgias had most to do with the beginnings of critical theory. Three propositions which he appears to put forward in his *Defence of Helen* are crucial.[15]

The first is that poetry is *logos echōn metron*, 'speech having (i.e. 'with') metre'. This is open to the interpretation that all that is needed to convert prose into poetry is metrical form. Such a view was common enough later. It was rejected by Aristotle in the opening chapter of the *Poetics*. It was also rejected by Horace:[16] if you break up the metre of *sermones* like Lucilius' or Horace's own, of course there is no poetry left; but do the same with some splendid piece of Ennius, and the *disiecti membra poetae* are recognisable enough. But did Gorgias

---

[13] *History of Classical Scholarship* i, 138.

[14] *Mor.* 715ᴇ (Lanata 206).

[15] Extracts in *ALC* 6–8; text in Radermacher, *Artium Scriptores*; see in general, V. Buchheit, *Das Genos Epideiktikon*, 30 ff.

[16] *Satires* 1.4.56 ff. (*ALC* 267).

really mean that metre alone turned prose into poetry? It is natural to ask whether he conceives the relationship between *logos* and *metron* as an internal one between wholly integrated elements of a whole, or an external one in which 'poetry' is simply the sum of the two. The safest way of answering this question is by looking closely at the context. Gorgias is 'defending' or 'excusing' Helen. One defence is that she was deceived by *logos*. Now for this to be an effective argument, *logos* should be represented as something she could not possibly be expected to resist. It has to be credited with the greatest possible emotional power. Now the emotional impact of poetry—its power to terrorise and sweep us off our feet—is, as Gorgias makes clear, universally acknowledged. *Logos* in general must then be seen to have the same force. The special characteristics of poetry and its difference from prose have therefore to be minimised. If this is best done, as it would seem, by treating *metron* as an external ornament, not affecting the intrinsic qualities of the whole, then this is how we should conclude Gorgias wished his statement to be taken.[17]

The second and third propositions in the *Defence of Helen* come from Gorgias' account of the emotional effect of poetry itself:

Those who hear poetry feel the shudders of fear, the tears of pity, the longings of grief. Through its words, the soul experiences its own reactions to successes and misfortunes in the affairs and persons of others.

We should note two points here: Gorgias' stress on the painful emotions of pity, fear and sorrow; and his recognition that the sufferings of others excite corresponding emotions in the spectators. We naturally think of Attic tragedy; but epic too, to judge from Plato's *Ion* (555c), was expected to have a powerful emotional effect on its audiences. Gorgias clearly anticipates one element in what is to be Aristotle's view of the characteristics that define tragedy: the emotions principally involved are pity and fear. But we have no reason to think that he defined the effect, as Aristotle did, as *katharsis*, or that he

---

[17] Isocrates, Gorgias' pupil, took a different view; see *Evagoras* 5, 11.

perceived that what has to be explained is the impact on us of events which we know to be simulated.

One other statement about Gorgias has to be added to this account of his views. It is reported by Plutarch,[18] in an antithetical and jingling sentence which is very much in Gorgias' manner. We are told that Gorgias described the deceit (*apatē*) of tragedy as one 'wherein the deceiver is juster than the non-deceiver, the deceived wiser than the undeceived'. This paradox amounts to affirming that poetic 'deceit' involves a voluntary move on the hearer's part. The illusion is the result of a contract; the audience is not under duress. Helen, on the contrary, was; she represents the victim of persuasion in the real world.

5

Thus, by the end of the fifth century, the foundations both of interpretative scholarship and of literary theory had been laid. The first had emerged mainly from concern with Homer, the second from reflection on the impact of Attic drama. But poetry was not the only art to invite reflection and discussion. The latter part of the fifth century was also the age in which the skills of persuasive speech were first systematically taught, by Gorgias himself among others. This, as we have seen and shall see again, was of decisive importance for all future literary understanding. At the same time, music, painting and sculpture flourished, all potential topics for the new spirit of questioning. Damon of Oa,[19] who is associated both with Prodicus and with Pericles, is said to have written—supposedly as early as the 440s—a fictitious *Address to the Areopagus* in which he discussed the psychological effect of music and the ways in which it could represent various states of character (*ēthē*). This remained a prime interest of musical theory: the different instruments, and still more the different 'modes', were held to have various powers over the emotions of the hearer. But music, though

[18] *Moralia* 348c (*ALC* 6). A similar argument in another sophistic text: *Dissoi Logoi* 3, 10.

[19] F. Lasserre, *Plutarque 'de la musique'*, Lausanne 1954, 54 ff., Wilamowitz, *Griechische Verkunst*, 58–66.

closely allied with poetry in many situations, was only incidentally a representational art, and did not offer a model of
mimēsis in the way that painting clearly did. If Simonides
really said that 'painting is silent poetry, poetry is painting
that talks',[20] he gave epigrammatic expression to an analogy
that was to have serious consequences in the history of criticism.
On the whole, ancient art criticism was naïvely realistic and its
influence on the understanding of literature often infelicitous.
But how little we know of the diversity of opinion there must
have been about such things is strikingly shown by an anecdote
dating from the middle of the fifth century. The poet Sophocles,
at dinner in Chios, admired the pretty boy who was serving
the wine:

'How right Phrynichus was,' he said to his neighbour, 'when he
wrote "on red cheeks shines the light of love"!' The Eretrian, who was
a schoolmaster, took this up. 'Of course, Sophocles, you are an expert
in poetry. But Phrynichus was surely wrong in calling the boy's
cheeks "red". If a painter were to use a red colour for them, the boy
wouldn't be a beauty any more . . .'
    Sophocles laughed. 'Then I take it, sir,' he said, 'that you don't
approve either of Simonides' much-admired line, "the maid from red
lips speaking"—or of Homer's "gold-haired Apollo". For if the
painter had made the god's hair gold and not black, the painting
would have been worse. And what about "rosy-fingered"? If you
dipped your fingers in rose colour, the result would be a dye-worker's
hands, not those of a beautiful woman.'[21]

The difference between poetical and graphic representation
was not made so clearly again in antiquity.

6

It has always seemed shocking that Plato,[22] the greatest literary
genius of the fourth century, the effective inventor and

[20] Plutarch, *Mor.* 346F (*ALC* 5).

[21] Ion of Chios fr. 8 von Blumenthal (392F6 Jacoby; *ALC* 4–5).

[22] P. Vicaire, *Platon: critique littéraire*, is the most useful survey, but the
literature is immense. A recent essay of distinction is Iris Murdoch, *The Fire
and the Sun* (based on her Romanes Lecture of 1976). See also J. Laborderie,
Le Dialogue platonicien de la maturité (1978) 71–89.

unequalled practitioner of a highly sophisticated genre, the philosophical dialogue, which may properly be regarded as the literary symbol of free inquiry, should at the same time have consistently advocated the most rigid and doctrinaire moral censorship of the arts. Clearly aware that excellence and correctness in poetry were distinct from excellence and correctness in other activities, he drew the conclusion that they must always give way to moral considerations. Poets could have no claim to knowledge; they peddled illusion and deceit. The better poets they were, the more likely they were to deprave.

It is easier to sympathise with his parallel rejection of rhetoric. We readily range ourselves against those who 'honour the probable above the truth', the 'flatterers' (*kolakes*) who cynically exploit the weakness of their fellow men. We enjoy it therefore when Plato shows us how absurd are the pretentions of the rhetoricians, how facile and easily parodied the tricks of their trade, how ridiculous their technical terms.[23] It is when— as in his *Gorgias*—he extends his condemnation to all social and political systems which rest on public persuasion that unease returns. The ancient debate over Plato's attack on rhetoric continued into the last ages of the ancient world. Aelius Aristides, summing up the rhetors' answer in the late second century A.D., produces the clinching argument:

Rhetoric . . . was invented . . . as a defence of righteousness and a bond of life for mankind, so that matters might be decided not by strength of arm or by weapons, not by numbers and size; in place of all this, Reason was to determine just solutions in peace and quiet.[24]

These Platonic attitudes, and our response to them, take us a long way from the ordinary levels of literary judgment. They represent the working-out of certain extreme positions. The *Republic* appears to sustain two propositions: that only 'knowledge of the Forms' possesses real validity, other kinds of human understanding being inferior in varying degrees; and that the principles of political life should be established on the assumption that we can find or create rulers who do in fact have both

[23] E.g. *Phaedrus* 266D.
[24] *Oration* 2.210 ff. (There is an English transl. by C. A. Behr in the Loeb *Aristides*, vol. i [1973].)

true knowledge and the ability to apply it to practical problems. The difficulty inherent in interpreting statements made in this context and as part of this model is that of assessing the element of fantasy and irony in it all. The more literally we take Plato's attack on the poets, the more plainly we have to confess that his political despair, in its search for scapegoats, led him to a total, one might almost say hysterical, rejection of a large element in the culture in which he was brought up. But this seems absurd. Perhaps it is only the lip-rejection common in radical thinkers. Irony abounds in the dialogues; perhaps it is here too. Something like this is P. Vicaire's conclusion, at the end of a very careful and methodical study. The irony, he says,

> touches other writers and the arts they practice, but turns back on to the philosopher himself, insofar as he consents to write; it is then the daily safeguard, the indispensable reservation, the means of freeing oneself from a universal weakness; more clear-sighted than the rest, conscious of the dangers he runs himself, the philosopher sets up this smiling, sometimes rather melancholy, defence, which allows him always to keep his distance.[25]

Plato's theoretical arguments, nevertheless, will concern us in their place, as will the replies and discussions which they excited. They touch on great issues: the poet's nature and commitment, and the quality and conditions of his *mimēsis* of the world. But Plato's own understanding of literature appears far more clearly in his pastiche than in his theory: in the speeches in the *Symposium*, especially Agathon's; in the mock funeral speech of the *Menexenus*; and in the Lysias parody in the *Phaedrus*. In most of these places, the overt criticism is of content; but content and treatment go together, and much of the fun is at the expense of stylistic mannerisms.

All these passages—indeed, almost all Plato's parodies—relate to what is called 'epideictic' oratory. This is an important but ambiguous term.[26] It is sometimes used to denote all oratory designed to provide a display (*epideixis*) of the speaker's

[25] Op. cit., 410–11. Such ambivalence and irony could well have been familiar to Plato's original readers; we may compare his contemporary Alcidamas' written attack on written composition (Radermacher, *AS* 135 ff.)

[26] On this ambiguity, see Menander Rhetor, ed. D. A. Russell and N. G. Wilson (1981), p. xx.

powers, not for any practical purpose; but sometimes also—as by Aristotle—exclusively for the oratory of praise and blame, designed as it is to 'display' the good or bad qualities of its subject. The first definition, the wider of the two, is the commoner and the more useful as a historical description; the second, probably the earlier, has a clearer logical character. In any case, this kind of work was a development of the sophistic period. Its importance for our theme lies in the fact that it is in some ways a half-way house between oratory and poetry. Its most obvious functions, praise and blame, were the traditional spheres of the poet, which the orator now claimed to take over. Its subjects were naturally taken from a wider range than those of forensic or deliberative oratory. Gorgias and his pupils Polycrates and Isocrates used mythical and fanciful themes. To show how Helen or Palamedes might be defended is not just practice for the courts. It involves an imaginative treatment of myth, and a degree of reflection on general issues of guilt and responsibility which would probably be out of place in practical oratory. The element of sheer play (*paidia, paignion*) was also large; encomia of Salt, Fever and Death were written primarily to display ingenuity and give the pleasure of paradox.[27] All such speeches are meant to have a permanent, not just an ephemeral, value. Hence they had to possess the accuracy of written style, so that the distant or future reader could not mistake the writer's meaning. And finally, many speeches are in Aristotle's sense 'mimetic', because they may deal with imaginary situations and imply the construction of a plot. This is true particularly of declamations, which, though not 'epideictic' in the stricter sense, are works intended for exercise and amusement rather than for real use.

There are thus many reasons for regarding 'epideictic' oratory as of special interest. We have seen how consideration of the conditions of declamation led 'pseudo-Dionysius' to some sort of general literary theory; we shall see later how other late rhetoricians embraced history, philosophy and all sorts of prose writing under the head of the 'epideictic' or, as they sometimes called it, the 'panegyric' kind.[28]

[27] See A. S. Pease, 'Things without honour', *CP* 21 (1926) 27–42.
[28] See Hermogenes, *De ideis* 389, 7 Rabe; below, Chapter X.

7

Plato did not teach rhetoric or regard it as a proper subject of study. His greatest pupil paid it great attention. Aristotle not only collected and studied earlier rhetorical *technai*, but himself wrote a *Rhetoric* which had an enormous influence on all subsequent work.[29] In its time, it was a highly original book, as we can see by comparing it with the only extant *technē* of the older tradition, the *Rhetorica ad Alexandrum*, whose survival is doubtless due to its being attributed to Aristotle himself instead of to his contemporary, Anaximenes of Lampsacus, whom there is good ground to consider its author. The basis of this book, as of early *technai* in general, is the breakdown of speeches into their constituent 'parts'—prooemium, narrative, argument and confirmation, epilogue—and the provision of appropriate precepts for each of these. This is a procedure which Plato ridiculed in the *Phaedrus*, and which Aristotle clearly thought unimportant. Their objection to it was sound and of wide application: knowledge of parts was only 'the preliminary to the art' (*ta pro tēs technēs*), for the art itself lay in knowing how to put the pieces together to form a coherent whole. This was as true of tragedy as of oratory; and the realisation of it is no doubt the reason why Aristotle in the *Poetics* shows so little interest in the analogous 'quantitative' division of tragedy into prologue, episodes, choral parts and *exodos*.[30]

At any rate, he organised his own *Rhetoric* on a different plan. Book I deals first with the kinds of argument used in persuasive speaking, and the difference between these and the arguments valid in dialectic—i.e. logical forms appropriate to philosophy and science. It then proceeds to describe the three main types of oratory—deliberative, forensic and epideictic—and the topics appropriately handled by each. Book II is concerned mainly with a psychological study of the emotions and characters of the speaker's audience; it is necessary, Aristotle holds, for the

[29] A convenient analysis of the *Rhetoric* in Kennedy, *Art of Persuasion*, 82–114.

[30] *Poetics* 12, where these parts are discussed, may well be spurious: cf. especially J. Vahlen, *Beiträge zu Aristoteles Poetik* (1914), 39; and most recently O. Taplin, *The Stagecraft of Aeschylus* (1977), 470 f. Cf below, Chapter X 2.

speaker to understand how and why people feel certain emotions, and what the objects of these emotions are. Particularly
important are anger, pity and fear. Books ɪ and ɪɪ thus
roughly fulfil the requirement for a 'scientific' rhetoric, out-
lined by Plato in the *Phaedrus*,[31] and are firmly based on the
ethics of the Academy. Book ɪɪɪ is about diction and arrangement; and it is the section on diction which is much the most
significant part of the whole work from the point of view of
criticism in general.[32] Aristotle gives an account of the development of prose style, and his views on what is good and what is
bad become apparent. Detailed criticism is concentrated
mostly on epideictic oratory, on Gorgias, Isocrates and Alcidamas. The great forensic and political orators—Lysias, Isaeus,
Demosthenes—are less prominent. Though the earlier part at
least of Demosthenes' career must have been known to Aristotle
when the *Rhetoric* was composed, he alludes to him only
once.[33] Politically, they were on opposing sides. And it seems
to be later—with the second-generation Peripatetic Hermippus
—that the story of Demosthenes' having been a pupil of Plato
becomes current;[34] and later still, perhaps not till the first
century B.C., that he comes to be regarded as 'the orator' *par
excellence*.

The general plan of Aristotle's *Rhetoric* became in fact the
pattern for most later handbooks. To its basic themes of invention, arrangement and style were added delivery (*hupokrisis*), which Aristotle had mentioned, and the pseudo-
science of mnemonics.[35] A system which began in a philosophical school, and in conscious opposition to the practice of
rhetores, thus came to dominate the rhetorical education of all
later antiquity. The sharp opposition between the Academy

[31] 271–2 (*ALC* 79–80).
[32] *ALC* 134 ff.
[33] 1407ᵃ 5.
[34] Plutarch, *Demosthenes* 5.7; Gellius 3.13.1–5. See A. S. Riginos, *Platonica*,
Leiden 1976, 135. That Demosthenes learned from Aristotle is an absurdity
rightly refuted by Dionysius of Halicarnassus in his Letter to Ammaeus.
[35] The basic texts for this are *Ad Herennium* 3.28–40, Cicero *De oratore*
2.350–60, and parts of Quintilian 11.2. See H. Blum, *Die antike Mnemotechnik*
(Spudasmata 15); and, for the later developments, Frances A. Yates, *The
Art of Memory* (1966).

and the schools of Gorgias and Isocrates, which had charac-
terised fourth-century educational debate in Athens, was later
much modified; in the end, Aristotle's successors seem to have
offered a type of training in general argumentation and
invention not so very different from that of Isocrates himself.

8

The *Poetics*—apparently earlier than the *Rhetoric* in its present
form—had no such spectacular fortune in ancient times. It did
not come into its own till the Renaissance; indeed, Greek and
Roman critics fairly consistently misunderstood or neglected
many of its essential doctrines.

This short, unique and very difficult book touches on many
topics. It begins with the general theory of poetry as a species
of mimetic art, and develops some of the consequences of this.
We are made to see how the growth of poetry from 'natural'
demands of human nature may be reconstructed, how its
principal genres arose, and in particular how tragedy began
and developed to the point where it fulfils its 'nature'. A large
part of the book is then taken up with Aristotle's analysis of the
elements of tragedy, the pre-eminence of plot, the subordinate
but still important parts played by character and ideas, and so
on. Chapters 19–22, which deal with diction, include a good
deal of what we should call grammatical theory, and are
relevant to poetry in general, and not simply to tragedy. At
chapter 23, Aristotle proceeds to epic, explaining the ways in
which it differs from tragedy, the excellence of Homer, the
proper approach to traditional criticisms of Homer, and
finally the reasons for regarding tragedy as superior to epic not
only in the vividness of the impression it makes but in its
greater degree of unity and concentration.

Now in much of this, Aristotle is responding to predecessors—
on the one hand, sophists and grammarians; on the other,
Plato. His brief, and not yet completely understood, allusion
to the tragic *katharsis*[36] of emotions as a familiar idea can easily
be seen as some kind of answer to Plato's insistence that the

[36] 1449^b 28. A recent valuable survey is A. Nicev, *L'énigme de la catharsis
tragique dans Aristote*, Sofia 1970.

emotional impact of tragedy was psychologically destructive. His assertion[37] that poetry is about 'generalities' (*ta katholou*), while history is about particular acts of individual people, implies a rebuttal of Plato's denial of the poets' claim to possess or impart knowledge. Plato had also proclaimed the superiority of epic, which he held to be less mentally disturbing than drama; Aristotle uses aesthetic criteria—especially the criterion of unity—to determine the case in favour of tragedy. It is the most singular achievement of the *Poetics*—seen clearly in this last argument—that Aristotle contrives, for the most part at least, to handle his subject in conscious isolation both from rhetoric and from ethics.

The section on comedy is missing. Reconstructions of it based on later texts are,[38] to say the least, speculative. But if we had it, we might well be in a position to say something of interest about the relation of Aristotle's theory to the practice of contemporary poets. The *Poetics* precedes the comedy of Menander, whose first play was produced a year after Aristotle's death; but no doubt Aristotle was familiar with the development of the comedy of everyday life in the preceding generation. The question is whether he in fact influenced it. Some features of Menandrean comedy make this seem quite likely; the importance given to plot-construction, the descriptions of characters and intentions, and the brand of humour. Aristotle in the *Ethics* contrasts wit with vulgarity, and what he commends accords closely with the practice of New Comedy.[39] Again, his pupil, Theophrastus, has left us a set of sketches[40] of human quirks and foibles which seems much more relevant to the portrayal of characters in comedy than to any conceivable need of the forensic orator or the moralist.

These scholastic works on rhetoric and poetics do not exhaust

---

[37] 1451^b 6.

[38] Extremely speculative is Lane Cooper, *An Aristotelian Theory of Comedy* (1922). For the 'Tractatus Coislinianus', on which this is based, see below, Chapter X 5, with Appendix, p. 203.

[39] *Eth. Nic.* 4.14. On this whole topic, see W. G. Arnott, *Menander, Plautus and Terence* ('Greece and Rome Surveys') 14 ff. and *Papers of the Liverpool Latin Seminar* 2 (1979), 343 ff.; F. H. Sandbach, *Gnomon* 39 (1967) 238 ff.

[40] The most recent annotated editions of Theophrastus' *Characters* are by P. Steinmetz (1960–2) and R. G. Ussher (1960).

Aristotle's contribution to the study of literature. When Dio Chrysostom[41] observed that *kritikē* and *grammatikē* began with Aristotle he was referring to the dialogues in which the philosopher praised Homer, and especially to *On the poets*, a substantial work in three books, which not only covered some of the same ground as the introductory chapters of the *Poetics*, but contained a good deal of historical and biographical fact and legend. Again, Aristotle's antiquarian studies were extremely important:[42] they included records of victories at festivals, *didaskaliai* in which the names of archons, poets, plays and chief actors were carefully registered. No one before Aristotle had attempted such documentation in anything relating to literary history. His researches became the basis of the official inscribed records that the Athenians erected in this period, and inspired similar records in later time. In this field, even more than in poetics and rhetoric, he opened up the way for Alexandrian and later scholars. Direct influence is less certain. Demetrius of Phaleron, a pupil of Aristotle and subsequently governor of Athens under Macedonian rule from 317 to 307, lived in exile at Alexandria, and was concerned with Ptolemy I's foundation of the Mouseion;[43] but what scholarly methods and approaches he, or anyone else, brought from the Lyceum to the new centre of learning in Egypt, must remain matter for conjecture.

---

[41] *Oration* 36.1.
[42] Pfeiffer, *History*, i. 79–84; Pickard-Cambridge, *Dramatic Festivals of Athens*, 68 ff.
[43] Fraser, *Ptolemaic Alexandria*, 314 ff.

CHAPTER THREE

Narrative: the Hellenistic Age from Aristotle to Horace

I

ARISTOTLE believed that tragedy can attain its proper effect simply by being read.[1] This is entirely consistent with his view of the predominance of plot over the other elements of a play. It is also, like his preference for written over spoken oratory,[2] characteristic of his age. In the Hellenistic age, a generation or two after Aristotle, the balance between speech and writing seems very different from what it was in the fifth or early fourth century. It is perhaps no great exaggeration to say that people stopped thinking of writing as simply the record of speech or song, and began rather to think of speech as a mode of performance, an actualisation of a written composition already existing in its own right and waiting for the performer. A pair of examples may help to point the contrast. In the sixth century, the poet Theognis promised his beloved Cyrnus an immortality which consisted of innumerable repetitions of his song at dinner through future ages.[3] On the other hand, the immortality of the Hellenistic poet, according to Horace, rests on poems that deserve 'preserving with cedar-oil and keeping safe in

---

[1] *Poetics* 1450^b 18, 1453^b 4, 1462^a 12.
[2] *Rhetoric* 1413^b 3.
[3] Theognis 237 ff. (*ALC* 3).

smooth cypress'.[4] The singer dies, the book preserves: 'still are thy pleasant voices, thy Nightingales, awake.'[5]

It seems natural that this way of looking at the written word should give new life to non-dramatic poetry. Tragedy and comedy lost their recent dominance. *Lesedramen*[6] for *côteries*, such as Alexandrian tragedians wrote, never had much life. They seem to have been exercises in dramatic rhetoric and *ēthos* rather than in plot-construction. Senecan tragedy is their direct descendant. The one condition on which, in Aristotle's view, they might have succeeded, was thus not fulfilled. Horace's *Ars*, based on Hellenistic sources, reflects these imperfections: he discusses consistency of character, techniques of chorus and messenger, and so on, but says nothing about probability and necessity in the plot, nothing about happy and unhappy endings, nothing about recognition and *peripeteia*. In any case, the social conditions which had fostered the Attic theatre, and were to give a brief heyday to the Roman stage in the second century B.C., seem to have been absent.

Lyric too had little chance of significant revival. The musical and metrical techniques were difficult, and soon forgotten. Scholarly interest in the various genres of lyric and in the interpretation of surviving texts did not lead to imitation. Only the simple personal lyric of the early Lesbian poets found imitators. Horace had some Hellenistic precedent in taking Sappho and Alcaeus as models, even for hymns and poems of state.[7] There remained elegy, iambic and above all the hexameter epic. The great scholar-poets knew and loved Homer and Hesiod. They also knew that they could not do the same thing.[8] Their epics, hymns, encomia and so on, shot through

---

[4] *Ars poetica* 332.

[5] W. Johnson Cory's famous rendering of Callimachus, epigr. 28 (=epigr. 2 Pfeiffer). The 'nightingales' (*aēdones*) are sometimes thought to be the title of Heraclitus' book.

[6] On this concept, see esp. O. Zwierlein, *Die Rezitationsdramen Senecas* (1966).

[7] Melinno's *Hymn to Rome* could be an extant specimen: E. Diehl, *Anthologia Lyrica Graeca* 3.315 f.; C. M. Bowra in *JRS* 1957, 21 ff. But the poem may be of imperial date, and its tone would suit the second century A.D.: see M. L. West, *Kyklos: Griechisches and Byzantinisches: Rudolf Keydell, zum neunzigsten Geburtstag* (1978) 107 f.

[8] So Theocritus 7.45: Hateful the workman who builds a house as big as

with allusive learning and civilised wit, were essentially new. It was natural that they should proclaim this, and adapt to fresh purposes the traditional statements of poetic intent that they found in Hesiod and Pindar.

Callimachus was the greatest of these men. His immense scholarly activity of classifying and authenticating texts extended over the whole range of literature, oratory as well as poetry. It is interesting that the greatest of later connoisseurs of rhetorical style, Dionysius of Halicarnassus, judged him incompetent in this field.[9] He was not a follower of Aristotle, but rather an opponent. He wrote 'against' the Peripatetic Praxiphanes,[10] a work in which he also praised the didactic poetry of Aratus' *Phaenomena*. He was in fact clearly opposed to much that Aristotle had advocated. Unity and size (*megethos*) were not, for him, qualities of literary significance; variety and perfection of finish were more important. The ideal came near to the portrait of Euripides' qualities that had been given by Aristophanes. Callimachus' main programmatic statements were seminal not only in Greek literature but even more in Roman. The image of the 'river of Assyria' bearing filth on its water, contrasted with the undefiled trickle of the holy spring, passed into the language of criticism.[11] 'Longinus' uses it in reverse to reject the whole ideal of perfectionist delicacy: it is not the little spring we admire, however useful its drinking water, but the mighty Rhine and Danube and the still mightier Ocean.[12] Other potent images appear in the prologue of Callimachus' *Aitia*.[13] It is the gods' business to thunder, not the poet's. Apollo's advice is to keep the poem 'slim'—fatness is all right for sacrificial animals, but not a desirable quality in poetry. It is the untrodden path, not the highway, which the poet's chariot must travel.

A touchstone of taste in Hellenistic times seems to have been

a mountain, and likewise those birds of the Muses who labour in vain by trying to crow down the Bard of Chios.'

[9] See Callimachus fr. 446–7 Pfeiffer.

[10] C. O. Brink *CQ* 40 (1946), 11–26.

[11] Hymn 2.105 ff. (Appendix, p. 180); cf. Propertius 3.3 (with M. E. Hubbard, *Propertius* 78 ff.).

[12] 35.4.

[13] *Aitia*, fr. 1.21 ff. (Appendix, p. 181).

the late classical (fifth-century) epic poet Antimachus of
Colophon, who wrote both love poetry and an epic *Thebaid*.
He had apparently been a favourite of Plato, perhaps because
of his high moral tone; later he was judged severe and chaste
(*austēros, sōphrōn*) by admirers, turgid and obscure by opponents.[14] These included the Callimacheans and, later, their
Roman imitators. Among those who concerned themselves with
Antimachus was Agatharchides of Cnidos, a historian and
critic who flourished in the first half of the second century and is
of considerable interest in the history of taste.[15] Agatharchides
wrote a synopsis (*epitomē*) of Antimachus' *Lyde*, which was an
elegiac poem in several books, containing apparently a series of
romantic and mythological stories. So presumably he admired
this. He also made a severe attack on the orator and historian
Hegesias of Magnesia,[16] who was later much attacked by
classicising critics like Dionysius (and even 'Longinus'), though
he had himself claimed to be an imitator of the simplest of the
Attic orators, Lysias. The burden of Agatharchides' attack is
in fact very like that of these later writers: Hegesias' comments
on the sack of Thebes are said to be frivolous and unreal, those
of Stratocles and Demosthenes dignified, serious and far
worthier of the occasion. It looks as if a certain strain in
rhetorical criticism with which 'Longinus' and Dionysius make
us familiar in fact goes back much earlier. But we hardly know
enough about Agatharchides to make a coherent picture of his
attitudes and their relation to those of his contemporaries.

   Hellenistic poetry, however, has another characteristic important for our theme, in addition to its emphasis on craftsmanship and on the avoidance of the well-trodden way. The possibility of some kind of vernacular poetry was alive in the fourth
century, for the gap between the language of New Comedy and

[14] B. Wyss, *Antimachi Reliquiae* (1936) collects 'testimonia': see esp. T15–23.
Particularly interesting references are Catullus 95.9, Dion. Hal. *Comp. Verb.*
22. Antimachus and Plato: A. S. Riginos, *Platonica* (1976), 167–9—though
she may well be taking too credulous a view of these anecdotes, the source of
which (at least in part) seems to be Heraclides Ponticus.

[15] Photius read Agatharchides (*Bibliotheca*, cod. 250). See Fraser, *Ptolemaic
Alexandria*, 540 ff.

[16] See Appendix, pp. 173 ff., and note the criticism of 'Longinus' 3.2, with
Russell's note *ad loc.*

that of ordinary speech does not look large. The metre of comic
dialogue imposes few constraints on speech rhythms. Not only
is the iambic, as Aristotle says,[17] the nearest of all metres to
speech, but the variety and freedom with which it was used by
Menander demonstrate an exceptional ability to combine
metrical regularity with the rhythms and intonations of ordinary speech. New Comedy does not read as though it was meant
to be declaimed. At a somewhat later period, the critic
Demetrius drew a distinction between the plays of Philemon,
which were good to read, and those of Menander, which were
better acted; he had in mind the frequent lack of connecting
conjunctions in Menander, which, he thought, 'stimulated
dramatic delivery'.[18] Frequency of connection makes for a fool-
proof written style; the opposite for the better reproduction of
natural speech. Menander's linguistic realism was very much
a temporary phenomenon of fourth-century Athens. The
literary conditions of the following period ruled out its con-
tinuance. Even humorous and satirical poetry was now composed in dialects based on older literary models and was not
meant as a reproduction of anyone's actual speech. The
reasons for this are complex. To the old tradition of the special
language of poetry was added the need for a literary language
understood by all persons of a certain culture, whatever their
origin. And the origins of potential readers were now very
various; Greek literary education was spreading rapidly
through the newly Hellenised regions of Asia Minor, Syria and
Egypt. The forces that encouraged the growth of a *koinē* for
everyday needs of trade or administration also strengthened the
tendency to distance poetry from vernacular forms of expression
altogether.

2

The unphilosophical 'craftsmanlike' attitude of Callimachus,
to whom no distinct literary theory can be attributed, ran
counter to some important tendencies of the Hellenistic world.
More and more educated men were undergoing training in

[17] *Poetics* 1449^a 24.
[18] *On style* 193 (*ALC* 207).

philosophy—in Plato's sense rather than in Isocrates'—and becoming adherents of one or other of the great schools. Such adherence might—especially with Epicureans—involve a commitment both to a way of life and to groups of like-minded persons. According to Cicero,[19] a man's choice of philosophical school even affected his oratorical style. The Stoics were too much concerned with dry logic, Epicureans were quite unsuitable reading for an orator, the Academy and Lyceum had the advantage of making their members read Plato and Aristotle, writers whose style was good to imitate. Now these philosophical schools—with the exception of the earlier and more wholehearted followers of Epicurus, who had brusquely rejected the whole traditional *paideia*—concerned themselves, not only with logic, ethics and physical science, but with the principles of rhetoric and poetics. It is thus here that we have to look for developments in critical theory, as distinct from movements of taste, in this period. The almost total loss of the prose literature of the age—a loss directly due to a subsequent revolution in taste, the classicizing movement of the first century B.C.—makes the search hard; but some facts are clear.

Our greatest loss is probably that of the literary works of Aristotle's immediate successor, Theophrastus.[20] His part in the transformation of Aristotle's theory of diction into the common 'three-style' theory of later writers is uncertain; but he certainly wrote on this subject, as he did on other topics of rhetoric and on history. Another early Peripatetic, Aristoxenus of Tarentum, wrote on music, and continued a line of thought familiar from Plato and from Aristotle's *Politics*, according to which changes in musical and literary taste are closely linked with the decline of moral values and social institutions. Somewhat later, Neoptolemus of Parium, famous as the alleged source of Horace's *Ars poetica*, seems to have written a handbook of poetics which transmitted many of the simpler and more factual parts of Aristotle's treatise with an admixture of

---

[19] *Brutus* 118 ff.

[20] Fragments of Theophrastus 'on diction' were collected, very uncritically, by A. Mayer (1910). See O. Regenbogen, *RE* Suppl. VII. 1522–32; F. Wehrli, *Die Schule des Aristoteles*, 'Rückblick', 121 ff. On the 'three-style theory', see below, Chapter IX 6.

rhetorical doctrine about invention and style.[21] But in the later Hellenistic period, the school evidently declined. Some of the antiquarian and biographical work which is associated with it is of a low level, gossipy and credulous: Satyrus' *Life of Euripides*, a dialogue in which Euripides' character and activities are for the most part inferred from passages in the plays, is a revealing example of low-grade popularisation.[22] We should remember that the texts of Aristotle's esoteric works were at any rate not commonly available or read until the first century B.C.[23]

However, one of the few surviving classics of Greek criticism perhaps fits into our narrative somewhere here. The Demetrius who is the author of the treatise *On style* is certainly not Demetrius of Phaleron, Aristotle's pupil, to whom it is traditionally attributed: it is later than the third-century poet Sotades (189). On the other hand, the Peripatetic connection is fairly clear: Aristotle, Theophrastus and Praxiphanes are mentioned, and the discussion of the periodic sentence, as well as the scheme of four basic styles with their perversions, suggests an independent elaboration of Aristotle and Theophrastus. Unlike Dionysius, 'Longinus' and all the later rhetors, the author draws particularly heavily on fourth-century writers, including some who are fairly obscure, and gives no special place to Demosthenes among the orators.[24] The first half of the first century B.C. perhaps fits the facts best; at any rate, the book seems independent of Dionysius, and yet is sufficiently backward-looking or 'classicising' in tendency to contrast the 'ridiculous' lack of taste in 'present-day orators' with the taste and sureness of touch exhibited, for example, by Plato.[25]

[21] Evidence and discussion in C. O. Brink, *Prolegomena*, 90–150.

[22] Ed. G. Arrighetti (1964). For Satyrus' place in the history of the biographical tradition, see now M. R. Lefkowitz *GRBS* 20 (1979) 187 f.

[23] How far they then became commonly known is very doubtful. Knowledge of Aristotle in writers of the Roman period, if we exclude professional philosophers, is usually confined, it would seem, to the Dialogues and to mostly indirect acquaintance with the works on natural history.

[24] See especially 240 ff., 250 (hostile to *On the crown*, later the universally acknowledged masterpiece), 265.

[25] 287.

3

Stoic thinking impinges on criticism in somewhat different ways. The Stoics were the founders of formal grammar and linguistics.[26] They had theories of the origin and development of language, and in particular of tropes and figures.[27] The discussion of change and innovation in vocabulary which Horace transmutes into poetry in *Ars* 47 ff. is of Stoic inspiration. They also paid attention to rhetoric, and held a characteristically rigorist view of what it ought to be; by 'knowledge of speaking well' they meant no less than 'knowledge of speaking the truth', and this was an accomplishment only to be realised in the perfect *sophos* who could never be expected on earth. Approximations to the ideal were however possible; the Stoic disciple was expected to do his duty in public life, and therefore to use rhetoric honourably, to be in fact, in the Roman formula, *vir bonus dicendi peritus*. So, although their theory was of no use to the orator—an 'art of becoming dumb', as Cicero called it[28]—they did in a way encourage rhetoric as a means to the fulfilment of a proper duty. From this point of view, rhetoric could not be a mere matter of tricks; it necessarily involved the character and moral outlook of the speaker. The conflict which Plato's attack on rhetoricians had produced could thus be resolved. The moralist imposed conditions on the rhetor which the latter found acceptable; 'philosophical' rhetoric became the basis of Cicero's—and later Quintilian's—very practical thinking about the ideal orator, and also a key slogan in Dionysius' rejection of Hellenistic fashions and re-establishment of classical norms.[29] Stoic attitudes were by no means the only factor in this—we have already seen how Aristotelian teaching in argument tended the same way—but they were undoubtedly an important one.

Stoic views of poetry were also influential.[30] Cleanthes used

[26] General account in G. Murray, *Greek Studies*, 171 ff. The standard work is K. Barwick, *Probleme der stoischen Sprachlehre und Rhetorik*, 1957.
[27] Barwick, 85–7.
[28] Cicero, *De finibus* 4.10.
[29] Dion. Hal. *De antiquis oratoribus* 1 (*ALC* 305).
[30] P. de Lacy, *AJP* 69 (1948), 241–71; Grube 136.

verse, as in his famous *Hymn to Zeus*, to convey philosophical
teaching, adapting the mythological detail of the god wielding
the thunderbolt to express, almost without concealment, the
profound doctrine of the universal creative fire. In their desire
both to maintain the tradition of reading the old poets, and to
use poetry as a propaedeutic for philosophy, the Stoics naturally
inclined to favour allegorical interpretations. Many later
allegorisations of Homer, both moral and scientific, are of
Stoic origin. Strabo, in a passage of obviously Stoic colouring,[31]
argues for the factual basis of Homer's geography against the
astronomer and poet Eratosthenes, who treated poetry as
'amusement', and thought you could as soon identify the
scenes of Odysseus' wanderings as 'find the cobbler who
stitched up the bag of the winds'. The Stoics therefore expected
poetry to have a moral or factual significance—in Posidonius'
definition[32] it involved 'imitation of things divine and human',
in other words the activities of all the rational beings in the
universe—and, presumably, regarded versification and euphony as means to this end. According to Ariston of Chios, as
represented by Philodemus, a poem might be good in content,
but bad in 'composition' (*sunthesis*) or vice versa, deficiency in
either being enough to condemn the whole.[33] This suggests a
sharp distinction of form and content, like Plato's distinction
between 'what is said' and 'how it is said'. Form would be
judged by the ear, content by reason. But it is not at all certain
that this was the universal Stoic view. Both Ariston himself and,
later, Crates of Mallos attached great importance to euphony.
Moreover, Stoic theories of language emphasised the imitative

---

[31] 1.2.3–9 (*ALC* 300 ff.).

[32] Diog. Laert. 7.60 (= F44, Edelstein-Kidd): 'A poem (*poïēma*), as Posidonius says in his Introduction "on diction" (*lexis*), is a material or rhythmical diction, with ornament (*kataskeuē*, exceeding the bounds of prose (*to
logoeides*); "rhythmical" . . . is, for example, "O mighty earth and heaven of
Zeus" A *poïēsis* is a significant *poïēma*, embracing an imitation of things
divine and human'. This passage has been much discussed; see e.g. C. O.
Brink, *Horace on Poetry, Prolegomena*, 65. (The difficulties are serious. As it
stands, (i) Posidonius apparently extends the area of poetry to cover non-
metrical rhythmical prose; (ii) he gives no example of 'rhythm' but only
one of metre. We may either (i) delete 'or rhythmical', or (ii) suppose an
omission in the text, giving the example.)

[33] *Philodemos über die Gedichte, Fünftes Buch*, ed. C. Jensen (1923), 32 ff.

relationship between words and the things they were invented
to represent. It would seem to follow that, in a good poem,
verbal form must be appropriate to content, and the judgment
whether this is so is one which cannot be entirely dependent on
the irrational criteria of sense. But how far any individual Stoic
theorists went in producing a theory of this kind is quite
uncertain.

Our difficulties over this are bound up with the problems
raised by Philodemus' book *On poems*, of which extensive fragments survive.[34] Philodemus, born in Gadara in Syria, was a
pupil of the Epicurean Zeno, and himself came to Italy in the
seventies of the first century B.C. He lived in the household of L.
Calpurnius Piso, the consul of 58, and continued to teach and
influence the Roman intelligentsia down to his death in the
thirties. Many of his books were found at Herculanum; the
decipherment and interpretation of them has been a preoccupation of scholars since the early nineteenth century. *On
poems*, Book v, like many Epicurean treatises, contains a
great deal of polemic against opponents, mostly unfair, but
comparatively little positive doctrine. There are, however,
points of great interest. Philodemus rejects any expectation
that poetry should have a moral or factual content, and any
allegorisation designed to produce this result. For him, it would
appear, it is not possible for a poem to be both good in thought
and bad in composition; the two go together. Nor can composition be judged on irrational criteria. Interpretation of this text
is difficult; we can perhaps only say, in very general terms, that
Philodemus held that a poem should be judged as a whole, and
not on two separate counts of form and content; and this makes
a sharp contrast with critics of other schools. It happens that
Philodemus was himself a poet. His urbane and humorous epigrams are in a noticeably simple style—certainly if we compare
them with the exuberance of his fellow Gadarene, Meleager
—and it is tempting to see in this a reflection of his theory.

It is an intriguing thought that Virgil and his friends moved
in the circles around Philodemus, even if we cannot possibly

---

[34] Grube 193 ff. gives a summary of the main points; but work on Philodemus proceeds, and much of what is said here must be regarded as pro-
visional.

know what influence such instruction had. It is prudent to recall that Horace, who sometimes called himself an Epicurean,
presents in the *Ars poetica* an orthodox Peripatetic system,
drawing (we are told) on that same Neoptolemus of Parium
whom Philodemus treated as a specially vulnerable and incompetent opponent.

4

Philodemus, in establishing himself in Italy among Roman
patrons and pupils, was following a tradition established for
more than a century. Rome had become not only the political,
but the literary centre of the Greek-speaking world. We must
go back to see how this had come about.

The first development of Latin poetry took place in the late
third and early second centuries, a little after the time of
Callimachus and his contemporaries, but still in the great
Alexandrian age of science and scholarship. From the time of
Ennius, at least, the metre and linguistic habits of Latin poetry
were formed on Greek models. These models—Homer, the
tragedians and the poets of New Comedy—were known and
studied in the form in which Hellenistic scholarship presented
them. There was thus no pre-scholarly epoch in Latin literature, as there had been in Greek. Criticism went side by side
with creation from the start, and it was a scholarly criticism, involving close attention to linguistic and formal correctness.

Crates of Mallus, the Stoic theorist and grammarian, visited
Rome, as an ambassador from King Attalus of Pergamum, in
169.[35] He was forced to stay longer than he meant because he
broke his leg in a drain; he lectured, it seems, to audiences who
appreciated his scholarship. Crates was an allegorist—he appears to have been interested in the allegorical interpretation
of the Shield of Achilles as the kosmos[36]—and it may be that the
serious and philosophical tone of his teaching appealed to
Roman gravity. Certainly, his pupil Panaetius, a generation
later, won great success and influence primarily by his moral

---

[35] Suetonius *De grammaticis* 1–2.
[36] The shield of Achilles was a natural subject for allegory: Buffière,
155 ff.

teaching. But Crates will have found grammatical and scholarly interests already flourishing. The poets Livius and Ennius, both bilingual, had interpreted not only the Greek poets but their own Latin compositions. Other early *grammatici* revised and commented on Naevius and Ennius themselves. A tradition of close links between poets and scholars was established, and was always to be an important feature in the history of Latin literature. At a later period, Catullus and the *côteries* of fashionable poets in the late Republic had close links with *grammatici*. Their allusive and difficult poems demanded interpretation; the poet could hardly make his way without the scholar. A hostile critic wrote of Valerius Cato—himself a poet —as 'the Latin Siren, who alone both reads poets and makes them'.[37] Cinna's *Smyrna*, a notorious piece of perfectionist elaboration, was annotated by L. Crassicius, his *Propempticon* by Augustus' freedman, the Palatine librarian Hyginus. Parthenius of Nicaea, a Greek who had reached Italy as a prisoner of war in the seventies, was an influence on the generation of Cornelius Gallus and Virgil.[38] His collection of love-stories for the use of poets survives: they are learned, romantic, sometimes sensational, usually based on local legends or folk-tales. Also connected with Gallus—and incidentally with Cicero's friend Atticus, whose freedman he was—is Q. Caecilius Epirota, the first *grammaticus* to give public lectures on Virgil.[39] An event, perhaps, of some significance: it shows how scholarly criticism operated in making new poetry known and understood, and it opens the long association between scholarship and the national poet of imperial Rome which dominated Latin poetical criticism in later periods.

But this essentially Alexandrian tradition of scholars and poets in close *côteries* is not the only manifestation of Roman literary study in this period. The great polymath M. Terentius Varro[40] had, it seems, no such links. He followed many paths of Hellenistic learning, and adapted them to Latin use,

[37] Suetonius *De grammaticis* 11.

[38] See, e.g. M. E. Hubbard, *Propertius*, 10. f.; J. P. Boucher, *C. Cornelius Gallus*, (1966), 74; W. V. Clausen, *GRBS* 5 (1964) 181 ff.

[39] Suetonius *De grammaticis* 16.

[40] *Entretiens Hardt* 9 (1960), 'Varron', contains essays on various sides of Varro's activity. A brief account in Grube, 160 ff.

following in the footsteps of his teacher, the first great Latin philologist, L. Aelius Stilo.[41] Stoic linguistic theory was applied to Latin Greek stylistic discriminations to the classical poets of early Rome. Varro wrote lives of poets and discussed genres. He did this not only in his learned works but in his satires. Though we have only small fragments to go on, it is clear that, like his predecessor Lucilius and his successors Horace and Persius, he regarded literary comment as a natural part of the satirist's field. But whereas both Lucilius—who criticised the ornate tragic diction of Accius and perhaps inclined to simpler, more Attic tastes[42]—and Horace, who seems to have found Varro's placid acceptance of the old poets uncritical and unhelpful, took up distinct points of view in the literary controversies of their time, Varro seems outside them: idiosyncratic, old-fashioned, a man of learning and humour, not an adherent of any party.

The use of satire is significant. This was a genre in which the Romans rightly believed they owed little directly to Greek models. It was the form in which Horace, the poet-critic, chose to set out his authoritative reflections on the state of literature and the application of theory to practice. And we can perhaps now see, in the light of the history we have sketched, what it was that he inherited. On the Greek side, the background of the *Ars poetica* was principally an Aristotelian legacy. This is the origin of Horace's interest in the history and development of tragedy—although his theory was not the same as Aristotle's and seems based on different evidence about 'satyric' drama. It is also the origin of his treatment of the formal features of a play, and of character and language. But here again, as we have already observed, there is a divergence: Horace has no interest in plot-construction, 'necessity and probability', suspense or surprise. There was also, of course, an Alexandrian element in his emphasis on perfection in technique. Unlike Varro, Horace was not much interested in early Latin literature, and thought its popularity mistaken. He certainly learned much from the attitudes of Catullus, Calvus and their friends; but he combined

[41] Cicero *Brutus* 205; Suetonius *De grammaticis* 3.
[42] Grube 159; E. H. Warmington, *Remains of Old Latin* III (Loeb ed. of fragments of Lucilius), p. xvi, with references.

their insistence on craftsmanship with a degree of seriousness
and commitment to public morality which they would have
found at variance with their whole outlook. The *Ars poetica*
represents a balance between Rome and Greece, Callimachean
perfectionism and concern with the moral duty of the poet.

5

Meanwhile, Greek rhetoric had established itself as a part of
Roman education, though not without opposition. As late as
92 B.C., the rhetors were condemned by the censors as corrupters
of youth.[43] Roman public men frequented rhetorical schools in
Rhodes, Athens and Asia to gain skills they were denied at
home; yet by Cicero's time, not long after the prohibition of 92,
it was possible to acquire a very full rhetorical education without going away. This is how Cicero himself learned.[44] His own
youthful textbook on 'invention', presumably intended to
supply an educational need, shows that the basis of the subject
was held to be the doctrine of *staseis* (Lat. *status*), that is to say
the classification of the types of issue likely to be involved in
forensic cases.[45] This theory was associated especially with
Hermagoras of Temnos, whose work seems to have been influenced by Stoic logical methods.[46] But Cicero does not confine
himself to these technicalities: his preface, insisting on the
civilising functions of rhetoric and its subordination to moral
principles, has strong philosophical overtones.

The other Latin rhetorical treatise of this period is the *Ad
Herennium*.[47] This is more comprehensive in scope; in particular,
it deals with the topic which is most obviously common to
oratory and literature in general, namely style. The author invents his own examples of the three styles—the grand, the
middle and the plain (*gravis, mediocris, attenuata figura*)—and of
the faults that arise from unskilled attempts to achieve them—

[43] Suetonius *De rhetoribus* 1.
[44] *Brutus* 305–12.
[45] See below, Chapter VIII 3.
[46] D. Matthes. *Lustrum* 3 (1958) 58 ff., 262 ff.; and *Hermagorae Temnitae
Testimonia et Fragmenta* (1962).
[47] H. Caplan's Loeb edition is not only good in itself, but is in many ways
the most useful beginner's book for the study of ancient rhetoric.

turgid, flabby and thin writing (*sufflata, dissoluta, exilis figura*).
Crude as they are, these examples give us a clearer picture of
what was actually intended by the common terms of stylistic
description than we can otherwise obtain.[48] Caricature gives at
any rate a sort of understanding.

Cicero's later theoretical works are not school textbooks, but
adult, often highly personal, discussions, and highly wrought
(if hasty) literary compositions. They are among our main
sources for many rhetorical and critical themes.

The earliest—*De oratore* of 55 B.C.—is also the longest and
fullest. The key concept in this elaborate dialogue is that of the
'perfect orator', educated in philosophy and the liberal arts,
and the antithesis of the *vulgaris orator* of ordinary practice,
whose success rests on talent, diligence, imitation and some
knowledge of rhetorical techniques. Cicero himself, in his
earliest great speech, *Pro Roscio Amerino*, clearly contrasts himself in this way with the hack prosecutor, Erucius. In *De oratore*,
both in his own person, and in the speeches of Crassus and
Antonius, Cicero, now at the height of his own oratorical
career, sketches a very personal and individual view of the
whole subject. *Elocutio* occupies a good deal of Book III; and
the treatment is broad enough to include a number of topics
outside the range of earlier handbooks—*ēthos* and *pathos*,
humour, prose-rhythm.

The two later works—*Brutus* and *Orator*—show Cicero involved in a controversy which has wide-reaching, though uncertain, implications.[49] Some mid-century speakers, notably
C. Licinius Calvus, the friend of Catullus, saw the ideal of
'Attic' oratory in the plain style of Lysias and Hyperides. This is
a point of view which is associated with Caecilius of Caleacte,
whom 'Longinus' criticises for his excessive admiration of
Lysias; but it is not clear from what source the idea came to a

[48] Particularly amusing are 4.15 (frigid manner) and 4.16 (trivial manner).
[49] A good introduction to this topic, i.e. to the problems of 'Asianism'
and 'Atticism', is R. G. Austin's note on Quintilian 12.10.16 ff. Wilamowitz' classic treatment (*Hermes* 35 (1900) 1–52) is reprinted in R. Stark,
Rhetorica, as is A. Dihle's 'Analogie und Attizismus' (*Hermes* 85 (1957)
170–205). See also A. Dihle, 'Der Beginn des Attizismus', *Antike und Abend-
land* 23 (1977) 162–77; and T. Gelzer in *Entretiens Hardt* 25 (1979), 1 ff.

group of Roman orators in the latter years of the Republic. What they did was consciously to reject the fullness of style in which Cicero's own main strength lay. This is obviously something like the rejection by the poets of the same generation of the looser structure of earlier writing—and indeed something like Callimachus' earlier polemic against attempts to revive Homeric epic. Now in poetry, polemics of this kind produced no clear reaction—unless Lucretius' deliberate choice of archaic, even pre-Ciceronian techniques should be so regarded —for the idea that the craftsmanship of poetry should be perfect commanded natural acceptance. Once the charge of imperfection was made against a particular fashion, it was very difficult to answer. Indeed, it was perhaps only answerable in the terms in which 'Longinus' answers it, by observing that great genius can be pardoned a few faults and it is better to be a genius than an impeccable mediocrity. But oratory was quite different. It was a practical art, and its excellence could only be judged by its success. Antimachus, the connoisseurs' poet, might be satisfied with an audience of one, if that one was Plato; but orators cannot go on without an audience.[50] Now success with audiences, Cicero reasonably maintains, belongs not to the delicate Atticists, but to those who had the power to move and to command. He tells an old story to make the point.[51] A murder had been committed in a remote part of Italy; suspicion rested on some members of a company of *publicani*. Scipio's friend, C. Laelius, an orator in the plain style, was engaged to defend them. The consuls (it is 138 B.C.) twice delayed judgment. Laelius advised his client to try a different advocate, Galba. Galba took up the case, studied it for a day, and appeared in court in a highly excited state, accompanied by his secretaries, who looked as if they had been badly beaten up. He pleaded the case emotionally, and the *publicani* got off.

The precise relationship between the controversy in which Cicero is here engaged and somewhat similar confrontations of taste among the Greeks must, however, be judged problematic. Certain statements may be made about it with some confidence, but the picture as a whole remains vague. (1) Both Caecilius and Dionysius clearly associated the styles they regarded as

[50] *Brutus* 191.   [51] *Brutus* 85 ff.

corrupt with 'Asiatic' oratory, which they represented as the work of half-Greeks of impure tastes and imperfect knowledge of the language. (2) For Cicero, on the other hand, the *Asiaticum genus* is rather the kind—or kinds—of writing practised by orators of the schools of Asia. It is not necessarily all bad. For some of these people, indeed, he has modified praise: Hierocles and Menecles of Alabanda are *ut Asiatico in genere laudabiles.*[52] (3) Now Calvus and his friends clearly disapproved of Cicero; indeed they seem to have used the term 'Asiatic' of his style.[53] (4) Moreover, Dionysius of Halicarnassus, in the preface to *De antiquis oratoribus* which sets out his position on these matters, both attributed the bad features of Hellenistic prose to 'Asiatics' and assigned the improvement in taste which he felt he was witnessing to certain leading men among the Roman governing classes. We do not know who he means; but the circle of Calvus and the oratory of Messalla, Tibullus' patron and the translator of Hyperides, naturally come to mind.[54] It is interesting also that 'Longinus', who opposes Caecilius and his idolatry of Lysias, appears at the same time to rehabilitate Cicero.[55]

This controversy between a 'fuller' and a 'purer' ideal of oratorical style was relevant both to Greek and to Latin writing. Indeed, there has been much dispute as to whether its origins are Greek or Latin. But it is, I think, important to remember that it is quite distinct from the peculiarly Greek phenomenon of linguistic Atticism. This was the rejection of certain features of the common literary language of the Hellenistic age in favour of a closer imitation of classical Attic, both in vocabulary and in syntax. In Dionysius, this inclination is only beginning; it reached its full development much later, in the second century A.D.

This movement, which aimed at the establishment of a 'pure', timeless Greek which could withstand change and development, only incidentally touches the choice in taste between the 'grand' and the 'simple', the overwhelming and the delicate.

[52] *Brutus* 325.
[53] Quintilian 12.10.12.
[54] For Messalla, see Quint. 12.10.11, 10.1.113; H. Malcovati, *Oratorum Romanorum Fragmenta*, no. 176.
[55] 'Longinus' 12.4.

The correct reproduction of classical vocabulary and grammatical usage is a necessary but not sufficient condition of
the kind of 'correctness' and 'purity' demanded by 'Atticist'
taste. The Greek linguistic movement, however, did have some
Latin analogues later on, in the second century A.D., though the
Latin situation (as Horace saw)[56] was quite different. There
were archaists who followed Sallust, grammarians who tried to
fix forms and usages on the basis of the older authors. If
Caesar's *De analogia* (as is often thought) is an answer to
Cicero's more carefree attitude to the basic virtue of *Latinitas*,[57]
we have an example of grammatical theory allied to a movement in taste; this is something we cannot parallel on the
Greek side. But the interaction between Greek and Latin literature and between theory and movements of taste in the age of
Cicero is still very imperfectly understood; and a somewhat
confusing picture is probably the best that can be had.

There is, however, another feature of Cicero's *Brutus* which is
easy to grasp, and clearly important. This is the amount of
personal criticism of individual orators which it contains. It
may well be that here is something peculiarly Roman. The
whole man matters—his personality, his career, as well as his
style. Cicero talks of orators as persons; it is natural to contrast
his method with the more scholastic attitude of Dionysius, who
describes the features not of Plato but of Plato's diction (*lexis*),
and comes almost to personify this.[58] But Roman persons are
important in themselves: their *cursus honorum*, the exact dates of
their activities, their actual relationships, all matter. We see
this in the dialogue-form itself: Plato is careless of time and
place, Cicero places his fictitious conversations at precise historical moments. Nor did this concern with biographical
accuracy and rounded portraiture cease with the extinction of
the Republic: the elder Seneca's sketch of Porcius Latro[59] has
the same quality, Tacitus' *Dialogus* shows the same precise
concern with dramatic date.

[56] This is the burden of the 'Letter to Augustus' (*Epistles* 2.1).
[57] See *De oratore* 3.48–9; *Brutus* 252–3; Suetonius *Julius* 56.
[58] *De Demosthene* 5–7, *Ad Pompeium* 2–4 (*ALC* 309 f.).
[59] *Controversiae* 1 pr. 13 ff.

CHAPTER FOUR

Narrative: the
Roman Empire

I

THE establishment of the principate and the flowering of
Augustan poetry mark a break in the conditions of Roman
literary life. Where there was previously only the patronage of
the nobility, there is now also the magnet of a court. Where
there was national confusion and despair, there is a new sense
of direction and purpose. The arrival of Dionysius of
Halicarnassus in Rome around 30 B.C. happens to coincide with
the establishment of this new order.

We may of course be exaggerating Dionysius' real importance, but the accident of time has made him the one critic and
theorist of the age whom we can fairly say we know.[1] His tastes,
his friends, even the course of his literary development are not
entirely hidden. He worked in Rome at least till the publication
of his history of early Rome, or a large part of it, in 7 B.C.: this
was the work he regarded as his chief claim to fame, his critical
work being rather the outcome of teaching. We have already
had cause to draw attention to the very important programmatic preface to his book *On ancient orators*, in which he proclaimed the restoration of a genuine 'philosophic' rhetoric,
under the beneficent lead of distinguished Romans. This book
sets out to describe the qualities of the classical orators and, in
particular, 'what should be accepted or rejected in each'; they
are studied as models for imitation. Since Dionysius promises a
similar book on historians, it is clear that he regards these also

[1] Best general account; S. F. Bonner, *Dionysius of Halicarnassus* (1939).

as possible models. In his treatise *On imitation*, a fairly early work, of which extensive fragments survive, he extends the range even further, including poets and philosophers.[2] But this does not necessarily mean that he regards himself either as advising writers other than orators and historians, or as thinking of oratory as itself now a scholastic activity, centred on the increasingly popular practice of declamation and on the epideictic mode. He does however take a view of his task which makes it different from that of the ordinary rhetor. He takes the basic exercises and all the theory of invention for granted, and concentrates very heavily on style. He calls the subject *politikē philosophia*,[3] a phrase that recalls Isocrates. And he is extremely interested in problems of authenticity, devising and carrying out scholarly inquiries into the dates and authorship of speeches, and criticising his predecessors in this field.[4]

Dionysius comes closer to modern ideas of a literary critic than any earlier writer. He excels in close observation and the analysis of stylistic effects. His critical vocabulary, largely metaphorical, is extensive and much of it unparalleled before him. His peculiar gifts are best displayed in his most original, and least rhetorical, work, *On the arrangement of words*. This is a study of the kinds of word-order conducive to particular kinds of literary effect—harshness, smoothness, or any gradation between. Dionysius rejects any attempt to determine word-order by general logical or grammatical considerations, and bases his discussion on an analogy with building: we have to consider how the units of our construction, words, clauses and sentences, are best fitted together to give a 'beautiful' and 'pleasing' effect. His examples include poetry as well as prose; indeed, some of his most telling discussions are of Homer, Sappho and Simonides. Much of what he says concerns the sounds of language, and the way in which they can be treated as musically expressive. Some of his points seem sensible: it makes sense to say that a preponderance of short words makes for slowness and roughness because of the pauses in pronunciation between

[2] This book was Quintilian's main source in the Greek sections of his survey of authors to be imitated, 10.1 (*ALC* 380 ff.).

[3] *Ant. orat.* pref. 2 (*ALC* 305).

[4] See below, Chapter XI 1, for his method in *Dinarchus*.

them. But much seems unconvincing, even allowing for our difficulty in matching what he says with the phenomena he describes, of which we can only have a very imperfect grasp. Thus, in his famous analysis of Homer's description of the rock of Sisyphus,[5] he sees clearly that the speed is changed in a line or two from the slow tempo where Sisyphus pushes the stone up, to the rapid rattling of its downward acceleration; but his idea that the difference is due largely to the greater number of monosyllables in the first part neglects altogether the metrical consideration that the line beginning

autis/epeita/pedonde/kulindeto . . .

has three successive trochaic caesurae. Again, the idea that 'contracted' grammatical forms are appropriate to disparagement or to 'small' things generally, while 'expanded' forms amplify the sense, is a singularly naïve variant of the basic fallacy in ancient doctrines of literary appropriateness, namely the demand that 'big' things should be expressed in correspondingly 'big' words.

Dionysius is essentially a teacher, and he is a good one. His pupils were lucky, and their taste was sensibly developed. He has obvious faults: we see much that is mechanical in his stylistic doctrine, and he works with no very consistent theory of the principles of literary judgment. But his moral emphases are refreshingly subdued; and his attention to detail and open acknowledgment of the importance of trained taste even when it cannot render a reason, are positive and attractive features. He is not unworthy of the age of Virgil and Horace.

2

Some connection between Dionysius and Caecilius of Caleacte is established by the former's reference to his 'very dear' Caecilius as sharing the view that Demosthenes imitated the thought and argumentation of Thucydides.[6] Caecilius is also the professed opponent of 'Longinus'. But the date of *On sublimity* remains uncertain; there is nothing in the practice of

---

[5] *De compositione verborum* 20 (*ALC* 335).
[6] *Ad Pompeium* 3.20 = Caecilius fr. 158 Ofenloch.

ancient polemic to preclude a sharp attack on an author some
centuries old, and the traditional attribution to the third-
century Longinus, the pupil of Plotinus and chief minister of
Queen Zenobia at Palmyra, cannot be ruled out on these
grounds alone.[7] The best reason for ruling it out, and asserting
that the work belongs (as is generally held) to the first century
A.D. and not the third, is rather the 'lament for freedom' in the
closing chapter, which has very much the air of certain first-
century speculations on the moral and literary consequences of
replacing republican by monarchical government. The *com-
munis opinio* that it is a work of the first century, somewhere
between the age of Dionysius and that of Pliny and Tacitus, remains the most reasonable view. Parallels with Pliny[8] are indeed
particularly close; yet there is really nothing in the book which
necessitates a date later than the first decades of the Christian
era. Like Dionysius, the author presupposes a general com-
petence in rhetoric, and addresses himself to the problems of the
orator who writes for posterity. Like Dionysius again, he draws
extensively on poetry for his illustrations. Moreover, he too is
concerned with a Roman audience; like Caecilius—and unlike
the more modest Plutarch[9]—he is prepared to discuss the merits
of Cicero. The work is certainly polemical; Caecilius admired,
excessively in 'Longinus'' view, the pure Attic virtues of
Lysias; at the same time he despised Plato, whom our author
admires greatly. This opposition to a view of literary excellence
which 'Longinus' regards not as a valid alternative to his own
but as a completely false trail, leading to something both tech-
nically and morally inferior, is set out in the form of a set of
rules for producing a certain tone of writing, *hupsos* or 'sublimity'. This tone is not thought of as entirely constituted by
verbal features. It involves also choice of subject and especially
a high level of emotion. The polemic against Caecilius concentrates on his failure to discuss emotion in this connection at all;
but 'Longinus' does not himself succeed in giving a clear account of the relation of emotion to other factors in good writing.

[7] A recent advocate of a third-century date is G. W. Williams, *Change and
Decline* (1978), 17–25, but he advances no new argument.
[8] Especially with *Epist.* 9.26 (*ALC* 429).
[9] *Demosthenes* 3.

His liking for Plato in fact leads him to try to embrace under the one head of *hupsos* both an emotionally intense rhetoric, like that of Demosthenes, and a more ornate and diffuse kind, represented by those parts of Plato which the school of Dionysius most disliked—the elaborate imagery characteristic of *Laws* and *Timaeus*. It is in keeping with his admiration for Plato that 'Longinus' adopts a strongly moral stance: only 'greatness of mind' can ensure 'greatness' in writing.

'Longinus' alludes to other books he has written, not now extant: one on Xenophon, two on the arrangement of words.[10] To judge from the book we have, these must be accounted a great loss; no other Greek critic has anything like this unknown author's freshness, enthusiasm and vigorous expression.

3

But we must return to the historically securer ground of Augustan Rome, with its busy and varied literary life. The poets continued, as in Hellenistic and Republican times, to write about themselves and their art. They proclaimed their inspiration and special gifts—dreams, visions, meetings with the Muse, withdrawal into solitary places. They modestly asserted the Callimachean principles that conveniently forbade them to attempt epic; how far their professed reluctance for this task is evidence for pressure from above to undertake it, and how far their stylised refusals (*recusationes*) are merely an elaborate form of flattery suitable to the material of the pastoral, lyric or elegiac poet, are debatable questions. From our present point of view, it is sufficient to say that they were asserting, as was Callimachus, that there was valid poetic value to be found in styles and genres which did not aim at traditional forms of grandeur, but unfailingly at perfection of technique. Perhaps Horace's 'Pindar ode' should be singled out:[11] in showing the inimitable qualities of Pindar's art, he reviews the whole range of his writing, giving a sort of catalogue of the types of Pindaric poem; metaphors traditional in this context—the

[10] 44.12 also announces a separate work on 'emotions', a sequel (apparently) to *Sublimity*.

[11] *Odes* 4.2. Appendix, p. 192.

great river, the honey-gathering bee—are skilfully deployed;
and while it is difficult to reconstruct the situation presupposed
by the poem, it is at any rate clear that its main function is that
of defending Horace's choice of the form of personal lyric, and
its adaptation to public themes. In Horace's *Satires* and
Epistles, and especially the *Ars poetica*, something more than
defence is attempted: Horace sees himself as a leader of taste,
guiding Rome away from undue respect for her old literature,
and establishing a literary ideal which combines technical perfection with a commitment to an acceptable—but by no means
conventional—moral stance. Horace is uniquely articulate
among ancient poets in stating the principles of his life's work;
his often misjudged masterpiece, the *Ars*, is no versified treatise,
but an urbane, and characteristically understated, confession
of faith.

The princeps and his friends were intimately connected with
the literary world. Politics and letters were the common interests of the men who governed—as they had been in Cicero's
time. The cynical might say that literature was an extension of
politics. What we know of Augustus' own literary tastes suggests that they were conveniently in the middle of the road:
Antony's 'Asianism' was 'madness', the archaic tendencies of
Pollio or Tiberius no less to be despised. Yet Maecenas, who
had very different tastes, remained a friend.

Cacozēlia ('misguidedness') is a key term. Augustus contrasts
cacozeli with *antiquarii*.[12] Maecenas is the very type of the
cacozelus, with his affected vocabulary and weird word-order;
so it was doubly pointed when Agrippa (if indeed it was he)
attacked Maecenas' protégé, Virgil, as 'inventor of a new
cacozēlia'—not an obvious perversion of the grand or the simple
style, but a subtle evil, the strained use of ordinary words,
hardly noticed by the careless reader.[13] The term is, like all
words of abuse, ill-defined; but its moral overtones can be
clearly heard.

---

[12] Suetonius *Augustus* 86: on *cacozēlia* in general, see H. D. Jocelyn, *Papers of
the Liverpool Latin Seminar* ii (1979), 67–142; W. Görler in *Entretiens Hardt* 25
(1979), 176–211.
[13] 'Donatus' *Vita Vergilii* 44 (Appendix, p. 188).

4

We saw that Cicero, especially in the *Brutus*, wrote about public
men and linked their oratorical performance with their whole
personality in a way which seems characteristically Roman. In
the next generation, the relationship between oratorical skill
and the active life of affairs became less direct and more complex. This was partly the result of the political changes. Despite
Augustus' professions, there was no longer a *res publica* as
Cicero understood the term. It was much less useful to have
rhetorical skills to deploy in the pursuit of political influence.
So, instead of the portraits of advocate-politicians which we
find in the *Brutus*, we have the records of the declaimers set
down in the elder Seneca's collection of *controversiae* and
suasoriae. These were not, in general, people of great public
standing, though some were successful in the courts, and some,
like Ovid, were figures of note in the literary life of the period.
Their fame was due to their skill in the imaginary legal plead-
ings and political counsellings which were the common advanced exercises of a rhetorical education. Though these exercises had already a long history, it was in the second half of the
first century B.C. that they became, as it appears, a major
intellectual interest of an educated public. In the shrewd,
gossipy criticism of the elder Seneca, we have the entrée into
this world. If we are to believe him, it was only accident that
prevented him from coming from Corduba to Rome in time
to hear Cicero, in the last year of his life, 'declaim' with the
consuls of 43 B.C., Hirtius and Pansa. But he heard many
others, remembered it all vividly, and recorded it for the
benefit of his distinguished sons—one a provincial govenor, another the father of the poet Lucan, a third the great literary and
political genius of the Neronian age. Through them and their
contemporaries the traditions of the declaimers can be seen
influencing the whole course of first-century literature. In what
ways, and how profoundly, are matters of debate. Such exercises naturally encouraged certain qualities at the expense of
others: verbal point, memorable *sententiae*, elegant descriptions
and character indications, ingenious interpretations of situations which had been devised for their paradoxical potentiali-

ties. The whole thing was a game played without the constraints of real life, and so without the need for any serious judgment of argument or personalities. Its unreality was often castigated, notably in Petronius' *Satyricon*.[14] Its influence is undoubtedly to be seen in much Latin historical writing of the Empire, and probably in Greek as well. But there is no clear connection, as is often suggested, between this form of exercise and the special features of 'silver' Latin prose style: poetic vocabulary, excessive *variatio*, short rather than long sentences. If the spread of poetic vocabulary into prose has any *rhetorical* origin, it is to be sought rather in the practice of encomium, thesis and ecphrasis, all of which became standard preliminary exercises. *Variatio* in syntax, on the other hand, has its roots in Hellenistic and Roman endeavours to find alternatives to the periodic manner imposed by Isocrates and Cicero, which demanded great control and precision, and could never be quite safe from the risk of dullness. In any case, declamation survived its first-century critics; later examples, especially the Greek ones, are often more dignified and sober, more acceptable perhaps to teacher and parent. And it had, it would seem, some importance for literary theory. It was a form that required a certain degree of imagination, a certain sense of character; and we have seen that at least one rhetor of the imperial age was moved to formulate something like a general theory of literary judgment simply by the practical need to criticise these exercises.[15]

5

Seneca, 'the philosopher', in one of his letters, provides what Eduard Norden regarded as the most important contemporary document on the history of Latin prose in the first century.[16] It is not directed against the declaimers; perhaps he could not be quite as false as that to his father's passion. He takes up a position which is both Augustan and philosophical. Like Augustus, he sees the archaists and the innovators as alike

---

[14] Petronius 1–4 (*ALC* 361); cf. Quint. 2.10 (*ALC* 372); Tac. *Dial.* 35 (*ALC* 454).

[15] Above, Chapter I 4.

[16] *Epist.* 114 (*ALC* 362 ff); E. Norden, *Antike Kunstprosa*, 308.

'corrupters' of natural speech; like Plato, he views style as a reflection of moral character—*talis oratio qualis vita*. His prime example is Maecenas, whose affected composition and involved imagery are supposed to mirror his effeminate manners and disregard for the decencies of public life. From this, Seneca proceeds to generalise: rejection of normality, in language as in dress, buildings and food, is a manifestation of *luxuria*, that disease of affluence which classical moralists tended to make the cause of all evil. This 'luxury' is a social phenomenon, which can affect not only individuals but whole generations. It takes various forms: common to them all is the search for novelty. Archaic patina, poetic colouring, absolute conventionality are all false aims. But a distinction must be drawn between the initiator of a fashion, whose innovation is due to his desire to be conspicuous, and the followers, whose foibles are signs of the style of the age, and not of their own moral weakness. There are thus historical observations in Seneca's account—he illustrates his point from Sallust and his imitators—but the burden of the argument is moral; indeed the whole literary content of the letter serves as a prelude to the sermon on cupidity with which it concludes. The life of letters is of interest primarily as an analogy to the moral life.

Seneca, with his epigrammatic and often hyperbolical style, himself owes a great deal to the declaimers. His plea for simplicity, like his millionaire's plea for a simple life, is often taken for hypocrisy. This is unfair. His profession of writing as a philosopher, with more thought for content than for words, is valid up to a point; he makes no more attempt to avoid the manners of his upbringing and his circle than he does to exploit and develop them. Antitheses and rhythmical clausulae are things it would cost him an effort to avoid. He does not make the effort.

Quintilian, however, regarded Seneca's influence on the young in the same way as Seneca himself regarded the initiators of vicious fashions. The lost *De causis corruptae eloquentiae* perhaps went into this further; we can still read the eloquent attack in which Quintilian's review of useful authors[17] is made to culminate. Quintilian reacts against Seneca's carelessness, and

[17] Quintilian 10.1 (*ALC* 380 ff.). See below, Chapter VIII 4.

against the staccato quality of his style. It is something alien to the classicising, Ciceronian manner which he himself advocated; for, though by no means a strict archaist or anything like an 'Atticist', he looks backwards to the dignity, abundance and correctness of Cicero as the classical model for the Roman orator. In the course of making his point, he reviews the whole of Greek and Latin literature, in so far as it is useful for imitation; heavily dependent on Dionysius for the Greek, he strikes out on his own in Latin. His neat and sometimes suggestive characterisations are often of interest; one or two more extended critiques—especially those of Homer and Menander—illustrate clearly how rhetorical ways of thinking were used in the evaluation of the poets.

Quintilian's ideal was to some extent realised in his pupils. Pliny's *Panegyricus* demonstrates how a modernised Ciceronianism could be the vehicle of an encomium worthy not only of the emperor's dignity but of the consul who speaks it. Pliny also had a theoretical interest, revealed in one or two letters, notably in his reply to the friend who found fault with some of his bolder metaphors.[18] The defence rests on the example of Demosthenes. There are very striking parallels with 'Longinus', both in the general theory—'to be faultless is itself a fault'—and in the instances chosen to exemplify it. A common source is likely, and the close link between Greek and Latin literary taste in all this period is clearly and agreeably illustrated.

6

Quintilian and Pliny were 'classicists', not in necessarily preferring everything old to everything new, but in believing in a certain dignity and purity of taste, to be found in the old masters, and still achievable. They were not—despite Quintilian's strictures on Seneca—seriously engaged in a *querelle des anciens et des modernes*. We see this rather in another work of the late first (or early second) century, Tacitus' *Dialogus de oratoribus*.[19] This elegant and charming book—arguably superior in

---

[18] 9.26 (*ALC* 429).
[19] Ed. A. Gudeman (1894), W. Peterson (1893). See also A. D. Leeman *Orationis Ratio*, 321 ff.; C. D. N. Costa in *Tacitus*, ed. T. A. Dorey (1969), 19–34 and esp. R. Syme, *Tacitus* ii, 670 ff.

vivacity and interest to any Latin dialogue we possess, including Cicero's—reports two debates, supposed to have taken place among a group of friends in A.D. 73, a quarter of a century or more before the probable date of writing. One debate opposes the poet's vocation to the orator's. The other contrasts modern oratory with older forms. The two are connected. Maternus, the orator who chose to turn poet, is also the closing speaker in the second debate, advancing the view that oratory is unnecessary in a well-ordered state; eloquence is 'the nurseling of licence and the companion of sedition', and when the state is perfectly healthy, it will cease to exist. The perspectives of the dialogue are social and educational, rather than stylistic, especially in the more conservative speech of Messalla (24 ff.). It is the 'modernist' Aper who comes nearest to genuine criticism; he gives a hostile review of the Roman 'Atticists', though he qualifies it by some discerning admiration of parts of the work of Calvus and Caelius (21). It has been held that Maternus represents Tacitus' own views: the dialogue is said to be an apology for turning to history, on the ground that free eloquence is now no longer possible. This is unlikely. Tacitus had a distinguished public career, and the writing of history, to the Roman way of thinking, was a proper activity for the statesman, not an escape from the world.

7

It is not until the generation after Pliny and Tacitus that we find strong archaising fashions in Latin prose. This was the age of Gellius, Fronto[20] and Apuleius. All of these studied and admired pre-classical literature; Fronto admired Cato and Ennius, and thought Cicero not scrupulous enough in his choice of words. This movement is a Latin reflection of contemporary Greek 'Atticism'. Greek literature had become even more 'purified' and imitative since the time of Dionysius, and Greek criticism, in the first and second centuries A.D., was largely directed towards the analysis of classical texts with a view to imitation. *Grammaticus* and *rhetor* collaborated in presenting a

---

[20] Leeman, op. cit., 366 ff. Note esp. *Ad M. Caesarem* 4.3.1–7 (extract in Appendix. p. 189).

close study of the diction, figures and argument of the great exemplars—in particular Homer and Demosthenes. So, while Latin criticism was involved in discussions of contemporary trends, its Greek equivalent was much more scholastic and historical. Its perspectives were governed by the prevailing concept of *mimēsis*. It is thus very conservative. For example, Dio Chrysostom's analysis of the *Philoctetes* plays of the three tragedians is a piece of highly conventional writing, with hardly an idea that could not have come from Aristophanes.[21] Again, Plutarch's attack on the 'malice' of Herodotus[22] is purely scholastic—unless it obliquely hints at similar 'malice' in the sensational innuendos of writers like Tacitus. Both here, and in his preference for Menander over Aristophanes, Plutarch takes a moral stand. This is characteristic of him; it appears even more clearly in his ingenious educational advice on 'how young people should read poetry' without doing themselves moral harm.[23]

Yet Plutarch was an appreciative and well-read student of all classical literature. The 'sophists' of the next few generations, though loud in mutual reproach, offer little for our theme save partisan attacks on *cacozēlia*. The defence of 'rhetoric' against 'philosophy', so voluminously conducted by Aristides, is based on no critical principles. The criticisms of personalities and styles which are to be found in Philostratus' *Lives of the Sophists*[24] fall far short of the elder Seneca in vigour and interest. Perhaps the most important non-rhetorical work of the second century is Lucian's treatise on writing history;[25] humorous as it is, it preserves some old doctrine and sets it out with modest common sense.

The professional rhetors did better, especially in the detailed analysis of stylistic qualities. Nothing hitherto attempted rivals the subtle distinctions with which Hermogenes sought to define the various qualities which he supposed to be embodied in

[21] *Oration* 52 (*ALC* 504 ff.). See below, Chapter IX 3.
[22] *Moralia* 854E ff. Extract in *ALC* 534 ff.; trans. by L. Pearson (Loeb), latest critical text by P. A. Hansen (Amsterdam 1979).
[23] Menander and Aristophanes: *Moralia* 853A ff. (*ALC* 531 f.). On reading poetry: *Moralia* 14D ff. (*ALC* 507 ff.).
[24] E.g. 1.7, 1.8, 1.21, 1.22.
[25] Ed. H. Homeyer (1965); extracts in *ALC* 536 ff.

the perfection of Demosthenes and present in varying degrees
in other less balanced and versatile writers. The application of
rhetorical theories of invention to the criticism of poetical texts
also yields interesting material: the authors of the pseudo-
Dionysian treatises *On figured speeches* give a vivid illustration of
a certain style of Homeric study.[26] But, whether the point at
issue is one of style or of argument, the rhetorical critics of this
period, true to their kind, are critics of means and of detail, not
of ends and of overall impression. It is difficult to find in them
any kind of literary theory, even any great diversity of taste. It
is a mistake to elevate technical differences into divergences of
critical direction, as used at one time to be done with the comparatively well-documented controversy between Apollodorus
and Theodorus in the time of Augustus. Theodorus, it was
sometimes said, was a sort of proto-Romantic, in revolt against
the rigorous formalism represented by his opponents. This was
quite false; Apollodorus' view that every speech had to have a
fixed structure of prologue, narrative, argument and epilogue
may have been little more than a forceful, perhaps exaggerated,
way of making the case for rhetoric as an exact 'science'.[27]

The rhetorical criticism of all this period resembles much
modern criticism in deriving from the lecture-room and the
student's 'needs', not from the taste of the adult connoisseur.
There are of course differences: there was no developed sense
of historical period, only a vague contrast of old and new;
practical considerations of rhetoric dominated techniques of
interpretation; and the conservation of traditional moral
values was constantly in the educator's eye—indeed, the large
religious and social changes of late antiquity are hardly visible
in its archaising pagan literature. Nevertheless, analogies are
obvious: the common concept of a general education dominated by the study of inherited texts makes the second-century
scene in some ways uncannily familiar to those brought up in

[26] Below, Chapter VIII 5.
[27] The 'old' view is that of M. Schanz, 'Apollodoreer und Theodoreer',
Hermes 25 (1890). 36 ff. Cf. H. Mutschmann. *Tendenz ... der Schrift vom
Erhabenen* (1912), 53 f.: the debate between T. and A. is 'the same battle
which, in the field of grammar, took place between the supporters of Analogy
and Anomaly, in jurisprudence between "Sabiniani" and "Proculiani"'.

the shadow of the classical education of the English nineteenth century.

8

That these later ages produced a body of critical theory which went beyond the tacit presuppositions of rhetors and grammarians was due to the revival of philosophical interest in questions of literature and aesthetics. We saw that not only Plato and Aristotle, but the Hellenistic schools also, held theories of the nature and function of poetry. We have also had occasion to notice the links between rhetoric and philosophy forged by the rhetors' adoption of the general *thesis* as an exercise for beginners. This introduced a wide public to simple ethical and even scientific argument. In the period we are now considering, 'sophists' and 'philosophers' were often opposed, but there were distinguished examples of people who combined both careers. Plutarch is one; his own talents were perhaps less suited to the strains of sophistic exhibitions than he would have liked, but he evidently regards rhetorical skills as appropriate to the young, to be set aside in favour of philosophy in graver years.[28] Dio Chrysostom is clearly both philosopher and rhetorical virtuoso. Seneca himself exemplifies this all-round culture, reacting against his father, it would seem, by a flight into philosophy.[29] Apuleius combined sophistic and philosophical writing quite happily; Maximus of Tyre blended the two in his pretentious *Dialexeis*.

But the new development in the third and fourth centuries is the appearance of academic persons who were fully professional on both fronts. Longinus, that 'living library and walking Museum',[30] was a pupil of the great philosopher Plotinus. Porphyry and Syrianus, famous Neoplatonist philosophers, also wrote commentaries on standard rhetorical textbooks—Porphyry on his teacher Minucianus, Syrianus on Minucianus' more influential rival Hermogenes.[31] These philosophers are

[28] *Moralia* 959C: a speaker has 'stirred up his rhetoric after a long interval, to please the lads and join in their springtime'.

[29] *Epist. Mor.* 108, 22; *Consolatio ad Helviam* 17.3–4.

[30] So Eunapius *Lives of the philosophers*, p. 352 Wright (=456 Boissonade).

[31] Suda, s.v. Minucianus; J. Bidez, *Vie de Porphyre*, 30, 71*; Syrianus on Hermogenes *De ideis*, ed. H. Rabe (1892).

thus fully conversant with the latest developments in rhetoric, that is to say with all the refinements of *staseis* and *ideai*. Their technique of writing commentaries on rhetorical textbooks resembles their common philosophical activity of commenting at immense length on the basic texts of Plato and Aristotle. At the same time, they were concerned to interpret Plato's attacks on rhetoric and on poetry, and, so far as they could, to justify both their philosophical and their literary culture. Plato's own dialogues also presented a literary problem; and it seems to have been in connection with this that the nature of the 'unity in diversity' which a literary work should possess was formulated and discussed anew.[32] Finally, the Neoplatonists, at least from the time of Porphyry onwards, looked with awe on certain mysterious poetical texts, the theological poems of 'Orpheus' and the Chaldaean Oracles, and regarded these as offering evidence for the truth of their religious and metaphysical views. This may in part have been a response to the success of the Hebrew and Christian scriptures, also mysterious storehouses of hidden meanings; in any case, it had the effect of concentrating attention once again on the principles of allegory and on the problems of poetic truth.

This is the background to the most remarkable work of literary theory which we possess from the later ages of the ancient world: Proclus' commentary (or rather essays) on *Republic* ii, iii, and x. Proclus, the great systematiser of the school, was a pupil of Syrianus, whose views he largely reproduces, though adding much of his own. His system is based on Neoplatonist metaphysics; its object is to establish acceptable principles of allegorical interpretation, which can save Homer from Plato's attack. Perhaps the most interesting concept is that of the correspondence of different types of poetry with the different kinds of life of the soul. There are three of these: one in which the soul is linked with the gods and lives 'not its own life but theirs'; one in which it functions by reason; and one in

[32] Neoplatonist criticism has been less discussed than it should have been: see J. A. Coulter, *The Literary Microcosm*, Leiden 1976; A. D. D. Sheppard, *Studies on the 5th and 6th Essays of Proclus' Commentary on the Republic* (= *Hypomnemata* 61), 1980. F. Walsdorff, *Die antiken Urteile über Platons Stil* (1927), contains some material. Some brief specimens are translated below, Appendix. p. 178.

which it operates with imagination and irrational sensation and is filled with inferior realities. To these correspond three types of poetry: the inspired, the didactic and the imaginative. These were known not only to Plato, but to Homer, who symbolises them by the figures of Demodocus, Phemius and Thamyris.[33]

9

Proclus' elaborate theories of allegory look forward to the Middle Ages. Ambitious allegory was a feature of late antiquity: the search to find truth in the classical texts was immensely stimulated, first, by the example of the Jewish and Christian scriptures; and, somewhat later, by the desire of Christian scholars to find the lessons of their religion prefigured in the best of pagan literature. The re-interpretation of Virgil's Fourth Eclogue as a Messianic prophecy is the best-known instance of this latter development.[34]

But Christian attitudes to literature must remain outside our present scope. Allegory existed in the Hebrew as well as the Hellenic traditions on which Christian culture was grounded. Mediaeval allegory and symbolism has thus no simple origin in pagan antiquity. Pagan literature excited in the pious men of the early Church the same sort of mixture of joy and horror that they, like us, could detect in Plato. Augustine's confession of the magic of Virgil is an articulate expression of what many must have felt.[35] On the other hand, the scriptures themselves were disconcertingly barbarous: their homely and concrete imagery and the unclassical features of the translations both in Greek and in Latin, seemed to produce countless breaches of the simplest rules of decorum. Augustine was among those who faced this problem also. The Christian writer, he held, was

[33] Complete translation (French) of Proclus' Commentary by A. J. Festugière (1970); partial English version in Preminger, 310 ff. See below, Appendix, p. 199.

[34] See the texts collected in A. Kurfess, *Sibyllinische Weissagungen*, 195; 208 ff; 340 ff.

[35] *Confessions* 1.13 ' "One and one make two, two and two make four" was a hateful incantation to me, while the most delightful spectacle of vanity was a wooden horse full of armed men, the burning of Troy, and the shade of Creusa herself.'

always dealing with themes of the highest value, because the Christian message permeated all things in life. There was thus no hierarchy of themes, such as classical rhetorical and poetical theory always demanded. But there was a range of purposes: teaching, admonishing and arousing emotion were all things the preacher had to do, and they naturally required a range of styles.[36] The greatest literature of late antiquity was Christian: Jerome and Augustine have no pagan rivals in Latin, the Cappadocian fathers have much more to convey in their elaborate rhetoric than their master Libanius ever had. The literary attitudes and theories of the Christians are a fascinating and far-reaching theme; they owe much to their pagan environment, but add much also of their own.

[36] St Augustine *De doctrina christiana* iv is an important text: extracts in translation in Benson and Prosser, 273 ff. See E. Auerbach, *Literary Language* . . ., 25 ff.

CHAPTER FIVE

The Poet and his Inspiration

I

OF the main topics of discussion which can be seen running through this long and confusing history, I isolate first a group of themes relating to the poet and the nature of what he does. There is no doubt that poets in antiquity often spoke of themselves as inspired or possessed by a superior power, or that they often claimed (or others claimed for them) the functions and privileges of the teacher. In this and the following chapter, I examine the forms these two sets of claims took, and the problems to which they gave rise.

2

It seems to be the experience of poets in many societies that composition is something not altogether under the control of the conscious mind. It appears to be sudden, unanticipated and automatic. The process is exciting, and it leaves behind as evidence of its reality a sort of 'apport' (if we may use the language of psychical research), a product or *poïēma* which may even seem novel and unfamiliar to the poet himself. His thoughts 'wash over him like a flood' or 'bubble up . . . from the pit of the stomach'.[1] Much the same may be said of other arts, and perhaps of high levels of imaginative activity in spheres outside the arts altogether. But there is something special about the poet: he is, by tradition and in virtue of his

---

[1] These descriptions come (a) from the Eskimo Orpangelik quoted by C. M. Bowra, *Primitive Song*, 44; (b) from A. E. Housman's lecture on the 'Name and Nature of Poetry'.

skill in words, articulate about these things in a way that
painters and musicians are not; and he is often thought of as
akin to the prophet who claims to communicate God's message
to Man.

This inexplicable and mysterious element in poetical composition finds different explanations in different ages and
circumstances. When religious belief is strong, it is of course
regarded as a gift of the gods, vouchsafed to a man of special
merit, or as compensation for a defect like blindness, sometimes
momentary, sometimes the settled talent of a lifetime. When
belief is questioned by rational speculation, the disillusioned
and the sceptical, who no longer believe in prophecy or direct
divine intervention, naturally seek what they regard as more
plausible explanations. They find them in psychology or
physiology—for example, in an excess of hot black bile—and
they treat the claims of the poets with irony and ridicule. It is
easy, after all, to make fun of a notion of inspiration which, as
Hobbes observed, turns the poet into 'a Bagpipe', and the
effects of ecstasy are little different, to the sceptical eye, from
those of some form of intoxication.

Both these attitudes are found in antiquity. The first, in one
form or another, was the regular language of the early poets
from Homer to Pindar; it was reinterpreted, and given new
religious content, by the Neoplatonists a millennium later. The
second, more rationalistic, tendency prevailed in the time of the
Greek enlightenment and in the heyday of Augustan urbanity;
the humour with which Plato treats the rhapsode Ion and the
satirical treatment of Democritus in Horace's *Ars* are characteristic evidences of it.[2]

3

The history of these ideas begins with the programmatic statements of the early poets. The *Odyssey* is especially explicit.
'A god', or more specifically 'the Muse', gives Demodocus the
power to delight with song, and yet also blinds him. Phemius is
autodidaktos, 'self-taught', and a god has 'implanted' (*enephuse*)

---

[2] *Ion, ALC* 39 ff.; *Ars* 295 ff. (*ALC* 287).

many ways of song in his mind.[3] These descriptions denote a permanent gift; Phemius and Demodocus are professional bards, in whom the poet, no doubt, creates a fictional model for himself, with the honour and reward bards ought to have. To judge from the compliment Odysseus pays Demodocus on the accuracy of his account of the war of Troy, the gift is not only one of fine words but of truth and knowledge.[4] This is not surprising. The poet of the *Iliad* appeals to the Muses' knowledge when he invokes their aid at the beginning of the Catalogue of Ships,[5] and it is knowledge of the past and future that the Muses give to Hesiod when they inspire him with song.[6] It is indeed the prologue of the *Theogony* which gives the most explicit statement in early Greek poetry of the poet's divine call. The Muses both 'breathe song into' him, and gather for him—or let him gather[7]—the branch of bay, Apollo's sacred tree, to serve as the wand that symbolises his calling.

Now the poet shares this acquisition of knowledge beyond the ordinary reach of men with the *mantis* or *prophētēs*, the seer or spokesman of the gods. When Pindar[8] bids the Muse 'prophesy' (*manteueo*), and says that he will be her *prophatas*, he is not simply making a comparison between two modes of the relationship of man with the divine. He is saying that they are really the same: 'inspiration' gives knowledge to poet and prophet alike.

The emphasis in these early texts seems in fact to be on knowledge, that is to say on content rather than on form, if this later distinction may be imported. This is not to say that beauty of language, musical skill and the power to move the heart are forgotten. These are all important parts of the poet's activity, but it is primarily his superhuman knowledge which comes to him from without.[9]

[3] *Odyssey* 8.64, 22.342 ff. (For these and other passages, see *ALC* 1 f.).
[4] *Odyssey* 8.485 ff.
[5] *Il.* 2.484 ff.
[6] *Theogony* 21 ff. (*ALC* 2).
[7] The point depends on the reading in 31: *drepsasai* 'having gathered', or *drepsasthai* '(for him) to gather'.
[8] Fr. 137 Bowra (*ALC* 4).
[9] Prof. H. Lloyd-Jones points out to me that post-Homeric epic also is in general more factual than Homer, so that the relative 'non-factuality' of

There is thus a contrast between these poetical statements and the earliest theoretical discussion of these matters that we possess, namely two passages of Democritus[10] which later writers regarded as of special importance. One of these passages reads:

The things a poet writes, on the one hand (*men*), with *enthousiasmos* and holy spirit (*hieron pneuma*) are all very beautiful (*kala*).

The other appears to be from a context dealing with Homer's language:

Homer, having been allotted a nature related to the divine (*phusis theazousa*), fashioned (*etektēnato*) an adornment (*kosmos*) of expressions of all kinds.

In later times, it was supposed that the first of these passages meant that successful poems were only composed by lunatics, and that this justified neglect of art. Thus, Horace talks of Democritus 'excluding sane poets from Helicon', and Cicero offers as a paraphrase the proposition that there can be no good poet without *inflammatio animorum* and a sort of *adflatus furoris*.[11] But the passage does not entail this. Democritus was no atheist. *Enthousiasmos*, 'possession', will have had a more positive meaning for him than mere loss of sanity; he will have regarded it, no doubt, as susceptible of explanation in terms of his atomic physics. Moreover, as Democritus' ethical ideal was one of tranquillity, it is unlikely that it should have associated the production of something he greatly admired with the most extreme kind of mental disturbance. And the point of the passage seems in fact reasonably clear. Possession by the divine power is a necessary, though not a sufficient, condition for 'beautiful' (*kala*) poems. The second part of the sentence—whose existence is implied by *men*, 'on the one hand', in the extant extract—

Homer is perhaps an original development, 'the *teleutaion epigennēma* [Longin. 6] of the epic tradition.'

[10] Fr. 18 and 21 (*ALC* 4, Lanata 258 ff.). W. K. C. Guthrie, *History of Greek Philosophy* ii, 477 n. 2. Date uncertain; Democritus, born *c.* 460 B.C., is said to have lived to be over a hundred.

[11] *De oratore* 2.194; this interpretation is even less cautiously expressed in *De divinatione* 1.80—'no poet can be great *sine furore*'.

presumably said that what is not thus inspired is not 'beautiful'. The point is, what is denoted by *kala*? In itself, the word might apply to any kind of beauty or goodness whose value was self-evident and not conditional on consequences or utility. It seems unlikely that it should apply exclusively to content; indeed it is doubtful whether Democritus, any more than any other serious thinker since Xenophanes, could have regarded the mythical and moral content of the traditional poems as *kala*. Much more likely therefore that he is thinking primarily, if not exclusively, of beauty of form and language.

The second fragment, despite its obscurities, appears to support this view. It seems to state that Homer possesses a permanent endowment of nature (*phusis*), which bears some unspecified relationship to the divine. We have no clear evidence for the meaning of *theazousa*; we do not know, for instance, whether it is merely a high compliment, and possibly ironical at that, as the cognate *theios* ('divine') so often is, or signifies a nature peculiarly receptive of atomic effluences from the gods. Nor can we say for certain whether Homer's possessing such a nature is the cause of his fashioning his *kosmos* of words. If there were not this grammatical ambiguity, the point would be clear: grand language, rather than the truth of what is said, would be seen to be assured by the 'given' element in Homer's make-up. Since we cannot be sure, we must also keep open the possibility that there is here nothing but two distinct statements, one alleging Homer's divine nature, the other stating that he contrived by his skill the *kosmos* of words, the two together amounting to a description of what makes him a great poet. This would amount to the common later idea that the union of *phusis* and *technē*, *ars* and *ingenium*, is what produces perfection. Yet in this case also there would be emphasis on Homer's craftsmanship: he is a *tektōn*, like a builder or carpenter, whose art consists in putting things together into an ordered and beautiful structure.

The difficulties of interpreting Democritus, on the evidence we have, are insuperable. But there is one suggestive point to be added. The only later thinkers to discard the dichotomy of form and content, *lexis* and *legomenon*, which is taken for granted at least from Plato onwards, were certain Epicureans.[12]

[12] See above, Chapter III 3, on Philodemus.

These were in a sense Democritus' disciples. Perhaps his understanding of poetry also was not limited by this prevailing over-simplification.

4

Plato's *Ion*[13] is sometimes supposed to owe some ideas to Democritus. It is an early dialogue, of a pattern common in Plato's shorter Socratic pieces. Socrates is shown, characteristically, as exploding a false claim to knowledge. Here it is the claim of the rhapsode or professional reciter of Homer, who is shown to depend for his 'art' on 'divine dispensation', *theia moira*. If we are looking for reason and understanding, this is nothing to be proud of. Though it is the reciter who is formally on trial, the main points that are made are true also of the poet, who is linked with the rhapsode by the same 'magnetic chain' that links him also with his inspiring god. It would seem that, at this period, there still hung round the rhapsode something of the character of the creative poet, at least the potentiality of original composition. He is certainly a different sort of person, both in capacity and in status, from the fifth-century tragic actor who merely rehearsed the part he has learned, the poet being the teacher (*didaskalos*) of the performers. Though ironical in tone, the *Ion* makes important points. A striking comparison is made between lyric poets and Corybantic or Dionysiac dancers.[14] Socrates here illustrates poetical inspiration by comparing it with a well-known but disconcerting religious phenomenon, that of orgiastic groups, dancing and experiencing hallucinations or conversions when 'possessed'. He asserts the entire dependence, not only of lyric poets, whose music makes an obvious point of contact with the dancers, but of the epic poet too, on the displacement of the normal mind by an invading god:

A poet is a light thing, winged and holy, and cannot compose till god is in him and his wits out, and his mind no longer in him.

The kind of inspiration which Socrates describes in this

[13] *ALC* 39 ff.; Vicaire 33–5; H. Flashar, *Der Dialog Jon*, Berlin (1958).
[14] 534A.

passage is clearly something which comes unpredictably from without and does not produce any skill which can be generally applied or taught to others. The poet, in this argument, is a highly specialised creature, capable of creativity only in one genre, perhaps capable of producing only one good poem in a lifetime, 'like Tynnichus of Chalcis' with his one lovely paean. This makes poetical creativity a trivial incident of the man's life, however beautiful and enduring the *poiēma* it leaves behind.

In the *Phaedrus*, Plato returned to the theme of poetic irrationality, but in a different context and in a half-humorous, half-serious manner which is even more difficult to assess. The tone of the *Phaedrus* is detached, amused, noncommittal and provocative; it ranges over many subjects—love, rhetoric, immortality—and bewilders by its allusiveness and sophistication. One passage in particular takes up the theme of the *Ion*. Poetry is among the blessings that come to us from god-given madness (*mania*). It comes third in order among these good things, after the gifts of inspired prophecy and ritual purification. This 'madness of the Muses' seizes a 'tender and untrodden mind' (*hapalēn kai abaton psuchēn*), excites it to frenzy, and educates posterity by the splendour it gives to the 'deeds of the ancients' that are the subject of poetry. Only poetry written under the influence of this madness comes to successful fruition. Sane and sober *technē* gets nowhere. There is clearly an echo of Democritus here,[15] but the overall meaning of the passage is not wholly clear. The context is decisive for the interpretation, for it shows that the rhetorical need in the speech is to minimise the evils of *mania*. Socrates is engaged in showing that it is foolish to argue that one ought to 'show favour' to a person who does not love one, rather than to one's admitted lover, on the ground that the non-lover is sane and the lover mad. This is established by examples. Inspired prophecy is superior to divination by birds or other omens. Purifications and rituals which seem to render the participants 'mad' are in fact ways by which members of certain families have escaped hereditary evils. This is clearly—whatever its exact reference—

---

[15] The form of the sentence at *Phaedrus* 245A5 (*ALC* 75) closely resembles that of Democritus fr. 18.

a very forced argument. What comes next also should be taken
in the same spirit, as a rhetorical point supporting the paradoxical main proposition, not as something necessarily in accordance with accepted views or with any conviction Plato
might himself defend in a serious moment. The inspired poet
stands to the mere technician as the inspired prophet stands to
the mere augur. But the passage seems to say two things more.
On the one hand, the mind the Muse invades is 'tender and
untrodden'. The poet is innocent and ignorant; he is not
necessarily young (the Greeks did not think of poetry as particularly a young man's occupation), nor necessarily virtuous,
but he is impressionable. And he 'puts in order' or 'adorns'
(*kosmousa*)[16] the deeds of men of old and so educates (*paideuei*)
future generations. It is necessary for the argument that this
beneficial activity should be seen to be the result of *mania*. It is
this that has enabled the poet to do something that improves
the moral quality of life; the *paideia* intended must be the hand-
ing down to posterity of the examples set by great men of old.
In later antiquity, as we shall see, this passage was taken as a
serious Defence of Poetry, linking the notion of inspiration with
that of a didactic purpose. But its original intention may be
wholly ironical; there are, as often in Plato, fantastic features
in the argument, which seem to colour the whole; and the
closing words of the passage suggest that the whole paradox is
to be taken lightly:

He who, without the Muses' madness, comes to the door of poetry, in
the belief that he will be an adequate poet, if you please, by art alone,
vanishes unfulfilled, he and his poetry together, the sane man's
poetry at the hands of the madman's.

In fact, it is clear that Plato had no wish, in this or any other
context, to present a defence of poetry. He believed it to offer
no road to knowledge; and he entertains the idea that the poet's
activity involves an uncontrolled element, akin to ecstasy or in-
sanity, simply because it suits the general position he has
taken up.

Aristotle was different. He held poetry to be a serious thing,

[16] The range covered by *kosmos* and related words includes both 'order' and
'ornament'.

a road to understanding as well as to pleasure, in virtue both of its mimetic character and of its generality. Moreover, his scientific interests, which were fundamental to his whole intellectual approach, lay in medicine and biology and not, like Plato's, in mathematics. And his attitude to religion and myth was more detached. Plato fought a battle for the mind, in which irony and exaggeration were weapons. Aristotle saw the beliefs and practices of the vulgar either as merely silly or as objects of scientific curiosity.

Only once in the *Poetics* is there any allusion to the possibility that the poet may be 'mad'. The passage is famous, and also puzzling.[17] Aristotle is giving advice to the playwright who is at the stage of composing his plot. In doing this, the writer has to imagine the action on the stage: he needs to do this carefully, or disaster may follow—as it did for Carcinus, when he failed to see that the audience would be aware of Amphiaraus leaving the temple. He needs also, apparently, to think out the appropriate gestures and movements (*schēmata*). Genuine emotion, whether distress or anger, is also the most convincing. Given two people of the same natural talent, the one who actually feels anger, or some other emotion, will also 'put it across' better to others. This idea—originally emphasised, it would seem, by teachers of rhetoric—is here applied to the relation between the poet and the characters whose actions and emotions he represents. If he puts himself into the emotional state appropriate to them, he will be able to give them the right words and movements. The passage (as most often translated) continues:

This is why poetry belongs to the naturally talented (*euphuēs*) or the manic (*manikos*); for one of these is malleable (*euplastos*), the other out of his mind (*ekstatikos*).

This rendering implies that Aristotle accepted the insane and uncontrolled as one of two possible poetical temperaments. This is an unwelcome conclusion. Plato, as we have seen, used this notion only to underline the inadequacy of the poets, and Aristotle is concerned to make their defence. Moreover, *manikos* and *ekstatikos* imply total lack of mental control. This is not at

[17] 1455[a] 27 ff.

all what the tragic poet needs. He has to enter into the personality of his characters, and their circumstances, each in turn, as he writes the part. This is something dependent no doubt on much natural ability, and it cannot be learned; but it is also dependent on control and versatility. *Euphuēs* and *euplastos* are right descriptions of what is needed, *manikos* and *ekstatikos* are not. We should conclude that those critics who think—like the sixteenth-century Castelvetro—that Aristotle must have meant 'the naturally talented *rather than* the manic' are essentially right.[18]

A passage of the *Rhetoric*[19] seems to be the only other place where Aristotle himself entertains these ideas. Compound and extravagant words, he says, are appropriate in strong emotion; 'an evil heaven-high' is an expression that a really angry man may be pardoned for making. This is the sort of situation in which a speaker tries to make his audience 'possessed' (*enthousiasai*), and grandiose or jingling phrases come naturally to *enthousiazontes* and so occur also in poetry, for this too is *entheon*, 'an inspired thing'. Not much should be made of this; Aristotle is here using the language of 'enthusiasm' in a weakened sense. It is in any case odd, to modern taste, that his example of 'enthusiastic' language justified by emotion is from the end of Isocrates' *Panegyricus*, a work of polished prose which later taste understandably admired for its artistry and fullness rather than for force or passion. Our surprise, however, may be due to a failure of historical imagination: the balances and noble rhythms of Gorgianic and Isocratean prose may well have had a more powerful incantatory effect on contemporaries than we can see.

So far as the interpretation of Aristotle is concerned, the later Peripatetic text found in *Problems* 30.1 is of no relevance; but it has an importance of its own.[20] It lists the possessors of excessive and excessively hot 'black bile' as 'manic (*manikoi*), naturally talented (*euphueis*), amorous (*erōtikoi*) and easily moved to anger and desire; some also talkative'. There is no

---

[18] This view is that taken by Miss Hubbard in *ALC* 113 f.

[19] 1408[b] 11 ff.

[20] *Problems* 954[a] 32 ff. This text has been much discussed: see, e.g. R. Klibansky *et al.*, *Saturn and Melancholy*, 18 ff.

reason to think that the author is thinking particularly of
poetry; the only poet mentioned in the context is one Marakos
of Syracuse of whom we are told that he was actually a better
poet 'when he was out of his mind'. The implication is that this
was unusual; poets are not like prophets, who are 'out of their
minds' when they are foretelling the future, but talented persons
whose excess of black bile is normally at least in a 'mean state'
in respect of temperature. A great poet, like a great philosopher,
is an exceptional being; but his powers are not out of his control.

5

Philosophical attempts to give an account of the unexplained
element in poetic creativity were thus often rationalistic; they
invoked physiological or physical theories. But the poets of
course continued, throughout Hellenistic and Roman times,
to repeat their claims to divine inspiration. It was understood
that this was now largely convention. The battle with the
philosophers was over; poets' *sophia* could no longer pretend to
knowledge, and didactic poetry, in so far as it was instructive at
all in intention, was essentially a versification of knowledge ob-
tained from others. There remained the contrast between
poetry and the literature of real life, the central form of which
was oratory: poets' fantasies, their *licentia* (*exousia*) in subject
and in language and their special instinctive scholarship still
set them apart, and made the continuing use of the old symbolism still attractive and meaningful. Moreover, the life of the
poet could be seen as exempt from political troubles, a sort of
secessus akin to the philosopher's, but with less extravagant
claims.[21]

The imagery inherited from Hesiod and Pindar survived
long, and was much exploited. Callimachus meets the Muses,
Ennius dreams of Homer, poets drink of holy fountains and
wander in mountains and woods. Priest and prophet, the *vates*
is a man apart. It is indeed convention; but the human experience, we must suppose, continued. Poets went on reflecting
in solitude and could not explain their processes. George
Moore's advice, to 'dine in and often alone', if you want the

[21] So Maternus in Tacitus' *Dialogus* 11–13 (*ALC* 438 ff.).

Muse to visit you, would have rung true to Virgil or Horace.

It is interesting that the symbolism comes now to be used in the service of new literary ideals. It had already served a polemical purpose for Pindar, who derogates opponents by representing them as mere 'learners', who cannot prevail against the 'bird of Zeus'.[22] For Callimachus and his Roman imitator it served another end. Instead of appealing to the god for knowledge or for the gift of fine words, Callimachus makes Apollo counsel him to avoid magniloquence and the common path: the gods like a fat beast for sacrifice, but a fine-spun poem.[23]

Horace is perhaps the most instructive of the Hellenistic and Roman poets in whom to study the new uses of these symbols. He is much given to them. As a lyric poet, he dwells far from the common herd, Nymphs and Satyrs dance around him in the woods. Instead of dying, he will wing his way to heaven, transformed into a bird. Calliope comes down to visit him; he wanders in holy groves, and his whole life is under the protection of the Muses.[24] Yet Horace is also a literary critic, and on this level of discourse he treats the idea of inspiration with severe irony, if not contempt. It is he who most explicitly interprets Democritus as advocating madness as a qualification for poets. When he is speaking seriously, Horace evidently regards the 'given element' in composition—whether in poetry or in rhetoric—as *ingenium*, a concept not unlike Aristotle's *euphuia*. Good poetry in his view comes from the combination of this quality—it is essentially inventiveness—with a mastery of the art (*ars*, i.e. *technē*). But while native poetic ability, in Horace's criticism, is stripped of the trappings of inspiration and seen as a faculty of the reasoning mind, its partner, art, is seen as something more than mechanical skill in words, versification or obedience to genre-rules. It involves a certain degree of ethical knowledge and certain positive moral attitudes, notably the rejection of greed and shortsighted selfishness:

Once this rust and care for cash has tainted the soul, can we hope for poems to be written that deserve preserving in cedar oil and keeping safe in smooth cypress?[25]

[22] *Olympians* 2.88.
[23] See below, Appendix, p. 181.
[24] *Odes* 1.1; 2.19; 2.20; 3.4.
[25] *Ars poetica* 330 ff. (*ALC* 288).

This rationalising and moralising transformation of the traditional symbols of 'inspiration' is not confined to poets. It may be found, for example, in 'Longinus', though at first sight things look a little different. The frequency with which the language of *enthousiasmos* is used in *On sublimity* has often been noticed. It seems to suit the author's powerful, evocative and stimulating way of talking about literature. Some scholars have therefore seen in him an exponent of the position supposed to have been that of Democritus, that all good poetry depends on the impulse from without.[26] But this is a misunderstanding. For one thing, it is of course wrong to think of 'Longinus' as primarily concerned with poetry; his subject is emotionally persuasive rhetoric, and what he says about the poets is by way of illustration. Now we have already seen that it was common rhetorical teaching—adapted to the poet's situation by Aristotle—that the best way to move an audience is to enter into the appropriate emotion yourself and 'really feel it'. The feeling of the audience is the end, the feeling of the orator the means. Thus Plato ironically compliments the epideictic orators of the day by making Socrates say that, after hearing them, he is in a daze, and loses count of where he is for two or three days on end, fancying he may be in the Isles of the Blest.[27] Dionysius alleges similarly (and perhaps with the *Menexenus* and *Ion* in mind) that he feels 'possessed' when reading Demosthenes, and imagines himself as in the same state of mind as initiates in the orgiastic rites of the Great Mother or the Corybantes.[28] Plato was making fun; Dionysius, it would seem, is seriously describing the state of mind of a reader who responds to the emotive effects of classical oratory. In both, the language of *enthousiasmos* is used not of the writer, but of the hearer or reader to whom the speaker's passion has been transmitted. This is also the principal way in which this language is used in 'Longinus'.[29] The speaker must feel a genuine emotion, but it must be such that the audience will share it. It is this emotion which 'inspires'

[26] So F. Wehrli, in an important essay, 'Der erhabene und der schlichte Stil', *Phyllobolia für P. von der Mühll*, 1946, 9–34 (= *Theoria und Humanitas*, 1972, 97–120).

[27] *Menexenus* 235A-C.

[28] *Demosthenes* 22.

[29] See 1.4; 3.2; 8.1; 8.4; 15.1; 38.4.

speech. 'Longinus' uses the full gamut of the traditional vocabulary of inspiration and prophecy: *mania, pneuma, enthousiasmos*
and *ekstasis* are characteristic terms. He even uses it in an
additional and perhaps novel way, to describe the relation between a writer and his classical model.[30] So we have two stages:
the excitation of the writer's mind by emotion, and the consequent excitation of the reader's, which is the purpose of the
whole procedure.

But there is a complication. 'Longinus' has a further expectation: he requires that the 'emotion' shall be not only vehement
but of a certain moral quality. In fact emotion in itself, despite
his polemical insistence on it as an element wrongly overlooked
by his opponent Caecilius, is not in his view absolutely essential
to 'sublimity', which can actually exist without it; indeed some
emotions, notably pity and fear, are 'low', and so not related
to 'sublimity' at all.[31] This is why the personality of the writer
is important. He cannot be expected either to think grand
thoughts or to generate and excite grand emotions if he is
ravaged by desire for gain or money, or deaf to the calls of
honour and posthumous fame. The right attitude can to some
extent be developed by training and habit, but only on the
basis of a certain natural endowment.

No one would claim that 'Longinus' is clear of ambiguity or
confusion. But it is evident enough that the grandeur he is
trying to teach is conceived as the product of native endowment
shaped by a moral education which influences both intellect
and feeling; it is supposed to sweep away all petty thoughts, fix
the mind on large and noble issues, and encourage all sorts of
generous and powerful emotional reactions. So far as the interpretation of the 'given element' is concerned, this is not so very
different from Horace. Neither the 'given' nor the 'acquired' is
enough in itself, but perfection comes from their combination.
Both Horace's poet and 'Longinus' ' orator, if they are to have
the effect on their audiences which they desire, have to have
certain qualities of character. They have to be 'good' men, not
disabled by vice or meanness; and they have then to subject
their 'nature' to the demands of an 'art' which is far from being
a mere verbal technique. Moreover, neither the basic ability

[30] See 13.   [31] 8.2.

nor the acquired technique is thought of as something which might exist in a personality otherwise unbalanced, eccentric or inadequate. The mad poet and the deranged orator are simply failures.

CHAPTER SIX

The Poet as Teacher

1

THERE are obvious links between the notion of a poet's inspiration and that of his didactic or social function. We saw that in early times the value of the inspiration was in fact believed to lie in the poet's access to knowledge which the gods were willing to impart to mankind. We saw also that, in the moralising synthesis to be observed in Horace and 'Longinus', the poet's 'nature' is chiefly valuable as a guarantee of the efficacy and permanence of his works. No ancient account of inspiration or 'given element' makes the expression of the poet's individuality the important thing. The *poiēma* 'left behind' by the process of *poiēsis* is not the image of a mind, but a statement about the external world which will be of use to the rest of us, because it is so constructed as to impress or excite our minds.

2

But in what way is the statement meant to be of use?

When Aristophanes,[1] at the end of the fifth century, makes Aeschylus say that children have teachers to instruct them, while adults have poets, he is formulating a general idea which would have been widely accepted not only among his own audience but by many people at most periods throughout Greco-Roman antiquity: namely, that it is the poet's business to give instruction of some kind—whether in factual knowledge or skill, or simply in the art of living. But the contrast between children and adults would not have been so universally obvious. Not long after Aristophanes' time, in the course of the fourth

[1] *Frogs* 1055.

century, a secondary education in rhetoric and philosophy became common; and the pattern in the later ages of antiquity
was very much to relegate the teaching of poetry to the earlier
stages. Far from being the staple educational medium of the
adult, it became the staple fare of the child.[2] Accordingly, from
Plato onwards, philosophers concentrated their attention on
the effect of poetical fable on the young and impressionable.
Plato of course, at least in the *Republic*, was dealing with very
special children, the future guardians, who have to be brought
up to be superior to ordinary mankind. In this context, the
morals of the actual audiences of real life—including women,
children and slaves—are of no great concern. Plutarch's treatise
On listening to poets[3] presents a more normal and realistic picture.
He envisages young people not yet ready for philosophy but
capable of accepting general ideas which may prepare them
for it; due guidance and selection in reading poetry are therefore what is needed.

In modern times, it is hardly thought to be the business of
literary criticism at all to engage in this kind of exegesis, or to
draw overt moral lessons from the fictitious events of poetry.
But implicit in what Plato says is the proposition commonly expressed by saying that the poet should be 'committed' to the
aims of the 'society' in which he lives—or else be exiled from it.
Similarly, what Plutarch says implies the related assumption
that the study of literature is justified only as a part of moral
education. Both these views have been much in twentieth-
century minds.

3

But of course, it was by no means the universal view in antiquity,
any more than it is today, that poetry should be 'useful'.
There were always those who held that its effect was adequately
described as pleasure, and that this indeed was quite obviously
its aim. 'Poets compose for pleasure, not for truth,' says a fifth-

[2] *Strabo* 1.2.8 (*ALC* 304) appears conscious of this change. He observes that
'the ancients' believed that all ages could be trained through poetry. History
and philosophy appeared later. It was still true, in his view, that poetry had
a use for many adults, because philosophy was not accessible to them.
[3] Extracts in *ALC* 507 ff.

century text of sophistic origin.[4] Now whenever such a general
statement is made, on either side, it has to be seen as part of a
polemic. Unless poets claimed truth, this particular sentence
would not be worth uttering; and what makes the contrary
worth saying is the belief, often enough expressed, that poetry
is a delusion and a source of moral harm. 'Pleasure' and
'utility' or 'truthfulness' thus play the same sort of part in
attempts to define the purpose of poetry as 'art' and 'endowment' do in attempts to describe the capacity which produces it.
And just as *ars* and *ingenium* could be said to 'combine' to produce the perfect realisation of poetry, so a combination of
'pleasure' and 'utility' could be regarded as the wise poet's aim:
'he who combines the useful with the pleasant wins every vote.'[5]
This compromise, however, settles nothing. It is true enough in
the literal sense: it is often possible to put in something to please
various sections of the audience, including those who want solid
instruction and not just entertainment. But unless some attempt is made to describe the relationship of the two aims to
each other, no useful theoretical point is made. The idea that
the 'use' comes from the content and the 'pleasure' from the
sound of the words is one such attempt; it seems to have been
what the Hellenistic theorist Neoptolemus said of Homer.[6] But
it is of little avail, since it is clear that we must judge the invention of a poem by qualities of fancy, coherence and probability
which have nothing to do with its moral use. Better perhaps to
say that the intended aim is the promotion of virtue, and the
charm comes 'by accident';[7] this at least makes your priorities
clear.

4

The 'didacticist' position is perhaps always the product of a
situation in which poetry appears to need defence. In early
Greece, this happened when the myths which were the subject-
matter of epic came to appear improbable or morally reprehen-

[4] *Dissoi logoi* (90 Diels-Kranz) 2, 18 and 3, 17: Lanata 224.
[5] Horace, *Ars poetica* 341.
[6] *Philodemos über die Gedichte: Fünftes Buch*, ed. C. Jensen (1923), 33.
[7] So Aristides Quintilianus 2.6.

sible. Perhaps an art-form which is widely accepted, even if it is disliked by some and regarded as a vehicle of corruption, does not attract defences of this kind. Attacks on the moral danger of television, after all, are commonplace; but we have not yet got to the stage of saying that it *ought* to be instructive, as Plato said poets *ought* to teach, or indeed of allegorising the myths which it propagates. The illusion is still too strong. In the fifth and fourth centuries, poetry was already being allegorised, while rhetoric, the newer art, could only be attacked. In fact, the practice of relating poetry to other human activities and judging it by criteria applicable to actions began in Greece at an early stage. It is not indeed to be found in Homer; the statements about poetry in the *Odyssey* make no apology for the art. But it may well be present in Hesiod. At least, it is often held, as we have seen,[8] that there is a criticism of heroic epic in the words put into the mouth of the Muses in the *Theogony*: 'we know how to tell many lies that resemble the truth, but we also know how to tell truth when we wish.' Even if this interpretation is wrong, Hesiodic poetry is obviously much more factual in tone than Homeric, and thus appears more primitive; *Works and days* indeed is openly didactic in purpose, a Greek epic version of the literature of advice that had long been current in the older civilisations to the east of the Mediterranean world. In later legend, Homer and Hesiod were supposed to have competed at the funeral games of King Amphidamas of Chalcis. The assembled populace wanted the crown given to Homer, but the King who presided, the successor of Amphidamas, preferred Hesiod, because he encouraged agriculture and peace instead of war and slaughter. This significant story can be traced back at least to the fourth century B.C., to the sophist Alcidamas; it became classical.[9]

The first person on record to condemn the epic explicitly on moral grounds was, as we saw, Xenophanes. In his eyes, neither Homer nor Hesiod can be commended. Both attributed theft, adultery and deceit to the gods. They were proof that

[8] Cf. above, Chapter II 1.

[9] Lanata 122 (extract); O. C. T. Homer 5.227 ff. (complete text of *Certamen*); see esp. G. S. Kirk *CQ* 44 (1950) 149 ff; E. R. Dodds (*CQ* 2 (1952) 187 f.; M. L. West *CQ* 17 (1967) 433 f. and (for later influence on rhetorical writers) Themistius *Orat.* 30, with Downey and Norman's notes.

men did indeed make their gods in their own image. Who then
is the praiseworthy poet? Apparently, he whose after-dinner
song shows concern for virtue and the gods, and is not about
battles of Titans, Giants and Centaurs, nor about quarrels
(*stasias*) with no good in them.[10] Whether this last phrase
alludes to political lyricists like Alcaeus or, as seems more
likely, to the strife and wrath that are the subject of the *Iliad*, it
is clear that Xenophanes is recommending a style of poetry that
uses the social opportunities of performance for moral education.

So it was familiar doctrine by the fifth century that the
traditional subjects of poetry were immoral. Familiar too was
the related observation that poets were bound to be bad witnesses to fact, because they aimed to entertain. Herodotus can
say that Homer knew the story that Helen went to Egypt and
not to Troy, but suppressed it in his main narrative because it
was not so 'seemly' (*euprepes*) for epic.[11] It was, Herodotus believed, the true version of what happened, because if Helen had
really been at Troy the Trojans would surely have surrendered
her long before enduring a ten-year siege. But what exactly is
meant by saying this was not *euprepes* for epic? The notion of
'seemliness' is both moral and aesthetic.[12] When Herodotus explains elsewhere that a certain Egyptian religious myth is not
euprepes for him to tell, he seems to mean that it is a secret he
ought not to reveal.[13] But in the passage we are considering, the
force of the word seems mainly aesthetic: if Helen had not gone
to Troy, the war and all its sacrifices would have been about
nothing, and so no fit theme for heroic poetry.

5

These negative evaluations, moral and factual, evoked appro-

[10] Xenophanes, B2 Diels-Kranz. C. M. Bowra, *CP* 33 (1938), 353 ff.

[11] Herodotus 2.116. This theme also had a long history: cf. Dio Chrysostom
Or. 11 (*Troiana*).

[12] *To prepon* (*decorum*) is an extremely important concept both in ethics and
in criticism; a classic discussion is M. Pohlenz, '*To prepon*', *NAG* 1933 (*Kleine
Schriften* i, 100–39).

[13] 2.47. The myth in question is a characteristic 'secret doctrine', the reason
why pigs are sacrificed only to the Moon and to Dionysus on a certain occasion:
cf. Plutarch, *Isis and Osiris* 8 (*Mor.* 354A).

priate defences, the earliest attempts to justify the poetic inheritance. One such defence was to recite the civilising achievements of poets, in cult, law, and the arts of life: we saw this in Aristophanes and in Horace.[14] Another—to which we shall turn later—was to allegorise the objectionable stories and reveal their supposed inner meaning.

Plato knew and rejected both these lines of defence. His discussion of poetry in the *Republic* falls into two parts: Books II and III, where the outline of his recommendations is given; and Book X, apparently a later appendix, which explains the psychological and epistemological principles involved, in the light of the theories concerning the soul and the forms which are expounded in the central books of the dialogue.

In Books II and III he illustrates the kinds of topic which are unsuitable, being both untrue to the real nature of the gods and unconducive to virtue. Since God is assumed to be good and unchanging, stories in which divine action appears to be weak or ill-intentioned must be false. But Plato does not condemn these myths solely because they are false (378A); the decisive point against them is the moral one, for he believes they ought not to be disseminated even if they were true. Nor is it any use, in his view, using the defence of allegory (*huponoia*, 378E), because 'the young' cannot recognise this when they hear it. In this of course the preoccupation with the future 'guardians' is evident; but Plato's dislike of allegory is to be seen elsewhere also.[15] He rarely uses it himself, and then with irony;[16] his own myths have resonances and deeper significances, but not a 'hidden sense'. The construction of myths, according to the *Republic*, must be governed by certain guide-lines (*tupoi*), and these in turn are determined by the moral ideal appropriate to the guardians; concord, courage and control of emotion are the essential virtues. Thus nothing frightening about Hades is permissible, and no lamentations. Now Homeric heroes weep freely, and grief for the dead takes its course of due indulgence. So it does in most Greek communities of all periods. Plato is imposing a special, perhaps Spartan, ideal on his imagined

---

[14] Above, Chapter II 3.
[15] *Phaedrus* 229c ff.
[16] As at *Gorgias* 492.

élite. Theoretical support for these proposals is given by the doctrine of *mimēsis*, that is, the account Plato gives of the relationship between the real world and its counterfeit in literature and art. Discussion of this belongs to our next chapter; for the moment, it is enough to observe that Plato is convinced that poetry does affect our emotions, and that exposure to emotional circumstances represented on the stage or in fiction is likely to intensify our natural tendencies and weaknesses. Indeed, the better the poetry, the worse the moral effect.

6

This tradition had a long history, but was none the less sometimes an embarrassment to later admirers of Plato, such as Plutarch. In his treatise *On listening to the poets*,[17] Plutarch uses many of the examples given in the *Republic*; but his object is not to dissuade the young from reading classical poetry, but only to show how it may be read without incurring moral danger. He therefore draws an argument from the consideration that poetry is not concerned with truth but necessarily involves fiction, and urges that we can admire the skill of the imitation even when we feel disgust at the thing represented. He draws two other kinds of knowledge into the art of judgment: comprehension of the context and the person of the speaker; and historical understanding of the peculiarities of the poet's language and circumstances. All this is in the service of a somewhat prudish respectability, but Plutarch's enterprise is none the less of interest: it probably represents fairly accurately much educational thinking of the Roman period, and it entails considerable scholarly sophistication. In the preface to his life of Pericles, however, Plutarch makes a further point. It is to the effect that virtue in itself contains a tendency to incite us to emulate it. Hence the presentation of virtuous characters—such as most of those whose lives Plutarch elected to write— possessed an educational effectiveness derived from the subject itself.

Plato and his followers thus recognised the educational force of poetry. They believed that the praise and blame expressed

[17] See above, Chapter IV 7.

by the poets—and praise and blame were the essence of their work—were likely to be decisive in determining the moral attitudes of their readers. Poetry must therefore be controlled. If it was impossible to prevent poets from writing undesirable things, the dissemination of them must be checked; and if that in turn proved impossible, wise guidance to the reader might at least lead him to a harmless interpretation.

7

Aristotle's position on these issues is much more complex. The *Poetics* is concerned with the special excellence of poetry, what we should call its aesthetic qualities. Poetical correctness (*orthotēs*) is, he says explicitly, distinct from that of ethics or other skills.[18] The criterion of unity, one of the main grounds on which he prefers tragedy to epic, is a wholly 'aesthetic' one, with no significant moral overtones.[19] It is true that in distinguishing comedy from tragedy he rests on a distinction of good and bad not only in the subject, but in the personality of the poet.[20] This value-difference, however, ought not to imply a difference of intrinsic value between the two genres themselves. Aristotle ought consistently to hold that a comedy which achieves its end and 'proper pleasure' possesses as much poetical *orthotēs* as a similarly effective tragedy. We do not have his account of comedy, and so cannot say whether he actually did say this. But it would not be inconsistent with the historical speculations of *Poetics* 2. Comedy involves 'inferior' personalities, both as subjects and as composers. This does not affect the correctness or otherwise of any specific exercise of the comic poet's art. Yet when we read the rest of the *Poetics*, further complications appear. It would appear from chapter 15[21] that the artistic principle of unity justifies the imitation of wickedness if it is necessary for the overall effect of the play; in other words, poetical *orthotēs* here overrides moral. The requirement that characters shall be 'good' then applies to tragedy because

[18] 1460^b 23.
[19] 1462^b 3.
[20] 1448^a 16, 1448^b 25 ff., 1449^a 32.
[21] 1454^a 16 ff.

it is defined as having 'people better than ourselves' for its subject, not because it is expected of it that it shall afford lessons or
exemplars for our own moral behaviour. On the other hand,
Aristotle seems to have thought that the relation between the
poet and his audience was not only distinct from that of persuader to persuaded[22] but also from the relation of entertainer
to entertained. This is because he too regarded it as involving an
element of instruction, the transference not of attitudes and
opinions conducive to the speaker's interest, but of knowledge
and understanding valid in itself. It was Aristotle's fundamental
conviction that 'all men desire to understand'; poetic *mimēsis*,
which was concerned with generalities, was an aid to this end,
and so was 'more serious and philosophical' than the record of
individual facts which is called *historia*.[23] In other words, a fictional narrative of the right kind has a wider application than
a factual one, and is a more economical and at the same time
more penetrating way of helping us to understand the world
and the people in it.[24] There seems to be for Aristotle—as for
Plato—sharp opposition between 'pleasure' and 'utility' where
poetry is concerned; but whereas Plato surmounts the antithesis by identifying the right pleasure with that felt by the
mature and sober men of sense, Aristotle does so by arguing
that the pleasure of poetry includes that of learning. Poetry
thus does a service for the life of contemplation, rather than for
the life of action; and for Aristotle this was the higher manifestation of human potentiality. If poetry has a utility on the
practical level, whether technical or moral, this must then be
incidental. A puzzle does indeed remain. The effect of tragedy
in 'producing a *katharsis* of emotions' like pity and fear forms

[22] I.e. it is distinct from the orator's relation to his hearers; Aristotle regarded rhetoric as an art which could be used for various ends, good or bad,
and concerned himself, in the *Rhetoric*, solely with the means it employed,
seen as an autonomous system of principles and devices.

[23] 1451^b 6.

[24] Aristotle of course regarded the plots of tragedies as based on historical
events, and it would be unfair to him to say that he would exclude contemporary or near contemporary history as a possible theme for poetry. Thus the
tradition represented by the statement that 'Lucan is not reckoned as a poet
because he is seen to have composed histories, not a poem' (Isidore *Etymologiae* 8.7.10) is contrary to Aristotle's standpoint.

part of the definition of tragedy,[25] and one would think that the effect meant here is in some sense a moral one; but the notorious difficulties of this abrupt and oracular allusion to *katharsis* make it difficult to be sure what Aristotle meant and what relation the doctrine bears to his position on the issue we are here considering.

This position is indeed not easy to define. Certainly, Aristotle rejects any view which exposes the poet, *qua* poet, to criticism on moral grounds. He regards such criticism as beside the point. The poet's art lies elsewhere; any lessons we learn from him are incidental to it. Yet the subject of tragedy and epic— and Aristotle hardly considers anything else—is nothing but the sphere of human action, and this involves a moral differentiation both of the acts and of the agents. Moreover, Aristotle would not dissent from the traditional view of poets as purveyors of praise and blame, and thus inevitably of good and bad examples. But he attaches most importance, it would seem, to the consideration that the poet generalises and idealises, this process tending then to enlighten the understanding of the mature and balanced reader. It is as though he is seeking a justification of poetry as a worthwhile study not for ordinary people but for those capable of 'philosophical' enlightenment. This would be a direct response to Plato's *Republic*, and a defence (far more subtle than Plutarch's) of the study of poetry by the people who matter most.

8

Aristotle's doctrine on the relationship of poetry to truth was thus complex and difficult. Like much else in the *Poetics*, it was imperfectly understood in the Hellenistic age. Horace, who absorbed indirectly much Aristotelian doctrine, talks on the one hand of the need for the *doctus imitator* to understand *mores* and moral principles,[26] in order that he may be able to fashion consistent and appropriate representations of character, and on the other hand of the past services of poetry in civilising mankind.[27]

---

[25] 1449^b 27.
[26] *Ars poetica* 309 ff. (*ALC* 288).
[27] Ibid. 391 ff. (*ALC* 290).

But he does not make the characteristically intellectualising connection between the two. So the idea entertained by Aristotle, that poetry, in virtue of its imitative character, might have a special relationship with the rest of human life, distinct from and superior to that of rhetoric, was not pursued. On the contrary: the similarity which Theophrastus formulated[28] between poetry and oratory, namely that both were directed not 'at the facts' but 'at the audience', and so were not primarily concerned with truth, weighed much more heavily in the minds of all Aristotle's successors than any notion of their fundamental distinctness. The problem of the commitment of poetry to practical issues could thus only be discussed in terms which had no reference to this; this meant a simpler debate, on grounds familiar already in pre-Aristotelian thinking.

We find in fact two theories, crudely opposed to each other. On the one hand there were those who accepted the old view that the aim of poetry was simply 'pleasure', and identified this pleasure with 'beguilement' (*psuchagōgia*). This was the view of the principal Alexandrian scholars and poets: Callimachus and Eratosthenes both held it, so did Agatharchides of Cnidos,[29] who said clearly that it was wrong to blame poets for their myths and improbabilities because they aim not at truth but at beguilement. This view resembles Aristotle's position in asserting the autonomy of poetry and the impropriety of judging it on criteria not suitable to it. But it is really quite different. These writers (and especially Callimachus) were mainly concerned with poetical technique—metre and the placing of words, vocabulary and metaphor. The goodness of a poem rested on this, not on choice of subject. Of the philosophical schools, it was the Epicureans who came nearest to affording a theoretical basis for this attitude, the Stoics who most clearly opposed it.

Epicurus' hostility to poetry as a vehicle of instruction was so sharp that it is puzzling to find Lucretius actually setting out his doctrines in verse.[30] On the other hand, later Epicureans at

---

[28] Cf. above, Chapter I, n. 4. Appendix, p. 203.

[29] Cf. above, Chapter III, n. 15.

[30] The 'paradox' of Lucretius is discussed, e.g., by P. H. Schrijvers, *Horror ac Divina Voluptas* (1970), esp. 325 ff.

least were interested in analysing the mechanism by which poetry effected its beguilement, however trivial its object was. To the Stoics, at the other extreme, a poem was, of course, a verbal construct, giving charm and pleasure—but it was also 'significant' of the world of gods and men. If it is a good poem, it contributes to the good life. The general view of the Stoics may be seen in Strabo's polemic against Eratosthenes.[31] They held that Homer was (and intended to be) educative, and on more than one level. The poems were of use to farmers and geographers, as well as to mankind in general in a moral sense. The poet's skills were thus ancillary to educational needs. Cleanthes and (in a sense) Aratus and Manilius consciously used it to promulgate Stoic views of the universe. This attitude has affinities, of course, with Plato. But instead of following Plato in confining the legitimate uses of poetry to hymns and encomia, the Stoics fell in with the older tradition of allegorical interpretation. This was in accord with their similar conservative attitude to myth and cult; and it is largely through the Stoics that allegory became so very important in Hellenistic, Roman and indeed Christian times.

Some discussion of allegory is thus a natural pendant to the topics we have been considering.

9

Indeed, allegory has a relevance to the topics both of this chapter and of the preceding. Not only is it a way of investing the offensive or the trivial with acceptable and important meaning, but the fundamental idea that there are hidden significances in the poet's words accords well with the doctrine of divine inspiration. If God speaks through the poet's mouth, he may be expected to do so in oracular terms, unintelligible without a skilled interpreter. The Greeks were used to riddling oracles.

The long and complex history of ancient allegorical interpretation naturally lies beyond our theme.[32] It has to do with the history of religion and ethics more than with that of literary

[31] See above, Chapter I, n. 31.
[32] Besides Buffière, see J. Pépin, *Mythe et allégorie* (1958); *OCD*, s.v. Allegory

criticism. Nor is the nature of the supposed 'hidden knowledge' our concern: it might be scientific, moral, political or, in the Neoplatonists, metaphysical. The implications for criticism, it seems to me, are three:

(i) The first is to be seen in the argument for the plausibility of the method expounded in the early chapters of 'Heraclitus'.[33] This is based on the occurrence in the poets of passages that are obviously 'allegorical'. 'Heraclitus' finds these in the early lyricists: Archilochus and Alcaeus use images of storm and seafaring to denote political upheaval and danger. He finds them also in Homer himself, in the words of Odysseus about the wastefulness of war:

Bronze throws a lot of straw down on the ground, but the harvest is scanty . . .[34]

This last is also the grammarians' stock example of the trope *allegoria*.[35] It is on the way to being what we should call an allegory, but not yet an extended narrative. 'Heraclitus' in fact does not distinguish very clearly between different kinds of figurative discourse: his account includes not only allegories of the gods and the stories about them—Apollo is the sun, Athena wisdom, the binding of Hera the creation of the world—but the personification of Prayers (*Litai*) as lame, wrinkled old women, who cast down their eyes.[36] He has no theory to distinguish these obviously different things. What is important is that he argues from acknowledged imagery to the likelihood that there is more to be uncovered. The basis of the method is thus extrapolation from a (supposedly) known instance.

(ii) 'Heraclitus' assumes that what he is uncovering is actually the intention of the author. This seems to be the general as-

---

(J. Tate); *Princeton Encyclopaedia of Poetry and Poetics*, s.v. Allegory (N. Frye); C. S. Lewis, *The Allegory of Love* (1936); A. Fletcher, *Allegory* (1964).

[33] See Appendix, p. 190. F. Buffière's Budé edition of 'Heraclitus' (1962) is the most convenient.

[34] *Il.* 19.222.

[35] So in Tryphon (3.191 f. Spengel).

[36] *Il.* 9.502 ff. 'Heraclitus' (37) comments: 'Homer is a painter of human emotions, as it were, dressing up our feelings with the names of gods.'

sumption throughout antiquity. Homer was thought to have been fully conscious of all the moral and scientific facts that were read into him. In the last age of the ancient world, the same was said also of Virgil: Fulgentius[37] makes the poet himself reveal his hidden meanings, though emphasising that he was a pagan to whom the Christian revelation had not been vouchsafed. Without this assumption, the defensive object of allegory —which had developed largely as a response to attacks on immorality in myth and epic—could never have been attained. The only area of doubt seems to have been whether Homer's intention included the intention to teach: perhaps, it was suggested, he put things this way just for poetical effectiveness. Even Philodemus, who denied that poetry had a moral function, allowed that Homer 'knew the facts', but questioned whether he set them down 'for educational purposes'.[38] So, in so far as it used 'allegory' as a means of interpretation, ancient criticism was 'intentionalist'.

(iii) It follows that the ancient interpreters assumed that the authors they were expounding first formulated their message, and then gave it allegorical dress. This is to neglect a distinction between 'allegory' and 'symbolism', which is commonly stated in modern times. No one in antiquity seems to have had the idea that, instead of beginning with a message and embodying it in fiction, one might begin with a story or subject and treat it as a symbol of happenings or truths which have some formal resemblance to it. And this is odd. The practical and rhetorical use of mythical and historical *exempla* itself implies that the traditional stories contain as it were the potentiality of being applied in a great many ways. Again, some ancient poems strongly suggest that this is an intelligent approach to understanding them. It is difficult to think that Virgil did not have the trials and triumphs of all human life in view as his subject when he wrote the Georgics, or that the exploits and virtues of Aeneas do not somehow foreshadow those of Augustus, without there being the kind of equivalence between them that would lead us to speak of allegory.

[37] See Preminger 324–40.
[38] C. Jensen, *Philodemos* . . ., p. 7.

These considerations suggest that we have here another case of the inadequacy of ancient criticism, as the rhetors and grammarians practised it. Their principles of 'allegory', like their principles of style, could not do justice to the complex and sophisticated literature they were studying.

CHAPTER SEVEN

Mimesis

I

THE relationship between artist or work on the one hand and
the world of external objects on the other is very commonly
described in Greek by the term *mimēsis*, the Latin translation
of which is *imitatio*.[1] These are difficult words to interpret, and
they cover a number of confusions and ambiguities. But it was
hardly ever questioned in antiquity that they were appropriate
as a general description of what poets and artists do. Now
these words certainly indicate that the relationship was held to
be some sort of representation or copying. Whatever problems
are raised by this, the artist's product, the *mimēma*, could not
come into existence without a corresponding object outside, on
which it depends for its structure and characteristics. It is a
distinctive feature of ancient criticism that this was very widely
taken for granted. Indeed, opposing attitudes are very rarely
glimpsed. It was of course possible, within the framework of
mimēsis-theory, to allow for the possibility of reproducing your
own frame of mind. The letter-writer has to project his image
to his distant correspondent, and make it seem as if he was talking to him face to face; and Demetrius therefore says of the
letter—which had become a minor but significant literary form
—that it is an 'image' of the sender's mind (*eikōn tēs psuchēs*).[2]

---

[1] Of the vast literature, I single out: T. Twining, *Dissertation on poetry as an
imitative art*, appended to his edition of the Poetics (1789), and often reprinted
(see Olson); H. House, *Aristotle's Poetics* (1956); R. McKeon, in *Modern Philology*
34 (1936), 1–35; W. J. Verdenius, *Mimesis* (1953); G. F. Else in *Classical Philology*
53 (1958), 73–90; and most recently, J. Laborderie, *Le Dialogue platonicien . . .* (1978), 74 ff. and H. Flashar in *Entretiens Hardt* 25 (1979), 79 ff.
[2] Demetrius 227 (*ALC* 211).

But this is still a very long way from the Romantic concept of literature as motivated by the need for 'self-expression'. Again, ancient notions of 'imagination'—*phantasia*—are a long way from Coleridge; and the whole idea of the writer as somehow creating a new world, rather than merely offering a partial image of the world of the senses, is in general alien to Greek and Roman thinking. The man who sees with the eye of the mind, and penetrates depths unknown before, is the philosopher or scientist, not the poet or man of letters. Such passages of ancient literature as are sometimes alleged to represent the poet as a true creator turn out in fact not to say this at all: when Macrobius compares Virgil to the maker of the kosmos, he is merely making an analogy between the *concordia discors* of the elements that constitute our universe and the unity in diversity produced by Virgil's power of combining various styles in a single work.[3] In ancient thought, the myth-maker (*muthopoios*), even the maker of what we should call fantasy, produces a suggestive or distorted image of reality, not a structure that exists in its own right and for its own sake.

2

Of the various ambiguities inherent in the term *mimēsis*, two may be singled out. Thomas Twining, in his classic essay on 'poetry as an imitative art', pointed out that Aristotle in the *Poetics* used 'imitation' in two senses—'imitation in fiction' and the imitation of 'personative poetry', in which speech imitates speech—but neglected two others, both of which are clearly important in describing what poetry does: simple imitation by sound, and what Twining calls 'imitation in description', whether of natural objects or of mental states. These distinctions are important; the use of a single term to cover all kinds of mimicry and suggestive representation is bound to cause problems. But there is a second kind of ambiguity in the term which is also serious. *Mimēsis*, in Aristotle's account, covers two activi-

---

[3] Macrobius 5.1.18–19 (see Appendix, p. 196 and cf. also p. 179 on Plato); I say this to counter the remarks of E. Curtius, *European Literature and the Latin Middle Ages* (E. tr.) 444, a magnificent and deservedly influential book, very important to classical scholars.

ties which are radically different in intention. *Mimēmata* may be of two quite different kinds. I can copy somebody doing something for either of two reasons: in order to do the same thing myself, or in order to produce a toy or model of the activity. The first sort of 'imitation' is the principle of many human skills and artefacts; 'art imitates nature' by planting seeds and letting them grow, and in countless other ways.[4] It is also the basic procedure of human learning. Such *mimēsis* is obviously useful. The second sort occurs, say, when the painter paints a picture of a shoe, or the toymaker makes a miniature model; neither model nor picture will keep one's feet dry. To make any apologia for poetry, if it is regarded as a mimetic art, involves showing that the second kind of *mimēsis*, the making of models or toys, has a utility. Aristotle appears to do this in a special case by his psychological theory of the 'cathartic' effect of tragedy; but he also, in the early chapters of the *Poetics*, emphasises the value of imitation as a procedure of learning, as though the obvious utility of copying in this context might rub off, as it were, on what the poet does.

3

The verb *mimeisthai* and its cognates do not appear in the *Iliad* or the *Odyssey*. They may be onomatopoeic in origin, and it seems that they apply primarily to the mimicry of sounds. The composer of the Homeric hymn to Apollo describes the maidens of Delos as singing of 'men and women of old' and 'charming the tribes of men'. 'They know to mimic the voices and chatter of all men; a man would think he was talking himself, so harmonious is their beautiful song.'[5] Again, in Aeschylus' *Choephori*, Orestes and Pylades pretend to be Phocians, and propose to 'imitate the sound of a Phocian tongue'.[6] Of course, they do not do so, at least so far as the evidence of the text goes, for Aeschylus gives us no hint of Phocian dialect; and it is very

[4] This idea played a large part in many ancient theories of the development of civilisation. It was familiar to Aristotle (*Phys.* 199^a 15, *Meteor* 4.381^b 6, *Protrepticus* fr. 11 Walzer [= Iamblichus, *Protrept.* 9, 49 ff. Pistelli].)

[5] 158 ff. *Krembaliastus*, here translated 'chatter', is of uncertain meaning. The writer probably intends the unintelligible gibberish of foreigners.

[6] *Choephori* 564.

. unlikely that the actors introduced any identifiable oddities of
pronunciation. But, even in early times, this group of words has
a wide range; and there is nothing in our evidence for its use
that throws much light on the later theoretical developments.[7]

4

The first theoretical discussion we possess of *mimēsis* in connection with literature is that which we find in Plato's *Republic*.
Plato uses the concept as an integral part of his argument for
rejecting poetry, the moral grounds for which we have already
considered. He begins by isolating 'personative' poetry—to use
Twining's word—and assigning the name *mimēsis* especially to
this.[8] He distinguishes three kinds of story-telling: by simple
narrative, by *mimēsis*, and by a combination of the two. The
difference between drama and epic is the formal one that the
latter includes narrative in addition to direct speech. This
division is thus a classification of modes of imitation (in the
wider sense), not of subjects; it is exhaustive and *a priori*; and
it seems to attach unreal importance to the simple difference between direct and indirect speech, though we have to remember
that this kind of grammatical analysis was novel in Plato's time,
and that he himself clearly attached significance to the distinction in question.[9] In any case, the purpose of the move in the
total argument is clear. Those parts of literature—all drama,
and portions of epic—which directly impersonate characters
can, according to Plato, exert an extraordinarily powerful influence on the mind of the 'imitator'. It does us harm, in Plato's
view, to act the parts of women mourning or ill, in love or in
labour, or of slaves or wicked men. We are bound to ask, however, whether the spectator or reader of a play can really be
affected to the same degree as the actor. Plato seems to make
the jump from active participation to mere observation without

[7] Nothing can be learned from Lysias 6.51, though it has been much discussed; here *mimoumenos* seems to mean 'copying the real ceremonies' of the
mysteries, which Andocides impiously parodies.

[8] 392D (*ALC* 61).

[9] Cf. *Theaetetus* 142–3 (Laborderie, op. cit., 394 ff.) Plato draws attention
here to the way in which the conversation with Theaetetus has been written
down, viz. omitting the 'narrative' sentences ('he said' etc.).

explaining it. Two considerations may help here. One is that 'reading' poetry was a more active business in ancient times than we are inclined to think. It involved a good deal of histrionic play, as well as a good deal of vocal virtuosity. The throw-away manner in which some modern poets present their works would probably have seemed very strange and misguided.[10] The second point is that audiences were expected to participate in the feelings of the speaker in a more pronounced way than is usual today. The educated modern critic tends to be patronising towards simple folk who 'enjoy a good cry' in the cinema; but the audience that Plato envisages participates in the emotions of the stage or the recitation to the point of physical expression, and this indeed is a criterion of the performer's success.[11] Consequently, the ill effects of the *mimēsis* on the performer will be reproduced, not all that much weakened, on those who hear him.

When we turn to Book x of the *Republic*, we are faced with considerable difficulties. The discussion here corrects and supplements the earlier one. It involves the application of the theories of Forms and of the 'parts' of the soul set out in Books v–vii. This is natural enough, whether we suppose that the discussion in x was planned as part of the whole and deliberately postponed or that it is in fact a later addition to the original plan. The problem is that the distinction between personative and non-personative poetry is now dropped. Both are described as *mimēsis*, both are condemned on grounds that follow from that description.

Plato begins, this time, from an analogy with the visual arts. He assumes the painter wants to make a likeness, and that in order to do so he needs to know only what the thing looks like, not how to make it in reality, nor even how to use it. Similarly with the poet: he does not need to know how to make war or advise men, but only how to say the sorts of things that people

[10] This fashion (I think of Robert Graves in this connection) may be quite new. Surviving records of Tennyson certainly show a much more declamatory manner.

[11] Cf. Plato *Ion* 535 (*ALC* 44). Ion judged his success by the audience's tears. St. Augustine (*De doctr. christ.* iv. 53) perhaps remembered this passage when he recalled the way in which his own oratory moved a rioting populace to tears: applause would have meant mere pleasure, tears meant conviction.

say in circumstances of war or politics. He needs no real moral knowledge, but only the sense of what ordinary people believe. He is 'third from the truth', because the world of the senses is an imitation of the world of the forms, and he in turn imitates the world of sense. The poet thus does nothing which has value for the good life. Metaphysical and psychological arguments have combined to represent him as both fraudulent and dangerous.

5

This picture is indeed somewhat modified in other contexts. The acceptable poet of the *Laws* is a good man in his way: over fifty years of age, having served the state with credit, he is now allowed under licence to compose poems of praise and blame.[12] But Plato makes no attempt to describe what an ideal poet might be, even in the somewhat ironical way in which he sketched the ideal orator in the *Phaedrus*. We have no reason to think that he ever entertained the notion that poets and artists might aspire to copy directly the *ideai* of which objects in the visible world are themselves copies. Poetic *mimēsis* is firmly *mimēsis* of this world, involving no knowledge of higher things. The nearest he comes to suggesting another view is in *Republic* 401B, where we find grandiose language about the good artist who can 'track down the nature of the beautiful and graceful'. This presumably means that the artist has some power to recognise and reproduce goodness, and not merely to echo common illusions. He is perhaps on a level with the lover in the lower stages of Diotima's 'ascent' in the *Symposium*,[13] who pursues beauty without philosophical knowledge. The road to cognition of the forms, which would be the necessary preliminary to 'imitation' of them, lies through intense study of philosophy and mathematics; it has nothing in common with the ways in which poets and painters go about their thinking. So, though Plato likes the paradox of the 'philosopher king', and even hints at a 'philosopher orator', he does not envisage a philosopher poet.

But if Plato, as is commonly held,[14] never proceeded further

---

[12] *Laws* 8.829c.   [13] *Symposium* 201D ff.
[14] Some arguments to the contrary in Verdenius, op. cit.

in this direction, later Platonists did. We do not know when this trend began, but Antiochus of Ascalon in the first century B.C. 'had at least an intermediary rôle'[15] in establishing a higher view of artistic creation than that to which Plato himself adhered.

At all events, there is a fair amount of evidence later than Antiochus for an analogy drawn between the 'demiurge' of the world and the artist, according to which both contemplate their own thoughts in order to form their creations. The demiurge thinks the ideas, and models the sensible world on them. The sculptor Phidias (the traditional example in the argument) has in his mind *species pulchritudinis eximia quaedam*, as Cicero puts it,[16] which he contemplates as he works on his Zeus or Athena, and by which he guides his hand and skill. In this form, the analogy is associated with a metaphysical position different from Plato's: the Ideas, instead of having a wholly separate existence, have become the Thoughts of God. This was accepted doctrine among many Platonists of the first and second centuries A.D., though its origin is not clear.[17] The consequent aesthetic theory, in which the artist stands to his work as the ideas stand to God who thinks them, is not really a mimetic theory at all, but an expressive one, for the artist now brings something of himself to the light of day.

In Plotinus and the Neoplatonists, the metaphysics is again more complex, and the essential point that artist and poet derive their subject from something of a higher order than the world of the senses is much clearer. Plotinus puts it thus:

If anyone disparages the arts because they produce by imitating nature, we must reply: (i) that natural objects also imitate other things; (ii) that it must be understood that the arts do not simply imitate the visible, but ascend to the Principles (*logoi*) from which nature derives; (iii) that the arts produce much out of themselves, and add this where there is some defect, themselves possessing beauty;

[15] J. Dillon, *The Middle Platonists* (1977), 93 ff. On Antiochus see esp. W. Theiler, *Die Vorbereitung des Neuplatonismus* (1934), 17.

[16] *Orator* 8: 'In his mind there was an outstanding appearance of beauty, and he contemplated this and concentrated upon it so as to guide his skill and his hand by its likeness.' For the expression, cf. Pl. *Rep.* 484C.

[17] Dillon, loc. cit.; A. H. Armstrong, *Entretiens Hardt* 5 (1960) 393 ff. Seneca (*Epist.* 58 and 65) treats this as a well-known doctrine.

(iv) that Phidias made his Zeus on no sensible model, but apprehending what Zeus would look like, if he wished to appear to our sight.[18]

Later, in Proclus,[19] it is not only the highest but also the second or 'instructive' kind of poetry that has this relationship to a higher order: the 'instructive poet' knows 'the real nature of beings' and can provide 'recollection' of 'the eternal principles and various powers'.

This Neoplatonist approach was historically very influential, especially in the Renaissance. It has little to do with Plato; it would be truer to say that it is an attempt to justify poetry against his censure, by bringing together the concept of *mimēsis* and the poet's claim to superior knowledge, and revaluing them both.

6

Another reaction to Plato's radical views—and one that was well known to the Middle Platonists and to Plotinus and his successors—was that of Aristotle. In the analysis of *mimēsis*, as in much else, the *Poetics* gives the most sophisticated literary theory that antiquity has left us. Briefly, Aristotle's position is this:

(i) He accepts the classification of poetry as a mimetic art. For him, it is all equally so. The narrower sense in which 'mimetic' is distinguished from narrative does not concern him much. It is in fact simply a difference of mode, and there are other, often more important, ways in which one *mimēsis* differs from another. The chief of these are 'media' (*di'hōn*) and 'objects' (*ha*). Thus while drama differs from epic in mode, it has the same objects and uses the same medium, verse. The difference between tragedy and comedy, on the other hand, is one of object; and that between poetry as a whole and music or dancing one of medium.

(ii) The object imitated by poetry—as by dancing, for that

[18] *Enneads* 5.8.1. Cf. M. H. Abrams, *The Mirror and the Lamp*, 42, and A. H. Armstrong in *Cambridge History of Later Greek Philosophy*, 233.
[19] *Commentary on 'Republic'* i, 179.5 Kroll. Cf. above, Chapter IV 8.

matter—is human action (*praxis*). This involves intention, execution and outcome. A *praxis* is not just a happening—animals cannot 'act' (*prattein*), nor even children,[20] for 'action' is a complex whole into which feeling, character and rational thought all enter. The poet's primary work is therefore the plot (*muthos*) of play or epic; in this he constructs a representation of people performing actions of the kinds that people of their sort will naturally do, with the consequences that may be expected to follow. The *mimēsis* is thus an image of a *praxis*. This obviously applies to drama and epic; though Aristotle does not say much about other *genres*, such as lyric, he evidently held that the same account would hold of anything that could properly be brought under the head of *poiētikē*.

(iii) The portrayal of action involves the portrayal of *ēthē*, i.e. human manners and characters, and these are either 'good' or 'bad'. Poetry is therefore a representation of something morally differentiated, and its two main kinds can be distinguished, on the basis of their objects, on this principle: tragedy imitates 'good' characters and comedy 'bad' ones. It is not easy to interpret this position; there are pitfalls on either side. On the one hand, it is tempting to water the statement down, and say that 'good' and 'bad' are primarily social or political terms. There is plausibility in this. 'The better sort' is a common Athenian way of denoting the upper strata of society, and it is of course true that the personages of tragedy are heroes and princes, and those of comedy private citizens; Theophrastus[21] spoke of tragedy as comprising 'the circumstances of heroic fortune', and of comedy as 'a story of private affairs involving no danger'. Yet this social difference cannot be the whole story. Prominent among the characteristics of *ēthē* are what we should call moral virtues—justice, courage, moderation and so forth. The 'actions' of the persons in the play are partly determined by these, and partly by other, more external, qualities which also characterize *ēthē*, but do not appear to us as 'moral' at all—power, wealth, status or age. For Aristotle, as for most Greeks of his time, a certain degree of good fortune in these respects was necessary for human happiness, and their presence or absence affects the way in which an

---

[20] *Eudemian Ethics* 1224ᵃ 28.   [21] Diomedes *Gramm. Lat.* I.487.

individual behaves, and goes to determine what sort of person he is.

(iv) Aristotle[22] says that tragedy imitates people 'better than the present population' and comedy those who are 'worse' than these. Again,[23] poets imitate either things as they were or are, or as people say or think they are, or as they 'ought' to be. Yet again,[24] the poet is more 'philosophical' than the historian, because he is not concerned with individual facts but with generalities (*ta katholou*). All these statements make it clear that Aristotle's *mimēsis* is something very different from the strictly realistic copying or mimicry that is the basis of Plato's arguments. The result of the process, it appears, is often an idealisation or a generalisation—in comedy, a caricature—of the object perceived in life. The poet, like the painter,[25] can fill up deficiencies in his model, and show particular *ēthē* in a more complete form than we can ever discern them in the world in which we live.

(v) This generalising and idealising tendency in poetic *mimēsis* is to be connected with another aspect on which Aristotle lays stress: its instructiveness. We learn by imitating, and we enjoy the pleasure of recognition. But the recognition is not of identical objects, but of similar ones; to see likenesses, to sense the common features between events on the stage and events around us, is to enhance one's understanding and so to gain a little of the highest of human pleasures. It is fundamental for Aristotle that 'all men desire to understand'; by his interpretation of *mimēsis* he shows how poetry also may contribute to the fulfilment of the desire.

7

Mimēsis thus takes on a creative look; it supplements, improves and illuminates its ostensible models. But it remains of course wholly dependent on them for its initiatives. It cannot 'make

[22] 1448^a 17.
[23] 1460^b 8.
[24] 1451^b.
[25] Xenophon (*Memorabilia* 3.10.1–5) 'reports' a conversation in which Socrates convinces Parrhasius that by reproducing features of expression he can also represent *ēthē*.

that which it has not seen'. For the creative faculty of 'imagination' which can do just this, later writers used the term *phantasia*.[26] Now Aristotle did himself have a psychological theory of *phantasia*: it was a faculty set in motion by sense-perception, and subsequently reproducing, more faintly, the images presented by the senses.[27] But he does not connect this with any special activity of the poet or artist. Later philosophers, not only Stoics, used the term in various ways, and it came to have a use in literary theory. We find a distinction drawn between the kind of poetry which is 'imitative of reality (*alētheia*)' and of which comedy is a clear instance, and two other kinds: one in which 'reality' is 'imagined' (*kata phantasian tēs alētheias*), and one in which 'reality' is surpassed by the imaginative reach that invents monsters and marvels.[28] This way of speaking may well be Hellenistic.

But the most interesting uses of *phantasia* are to be found in the later rhetorical critics, Quintilian and 'Longinus'.

Quintilian[29] promulgates the conventional opinion that we must ourselves feel the emotions we wish to promote in others. How are we to do this, given that emotions are not in our control? By forming in our minds clear *phantasiai*—'visions'—of absent things; this means putting to practical use the faculty of day-dreaming and fantasy which we often employ in an idle moment. From vividness of vision will come vividness of expression, both in poetry (Quintilian quotes Virgil)[30] and in oratory.

'Longinus' uses the term *phantasia*, not in a general

---

[26] Cf. Philostratus *Life of Apollonius* 6.19 (*ALC* 552).

[27] See D. J. Allan, *The Philosophy of Aristotle*, 74 ff.

[28] Scholia on Hom. *Il.* 14.352–1. Such classifications are not uncommon. A somewhat similar one, for example, is reported by Sextus Empiricus *Adv. math.* 1.263: *historia* = exposition of true events; *plasma* = invention of probable events; *muthos* = exposition of fictions which never happened. This merely classifies the *content* of various kinds of literature, without saying anything about the mental processes of the writer.

[29] 6.2.25 ff. (see Appendix, p. 202).

[30] His examples are all of moments of what we should call pathos: *Aen.* 9.476 (the shuttle slips from the hands of Euryalus' mother when she hears the rumour of his death); 11.40 (Aeneas sees Pallas' wound); 11.89 (the horse Aethon weeps); 10.782 (the dying Antores remembers his home). So vividness is associated with emotion, especially grief.

philosophical sense, but in much the same way as Quintilian: it is exercised 'when enthusiasm and emotion make you seem to be actually seeing what you are talking about, and when you thrust it under the hearer's eyes'.[31] But he makes a distinction between 'poetical' and 'rhetorical' *phantasia*: the rhetorical kind is based on fact, and does not involve elements of the supernatural or what we should in general call 'fantasy'. When Euripides makes Orestes cry out at the vision of the Furies—'they're coming, they're jumping up at me'—'the poet has himself beheld the Furies, and almost made his hearers see what he imagined'.[32] When he makes Helios nervously advise Phaethon how to guide the chariot, 'the writer's soul mounts with him, shares his risks, and takes wing with the horses'; it could not have achieved these imaginative heights 'if it had not moved with equal pace in the course of those heavenly movements'.

The implications of this way of speaking of the poet's activities seem to be two: (i) he experiences a vision or emotional experience which depends on his possession of a natural capacity, but can be encouraged or induced; (ii) he reproduces this experience in a form which will then induce it in others. The notion of *mimēsis* is thus supplemented by an appeal to the rhetorical doctrine of emotions (*pathē*); and the whole process is coloured by the terminology of 'enthusiasm', to which Longinus is so much addicted.

8

We thus see, first, a broadening out of the concept of *mimēsis* from Plato to the Neoplatonists on the one hand, and to Aristotle on the other. The process comes to be conceived not as a copying of individual objects (as in Plato's arguments) but either as a reference to an ideal or as a generalised reproduction of human action. Secondly, the account of the poetic process

---

[31] 15.1.

[32] This at least is what the manuscript tradition of 'Longinus' (15.2) gives. But Manutius conjectured 'did *not* behold', and this (an easy correction) would make 'Longinus' agree exactly with Philostratus, and represent *phantasia* as a capacity which *supplements* the senses.

that is thus developed is supplemented by the concept of
phantasia, the mental power that can visualise what the eye has
never seen. At this point, writers like 'Longinus' and Quintilian
invoke also the rhetorical precept (known to Aristotle, and indeed commonplace) that a certain degree of emotional excite-
ment in the speaker is necessary for the adequate projection of
emotion to others.

It is natural to ask whether there are any links between this
complex of ideas and other ways in which we find *mimēsis*
terminology employed. There are two possible areas.

The first relates to the 'mimetic' use of language. This was
discussed in ancient theory in connection both with word-
groupings (figures and arrangement) and with individual
words and sounds. Longinus shows how asyndeta and hyper-
bata reproduce the haste, impediment and disorder of anxious
or excited speech;[33] Demetrius[34] and Quintilian[35] make the
point that 'small words' and short cola are more expressive of
small things. Some of this theorising is absurd; but the elaborate analysis by Dionysius of Homer's description of the rock of
Sisyphus is worth careful study.[36] Discussion of the association
of sounds goes back perhaps to Democritus; it is a main theme
of Plato's *Cratylus*; and the later rhetorical tradition, represented by Dionysius and Quintilian, makes a lot of it. In
Cratylus, R represents movement, because of the trill of the
tongue; PS, X, S, PH (an aspirated P) produce a sense of
agitation: D and T, in which the tongue rests against the teeth,
display rest; the long open-mouthed vowels A and E denote
size. This kind of theory, based on observation of the mouth and
tongue, does not say much about the aesthetic qualities of
sounds, and in this respect it differs from the precepts commonly given in the rhetorical tradition. For Dionysius, for
example, L is 'sweet', R 'noble', and S disagreeable if used in
excess: M and N make a noise like a horn; and the order of
euphony of the vowels is A E O U I—in other words, the
thinner, front vowels are the least attractive.[37] That poets use,

---

[33] 'Longinus' 19, 22.   [34] Demetrius 48.
[35] Quintilian 8.3.20 (on Virgil's 'exiguus mus').
[36] See above, Chapter IV 1.
[37] *De compositione verborum* 14.

or invent, words which reproduce or strongly suggest natural
sounds is an obvious extension of this way of thinking: Dio
Chrysostom discourses at length on Homer's *kanachē, bombos,
doupos,* and so on.[38] So we have two approaches to the sounds of
words: the mimetic and the aesthetic. In the practice of poets—
Virgil for example—we can see both in use. For our present
purpose, it is the mimetic that matters; Twining's 'imitation by
sound' was clearly recognised in antiquity, while Plato at least
tried to see an act of mimicry in the physical movements which
form the letters rather than in the resulting noise.

9

The second area to which the term *mimēsis* extends has at first
sight no more than an accidental connection with the main
sense of the word. It is that of the 'imitation' of earlier writers
by later. This is, in itself, very important in the history of
criticism. In classical Greek literature, lyric poets followed the
stories, and sometimes adapted the language, of epic, and this
fact was obvious and widely recognised; moreover, the development of the various genres proceeded by a process of improvement on existing models, and this too was recognised, not
only for drama, but for fourth-century oratory. When we come
to Hellenistic times, we encounter a literature which is almost
entirely 'mimetic' in this sense, deriving its inspiration not so
much from immediate predecessors as from much earlier
'classical' models. Roman literature, again, was, in most formal
respects, a reproduction of Greek. In these conditions, what
makes a work good or bad? It is possible to identify at least
some of the criteria which ancient critics used to distinguish
acceptable imitation from what they called 'theft' or plagiar-
ism (*klopē, furtum*).[39] These were, first, that the copy should be
acknowledged as a copy and be recognisable; secondly, that the
writer should stamp his mark on the material, and so make the
borrowing 'his own property'; and thirdly, that what was

[38] *Oration* 12.68 ff. (Appendix, p. 181).
[39] I have discussed this in more detail in an essay *de imitatione* in *Creative
Imitation and Latin Literature,* ed. D. A. West and A. J. Woodman, Cambridge
1979, 1 ff.

imitated should not be just some particular feature but a sign of a general excellence perceived in the model which could be achieved anew in a fresh setting. The links between this theory and the general literary theory of *mimēsis* are tenuous; but there is an important point of resemblance in the insistence on the need for general understanding of the model rather than mechanical or (as we might say) photographic copying. It is the practical criticism based on these principles which excites our interest; a fair specimen of it is to be found in the comparisons of Virgil and Homer which Macrobius inherited from earlier critics of Virgil. It is not an encouraging specimen. Macrobius offers little discussion of nuances or new arrangement; instead, forced logical or factual points form the staple of his comment.[40] Once again, we must admit that, in an important department of literary evaluation, the normal practice of ancient critics is quite inadequate for the literature they were considering. Only 'Longinus' relieves the gloom: he makes worthwhile points about the 'mimetic' relationships of Demosthenes to Eupolis, Euripides to Aeschylus, and Aratus to Homer.[41]

[40] See (e.g.) 5.13.31 ff., on Virgil's imitation of Homer's description of Strife. See also Appendix, p. 193 ff.

[41] 'Longinus' 16.3; 15.6; 10.6.

CHAPTER EIGHT

Rhetoric

I

THIS chapter is concerned not with the general question of the influence on literature of oratory and its theoretical counterpart, rhetoric, but with the more specific issue of the way in which rhetoric affected literary understanding and evaluation. I ask not what the rhetor taught the poet, but what he thought of him. These two questions are quite distinct. That this is a central issue should be clear from much that has been said above; indeed, it is pretty clearly a salient distinction of all criticism derived from the ancient model that the categories and presuppositions employed are largely based on rhetoric.

By 'rhetoric' here is meant a particular academic discipline, the subject taught under that name in Greek and Roman schools from the fifth century B.C. onwards, modified in mediaeval times, and largely revived in its older form by the humanists.[1] It enjoyed remarkable stability throughout the classical millennium. If the pupils of Anaximenes in the fourth century B.C. could have been transported eight hundred years on into the school of Libanius, they would not have found it entirely strange; the mass of new technical terms and distinctions to which their new teacher would have introduced them would hardly have obscured the familiar outlines of the basic exercises and lessons.

Like all educational 'subjects', rhetoric had vague boundaries. On one frontier, the rhetor held ground in common with the *grammaticus*. Correctness of speech—*Hellēnismos, Latinitas*—

---

[1] Brian Vickers, *Classical Rhetoric in English Poetry* (1970), ch. 1, offers a concise historical survey.

is the first of the rhetorical virtues of style; it is also one of the main objects of the grammarian's art. The study of the details of presentation and diction (choice and arrangement of words, and also figures), is vital to the orator; it is also wholly within the province of the *grammaticus*, since one of his prime tasks is to interpret in detail the classical poets who were the staple of education. On the other frontier, the rhetor disputed territory with the philosopher. He did this partly out of natural expansionism, adapting simplified philosophical *theses* as exercises in composition; but partly also as a measure of defence against the common charge that his art was indifferent, or even hostile, to morality. These areas of interest greatly extended the rhetor's concern with literature in general; and this in turn widened the influence of rhetorical thinking on the criticism of poetry and other literary forms.

Rhetoric claimed to teach 'persuasion'; this was how its teachers generally defined its end-product.[2] The rhetor accordingly saw the study of the poets and other great writers as a means to this end. Such study was supplementary to theoretical precept and to actual practice. In early times, it was merely a convenient ancillary; the pupil's existing knowledge of Homer and tragedy could be put to good use in helping him to frame a convincing speech. In later periods, however, in the Greek world at any rate, general literary study became even more important, because the pupil's exposure to effective oratory largely depended on his study of the classical orators, and it was in their language, not his own vernacular, that he was expected to compose. But the ostensible purpose of all the reading remained practical, and the sort of analysis of classical literature which was expected was determined by this.[3] Now—as we have seen—it is an inescapable presupposition of rhetoric that the speaker knows what he wants and has formulated to himself the message he wishes to convey; he has now to be shown what to say and how to say it in order to attain his end. The activity of composition, on this way of thinking, cannot be regarded as a process of self-discovery, or as an intellectual adventure

---

[2] Rhetoric is *peithous dēmiourgos*, 'manufacturer of persuasion': Plato *Gorgias* 453A (see E. R. Dodds' note); Quintilian 2.15.4 ff.

[3] Cf. above, Chapter I 3.

embarked upon in ignorance of its end. In a sense, everything has
to be settled before you put pen to paper. The content and form
of the speech depend on a preliminary assessment of the situation and of the character and attitudes of the persons who have
to be convinced. Any analysis of literature undertaken as part
of rhetorical instruction has therefore to expose the workings of
the writer's mind on these lines. This is a simple matter when
the object under examination is, for example, a speech in
Homer or Virgil, and it is this kind of material to which the
rhetorical critic is specially attracted. We see this attitude in
Quintilian's discussions of Homer, Euripides and Aristophanes; and there are good examples of 'practical criticism' of
the same kind in the later pseudo-Dionysian treatises on
'figurative discourses', and many echoes of it in the ancient
commentaries on Homer and Virgil.[4] The critic who reads and
comments in this way necessarily considers the situation, the
muthos or *hupothesis*, which the epic poet or dramatist has set up,
as something given, and not itself normally to be criticised—
just as the inventor (*fictor*) of a *controversia* is normally not to be
blamed for the foolishness of pupils' answers to the problem he
has set. So the kind of critique of plot on grounds of coherence
and appropriate ending which Aristotle practises in the *Poetics*
is absent from the rhetorical mode of criticism.

But of course it is not only the speeches in epic or drama
which are susceptible to the rhetor's procedures. Narrative too
is a technique studied by rhetors: clarity, orderliness and the
capacity to convince by an attractive, well-contrived—and
perhaps dishonest—tale are qualities which rhetorical teaching
naturally sought to develop. History is thus easily drawn into
the orbit of rhetoric, especially since the composition of
formal speeches had been commonly held to be a necessary part
of the historian's work since the time of Thucydides. The
analysis of Thucydides by Dionysius, able as it is, is very little
concerned with historical research.[5] At the same time, the third
main division of oratory—the 'epideictic' or 'panegyric' kind,
the oratory of praise and blame—easily embraced the subject-

[4] Some examples below, Appendix, p. 193.
[5] W. K. Pritchett, *Dionysius . . . On Thucydides* (1975) gives a very full
commentary and translation.

matter of most lyric poetry, for which indeed it was, historically speaking, a substitute. The extreme point of this development can be seen in Hermogenes, for whom the term 'panegyric' has come to include history, philosophy and poetry.[6] In the end, therefore, the rhetors took all literature as their province, and encouraged the kind of analysis and criticism that suited their purpose. This was to the detriment of aesthetic judgment, and more or less blocked the way to a historical view of literature. With the moralists—and ancient education was essentially moral—rhetoric maintained a complex relationship: on the defensive lest she be thought amoral, she presented herself more and more as the guardian not only of pure and effective language but of the highest moral values of the past.

2

How did all this come about? It was generally believed in the time of Aristotle that rhetorical teaching had begun in Sicily, in the aftermath of the fall of the fifth-century tyrannies in Syracuse and other cities. Democracy brought much litigation and political speaking; this in turn bred a demand for effective instruction in the skills of speech, on which property and life might depend. Corax and Tisias were remembered as famous teachers and innovators, though little is known of their doctrine. An earlier and more famous Sicilian, the philosopher Empedocles, was believed by Aristotle to be the first inventor; a later one, Gorgias of Leontini, is credited with the first teaching of the art at Athens. This last story is false, or at best a partial truth; but Athens, with its democracy and its jury-courts, was the natural scene for the rapid growth of the technique. It is clear from the earliest extant oratory, that of Antiphon, and from many features in Thucydides, Euripides and Aristophanes, that jurors, assemblymen and theatre-audiences all appreciated a certain professionalism. At its lowest level, this amounted to set forms of exordium and peroration, a recognition of the importance of the occasion and the courtesy due to the hearers. Dicaeopolis, the 'hero' of Aristo-

---

[6] Hermogenes *On types* 404, 5–21 Rabe (*ALC* 575 f.). Cf. below, Chapter IX 7.

phanes' *Acharnians*, is made to address his fellow-citizens with a
captatio benevolentiae borrowed from Euripides;[7] he proceeds to a
recognisable prologue and narrative, raises and answers objections, and builds up his picture of the situation in a passage
that could serve as a text-book example of what the rhetors
called 'amplification' (*auxēsis*). If we can infer from this that
political speeches in the 420s were habitually using these forms
—speaking, as Aristotle would say, *rhētorikōs* rather than
politikōs[8]—it would follow that the corresponding teaching was
known well before Gorgias' arrival in 427. As soon as these techniques became common, speakers in the courts often found it
necessary to disclaim special ability (*deinotēs*), as they would
disclaim any other unfair or 'undemocratic' advantage, such
as wealth or family. It always helps one's case to appear to be
fighting the superior advantages of a privileged adversary.[9]
Rhetoric thrived on the hostility it excited. What is believed to
be formidable is also believed to be important; and the undoubtedly fraudulent claims of the 'art' were sustained by the
convention of fearing the advantages it was supposed to confer.

For everyone knew that the gift of persuasion was a natural
one, and its exercise too subtle to be reduced to rule. Isocrates
makes it clear that practice and natural endowment are no less
important than precept, and even the best rules are made to be
broken if occasion (*kairos*) so demands.[10] Cicero often breaks
the simplest rules of arrangement because of the forensic situation. In fact, the history of rhetoric knows only one noted
master who deliberately set himself against irregularities of
arrangement: this was the Apollodorus of Pergamum who was
one of Octavian's teachers and is said to have insisted on rigid
adherence to the scheme of prooemium, narrative, argument
and epilogue. His successors refuted or neglected him. Why he

[7] *Acharnians* 497 ff.
[8] *Poetics* 1450[b] 7.
[9] See, e.g., Lysias 12.3, 17.1, 19.2. It became standard advice that the
orator should, in his opening, represent himself as weak, unprepared or un-
equal to his adversary. *Est enim naturalis favor pro laborantibus* (Quintil. 4.1.8–9).
[10] So Isocrates says (12.33): 'I perceive that I am going beyond the proportions prescribed for prooemia. But a sensible man ought not to be content
just with having more than anyone else to say about a given subject, but, in
any subject, to keep his eye on opportunity (*eukairia*).'

took this stand—if he really did—remains uncertain. Perhaps it was a reaction against the freer spirit of Ciceronian rhetoric, perhaps a counterpart in the sphere of invention and arrangement to contemporary 'Atticist' insistence on purity of language, perhaps merely an attempt to justify the claim that rhetoric was a science (*epistēmē*) not simply an art (*technē*). In any case, it was an eccentric view.[11]

Yet rhetoric was always a rigorous discipline. It had arisen in a period of unparalleled inquisitiveness and doubt. It encouraged hard thinking, verbal and logical ingenuity, and shrewd psychological observation. In its long centuries of arid scholasticism, it never quite lost its edge. It is therefore something of a misunderstanding when writers on ancient literature treat the influence of the rhetorical schools as entirely negative and destructive. The mistake, now less common than it was, comes partly from taking Plato's polemic as a decisive condemnation, partly from regarding rhetoric as basically an art of verbal embellishment, not of reasoning. It is obvious that rhetorical teaching helped to shape the work of many of the great poets and historians of antiquity, and that this formative influence was also an inhibiting one; but both the good and the bad in all this were due less to rhetoric's concern with the ornaments of speech than to the rational framework which she sought to impose on whatever theme or topic was handed her for treatment.

3

The conservatism of rhetorical teaching over such a long period makes it possible to give an account of it as a system, based on the late text-books which survive, without feeling that one's conclusions are likely to be fundamentally wrong for the earlier period. Quintilian is undoubtedly the best guide, the 'Ariadne's thread' through the labyrinth, as Richard Volkmann said in his still unreplaced survey of the whole field.[12]

[11] Cf. above, Chapter IV 7.
[12] *Rhetorik der Griechen und Römern*, ed. 2 (1885) p. vi: 'Einen erwünschten Ariadnefaden in dem krausen Gewirre rhetorischer Begriffe und Kunstausdrücke.' The recent compilations of Lausberg and Martin come nowhere near Volkmann's sane and alert understanding of the whole subject.

The classical division of the subject reflects a point to which I have already drawn attention more than once: the assumption that content and linguistic form are quite separate. 'Things' were the subject of that part of the discipline of rhetoric which was called 'invention' (*inventio, heuresis*), and embraced the procedures for 'discovering' what may usefully be said in a given situation. 'Words', on the other hand, were studied separately, under the two main heads of 'choice' and 'arrangement'. The concepts of 'arrangement' and 'figure' could clearly be applied both to 'things' and to 'words'; and it was in the discussion of 'figures' of thought and of speech that the rhetorical tradition came nearest to admitting that the two departments were not really separable. All these elements of the art depended on memory for their retention and effective use, and on delivery (*actio, hupokrisis*) for their acceptability to the audience. So a comprehensive course in rhetoric—as we can see in Quintilian's *Institutio*, a sort of teacher's manual—covered five main subjects: invention, arrangement, diction, delivery, memory.

The 'things' of which the orator had to treat might be either 'definite' or 'indefinite'. A teacher like Quintilian envisages his pupils as practising both types of theme: not only 'Is Manlius aiming at tyranny?' but 'Is the world governed by providence?' And whatever the subject, certain basic questions are the same: in order to develop this general theme we need to ask, for example, whether providence exists, what it is, and what sort of thing it is. Beyond this, the procedure depends largely on the purpose of the speech, that is to say, on whether it is forensic, deliberative or 'epideictic'. 'Epideictic' subjects involve both the actions of the persons praised or blamed and their consequences; the speech will be mainly concerned with the antithetical topics of 'honour' and 'expediency'. In deliberative oratory, we have to engage not only in these questions but in the question whether the proposed course of action is feasible or not. Obviously, study of the characteristics of the audience is particularly important, since the outcome rests on enlisting their sympathy. This is true also of forensic cases; but these may be much more complicated, for they may involve the organisation of many different debating topics into a single whole, directed to the achievement of the very specific goal of an acquittal or a conviction. Forensic oratory is thus seen as the crown of the whole art; the massive forensic speeches of Demosthenes, Aeschines and Cicero are the dominant models, to be studied and analysed in detail. It is therefore to forensic speeches that the fundamental analysis into parts best applies. This analysis goes back to the early days of rhetoric,[13] and, despite some vacillation of terminology, never changed in its essentials. There are always five main parts to a speech: exordium to conciliate the juryman, narrative to instruct, proof to establish your case, refutation to overthrow that of your opponents, and peroration to refresh the memory or excite the appropriate emotion—pity or indignation, as the case may be.

The most elaborate branch of the doctrine of 'invention', the theory of *status* or *stasis*[14]—'issue', 'standpoint'—also arises from forensic considerations, and primarily from the problems of defendants. There are traces of it as early as Antiphon's *Tetralogies*, but the main authority was the Hellenistic teacher Hermagoras,[15] until his work was replaced by the more elaborate systems of the Roman period. Essentially, the teacher aimed to suggest to his pupil a way of classifying the problem presented to him. Thus:

(i) If the matter at issue is uncertain—that is to say, if there is a question of fact—the case falls under the *status coniecturalis* (*stochasmos*). Suppose a man is discovered burying a corpse in a lonely place, and is accused of murder. We have to discover what actually happened.

(ii) But the facts may be clear; it may be quite certain that he killed the man. We must then ask whether his action falls under the definition of murder, and was not, for example, homicide committed in self-defence. This is the *status definitivus* (*horismos*).

[13] It is even attributed to Corax (*Prolegomenōn syllogē* 67.3 Rabe = Radermacher, *Artium scriptores*, в ıı 7).
[14] C. S. Baldwin, *Ancient Rhetoric and Poetic*, 49 ff., 74 ff., gives a useful summary in English. See also Kennedy, *Art of Persuasion in Greece*, 300 ff.; Martin 28 ff.; Volkmann 38–92; M. Lossau, *Untersuchungen zur Antiken Demothenesexegese*, 113 ff. Quintilian 3.6 offers his 'Ariadne's thread'.
[15] See above, Chapter III, n. 43.

(iii) It may indeed have been murder—but all the same it may have right: the victim may have been a would-be tyrant. So we have to ask after the quality of the act—was it just or expedient or not? This is the *status qualitatis* (*stasis poiotētos*).

(iv) And finally, in despair as it were, the defendant may plead that the court is not competent: this is the *status translativus* (*metalēpsis*).

Many other terms and refinements are found and rhetors engaged in stirring controversy over them. We need not dwell on them here, for this kind of thing, however much it encouraged shrewdness in the analysis of situations, has little bearing on the criticism of poetry or non-rhetorical prose.

These matters of 'invention' occupy the central books of Quintilian's *Institutio*; it is his summary that has guided us so far. From Book VIII onwards, he concerns himself with style, which he regards as both a more difficult and a more necessary subject.[16] Stylistic failure, not failure in argumentation, has, in Quintilian's view, produced the *corrupta eloquentia* against which he is campaigning. From our present standpoint, it is very interesting that a teacher of rhetoric should say this. It seems to be characteristic of the imperial period. Rhetoric, in Quintilian's hands, is evidently no longer a purely vocational training; it has acquired much of the character of a general literary education, with a strong ethical element, and it seeks to impart a type of literary taste and practice which reflects sound moral attitudes. This is not done, however, by confining the student to books of acknowledged moral value, for that would not fit in at all with the core of the curriculum, the rhetorical masterpieces occasioned by the chicaneries and evasions of ancient Athenian assemblies and courts. Instead, it is done by drawing the pupil's attention above all to style, and associating stylistic 'good' and 'bad' with moral qualities. So it is not only the study of historical events and personalities, but even more the formal study of classical writings, that becomes the main vehicle of moral indoctrination. This consideration perhaps also helps one to understand 'Longinus'.

[16] 8 pr. 13.

4

We shall return to style later. Meanwhile, there are still some points to be made about the ways in which the theory of 'invention' might affect the appreciation and understanding of the poets.

These points are perhaps most clearly made by adducing examples. I select first one which illustrates the way in which the expectations aroused by rhetorical teaching about the shape and form of a speech affected the judgment passed on poems. Quintilian's famous chapter on authors to be imitated contains a particularly elaborate discussion of Homer, the universal genius and 'inventor of rhetoric', in whom all virtues can be seen. Here, Homer is alleged to be capable both of elevation when the subject requires it, and of 'propriety' where elevation is out of place. This is an Aristotelian touch: the poet's language must never be 'low', even when his theme is an everyday one. Homer in fact combines in himself the capacity for the most diverse qualities: richness as well as compression, charm as well as gravity, abundance as well as conciseness. Naturally, he is a model for the kinds of epideictic discourse which one might expect to find in poetry; but he can also teach deliberative and forensic skills, witness the Embassy in *Iliad* ix and the debates in *Iliad* ii. He has a comprehensive range also in emotional tone, encompassing both *pathē*, the stronger emotions, and *ēthē*, the milder traits of manners. In 'Longinus', these two qualities are attributed to the *Iliad* and the *Odyssey* respectively; Quintilian apparently makes no such distinction, and all his examples are Iliadic. He proceeds then to enumerate the traditional five 'parts of a speech' and to show how Homer offers models of all. In this he doubtless follows an established tradition for the praise of Homer's prologues is to be seen also in Horace,[17] though Quintilian gives it a more conventional turn. Homer, he says, illustrates to perfection the rule that the prologue must make the hearer *benevolum attentum docilem*, welldisposed, alert and ready to learn. The virtues of narrative —vividness and conciseness—are also perfectly illustrated by

[17] *Ars* 137 ff. (*ALC* 283).

such incidents as the death of Patroclus and the battle of the
Curetes and Aetolians. The value of his argumentation—the
next main point—is proved, Quintilian thinks, by the frequency with which technical writers draw on him for examples;
and finally no epilogue could ever equal the prayers of Priam
to Achilles.[18]

This encomium is a tour-de-force; it is meant as a serious en-
couragement to the young orator to go back to the reading of his
childhood, and look at it afresh in the light of his adult needs.

5

My second example is of a different kind. It concerns not the
parts or elements of a speech or a poem, nor the stylistic
qualities, but what is called the 'figure' (*schēma*); the question
at issue is the relationship between *prima facie* form and underlying purpose. Teachers of rhetoric were as we have already
observed especially interested in the complexity of theme to be
found in forensic speeches. Analysis of the purpose and execution of the famous orations of antiquity, especially those of
Demosthenes, was a favourite pursuit of the schools; and the
kind of analysis which was developed could be easily extended
to other branches of literature. There was, for example, considerable debate about what were called 'figured' speeches (*logoi
eschēmatismenoi*), in which the ostensible intention of a piece
could be held to be different from the real one: Demosthenes'
De corona, for instance, was not only a defence in court, but also a
deliberative and encomiastic oration, and these latter aspects
were in some ways more important than the nominal purpose.
It was clearly possible to apply this sort of technique to non-
oratorical literature. A late rhetor—one of the authors of the
Art of Rhetoric attributed to Dionysius, though not the author of
the chapters on declamation to which I drew attention in
Chapter I—composed two short treatises on 'figured speeches'
(*logoi eschēmatismenoi*), in which he speculated in quite interesting ways on the whole subject. His analysis of a play of

[18] 10.1.46 ff. (*ALC* 387 f.). 'Patroclus' death' is the beginning of *Il.* 18; 'the
battle of Curetes and Aetolians', *Il.* 9.529 ff.

Euripides, *Melanippe the Wise Woman*, illustrates his method.[19] In this, he says, there are two figures (*schēmata*), one of the poet's, and the other the character Melanippe's. Euripides, being a pupil of Anaxagoras, wished to present that philosopher's views on creation to the public. He does so in a speech of Melanippe, and 'covertly conveys' (*ainittetai*) his respect for the doctrine and his teacher by making Melanippe preface her exposition by saying

> 'Not mine the tale—I had it from my mother.'

This is a sign to the audience, it appears, that the doctrine is venerable. At the same time, the character Melanippe is herself employing a 'figure'. She has exposed her children (who are Poseidon's) in her father's cowshed, and they are found being suckled by a cow and guarded by the bull. Her father takes this as a supernatural event, decides to burn the children, and orders her to prepare them for death. To save their lives, she demonstrates scientifically that no miracle has taken place; so she accomplishes her end not by a direct plea but by this 'scientific discourse in didactic form'. The orator, it would appear, can learn from this also; he need not put forward his case directly, but may let conviction come of its own accord from what appears on the surface to be discourse of a different kind.

6

In another passage, a little later on, the same rhetor links Xenophon with Homer.[20] His text is the passage in the *Anabasis* where the Greek soldiers come to suspect that the expedition is against the King, and are unwilling to go further. Their general Clearchus undertakes to deal with this situation. He addresses them, promising to follow the soldiers everywhere, but arguing for the necessity of staying where they are. The rhetor notices the similarity between this and the scene in Homer where

---

[19] [Dionysius] *Ars rhetorica* 8.10, 308.23 ff. Usener-Radermacher. Cf Eurip. fr. 480 ff. Nauck.

[20] Ibid. 8.11, 310.7 ff. The reference is to *Anabasis* 1.3.3–6, and *Iliad* 9.434–523.

Phoenix asserts that he will go where Achilles goes, and cannot be separated from him, this being part of Phoenix's attempt to persuade Achilles not to leave the army. 'Nominally he shows why he himself must stay, but in fact he is asking the return of the favours he did Achilles in rearing and educating him, and also doing a favour to Agamemnon.' Since Achilles answers this by saying

> 'Do not break my heart with your grief and complainings,
> Doing Agamemnon a favour',

he shows that he has seen through Phoenix's device. This means that Homer—once again the rhetors' master—has let us also see what is happening: he 'reveals the art of the first speaker in the speeches of the respondents'.

Such discussions, not uncommon in ancient commentaries on Homer, are difficult to follow unless one reads the texts closely; but they are undoubtedly acute and, within their limitations, must have helped to sharpen the perceptions of the reader.

7

What Homer was to the Greeks, Virgil became to the Romans. His commentators adopted similar techniques. Thus, when Juno begs Aeolus to raise a storm and wreck Aeneas' fleet, promising him the nymph Deiopea in return,[21] this is seen as an illustration of a rule of 'invention': if you make a request, it must be within your power, just and reasonable and you must offer remuneration. Again, things are sometimes found in the poet which appear to go against the usual rhetorical rules. When Aeneas,[22] in the middle of his narrative of the Sack of Troy, cries 'Alas! It is wrong for anyone to trust the gods against their will' the commentator offers an excuse. Normally, a general statement with no reference to the special circumstances would be a fault. But here it is appropriate. It applies to the captivity of Cassandra, shortly to be mentioned: she had trusted in her position as priestess, and is to be brutally deceived. It also serves as an argument to show that the Trojans could not have

---

[21] *Aeneid* 1.65, with Servius' comment.
[22] *Aeneid* 2.402.

won however bravely they fought; and Aeneas' narrative of defeat needs this if he is to maintain his prestige as a fighting man.

Comments on the actual form of speeches are also common. There is a very beautiful and moving speech of Anna to Dido near the beginning of the fourth book of the Aeneid, in which she delicately urges her sister towards marriage with Aeneas.[23] Servius' rhetorical comment is unusually detailed. He regards the speech as a complete *suasoria*, in which the speaker removes objections to the proposed course of action, demonstrates its expediency (honour hardly comes in!), and presses the case by an appeal to fear. He points out that Anna begins by demonstrating her love of her sister—

> O dearer to your sister than the day—

and then proceeds at once to the heart of the matter. What follows is a very close analysis, following a set form of approach:

> Then she takes up the various aspects of the question: (i) Dido's personality: should she take another husband because she has lost one? 'Do you think ashes and buried spirits care for this?' (ii) Aeneas' personality: 'Will you fight even a love you like?' (iii) Place: 'Do you not consider in whose country you have settled?' (iv) Fear: 'Why should I tell of wars rising out of Tyre and your brother's menaces?' (v) Expediency: 'What a city will you behold here!' (vi) Method: 'Extend his welcome, make reasons for delay.' (vii) Conjecture about the gods' intention: 'I think it is with the gods' favour . . . that his ships came this way.'

Somewhat similar is the discussion of Aeneas' reply to Dido later on in the same book.[24] This is in terms of *status* theory: Aeneas uses the *status* of excuse (*status venialis*),[25] putting the responsibility for his departure on the gods, but it also involves a point of 'definition': he removes the objection that he is 'running away' by calling it 'departure'. We know that certain teachers of rhetoric, by name Titianus and Calvus, perhaps in

---

[23] *Aeneid* 4.31 ff.
[24] *Aeneid* 4.333 ff.
[25] For this see, e.g., Hermogenes 39, 11; 72, 2 Rabe; Halm *RLM* 93, 32 ff. (Fortunatianus).

the second century A.D., used Virgil extensively in their teaching, and were particularly concerned to illustrate *status* theory from him.[26]

Restrictive and mechanical as much of it is, such criticism had a long history. It persisted in the Renaissance commentaries, and especially in the great and influential work of the Jesuit La Cerda.[27] Something like it is common in modern analyses of classical texts; and the techniques of the ancients still have something to teach.

[26] Servius on *Aeneid* 10.1 f.
[27] First published Madrid 1608.

CHAPTER NINE

Theories of Style

I

ANCIENT theories of style grew up almost entirely in the context of a certain kind of rhetorical instruction, or perhaps one should say philosophical rhetoric. The third book of Aristotle's *Rhetoric*, and the lost work of his pupil Theophrastus, represent the earliest attempts to set out the principles. One of our most important sources, the surviving treatise of Demetrius, is in the same tradition and has a strong Peripatetic strain in it. Stylistic theory was of course of general literary concern and dealt with poets as well as with prose-writers; but it is important to remember that its origins were rhetorical, and its purposes primarily normative rather than descriptive. Its most elaborate achievements, such as the refined sophistries of Hermogenes, are manifestly part of the rhetorical teaching programme of an archaising age.

'Style' is a term of which any critic must formulate his own definition, in accordance with the needs of his own way of talking about literature. But however it is used, it implies a contrast with an element of content, and the assumption that the message might theoretically at least have been conveyed in some other way. The more sophisticated the theory, and the more attention it pays to poetry as opposed to ordinary speech, the less clear this distinction becomes, and the less certain it seems that one can really talk about the matter of a piece of discourse without the 'style' that gives it form. In antiquity, a fairly naïve view of these matters prevailed. This accords with the dominant assumption that the rhetorical use of language was to communicate a known message, and that poetry was mimetic only and so secondary to the real world.

What the Greeks called *lexis, phrasis* or *hermēneia*, the Romans
called *dictio* or *elocutio*: they meant, quite simply, the verbal
dress of thought. The metaphor commonly used to express the
relation was indeed that of clothing or ornament.[1] This was no
doubt simple-minded. But it is not true that ancient writers
saw no difficulty in the matter; on the contrary, the incon-
veniences of fixing a frontier between the *lektikos topos* and the
pragmatikos topos were often felt. The complexities of the doctrine
of 'figures' are evidence of that. And it is certainly true of
Demetrius and Hermogenes, and indeed of 'Longinus' and
Aristides and the whole tradition which they represent, that
they do not think of *lexis* as a wholly independent thing. All
these writers agree in denying, in their practice, that the
charaktēres logōn ('types of discourse') are wholly definable in
terms of vocabulary and word-order. Content comes into it
also. To achieve a certain effect, the writer needs to control his
choice of thought, his handling, his figures and finally his diction and his arrangement. There is a good deal of understanding, in practice, of the organic connection between form and
content. This connection is indeed seen in terms of the doctrine
of decorum, and of the assumption that 'great words suit great
things, and little words little things'. I suggested above[2] that
this was something which seriously limited the power of the
ancient critics to see their literature clearly. It did however
save them from an opposite error, to which their highly verbal
culture might well be thought prone, namely the evaluation of
literature solely by the quality and harmony of its words.

There are two general observations which may be useful in
helping to define the characteristics of the ancient doctrine of
lexis, and to clear it of some associations which attach to the
modern term 'style' but are not relevant to ancient ways of
thinking. The first is that these terms *lexis* and *phrasis*, *dictio* and
elocutio show no metaphorical extension at all; the English
word 'style' by contrast, though originally just the characteristic

[1] So Quintilian 11.1.3, on inappropriate style: 'Men would similarly be de-
formed by necklaces and pearls and long dresses, which adorn women; nor
would the robe of the *triumphator*, than which one can think of nothing more
august, suit women.' We should recall also the *kosmos epeōn* of Democritus
(above, Chapter V 3).
[2] Chapter I 3.

movement of the pen, extends, in common usage, to all sorts of activities.[3] 'Style of life' is a metaphor unthinkable in Greek or Latin. Secondly: 'style' in modern usage is very much an individual matter. We think of it as a kind of finger-print, unique to every individual, and interestingly unique to every interesting individual. Something like this is of course found in antiquity. The style of a great examplar, Lysias or Demosthenes, is naturally called the 'Lysian' or 'Demosthenic' *charaktēr*. The fact that sensitive critics sometimes felt sure enough to identify authors by their style points the same way. Yet the maxim, *talis oratio qualis vita*, a way of saying that 'speech reflects life',[4] seems to be of a different application altogether. It asserts that speech is an indication of the moral characteristics of the speaker, marking not his individuality, but his type. This is in accordance with the general ancient view of character, as we see it for example when we observe the biographies of Plutarch and the ways in which they differ from the individualised biographies of modern times;[5] there is nothing surprising in finding this attitude prevalent in views of literature as well as in views of life and morals.

2

A word of warning is also necessary. We are very remote from these languages, and our sensibilities, however carefully trained, are very imperfect. We have therefore often to take it for granted that words actually made the impression they are said by our sources to make. Now this is not at all a safe assumption; Hermogenes lived five centuries after Demosthenes, and he (like the rest of the rhetors) was in business to give confident judgments, even if they were not always based on a sound sense of the classical language. Consequently, the discrimination of styles in Greek and Latin, one of the main achievements claimed by the critics of antiquity, is easier to admire than to evaluate.

[3] *N.E.D.* s.v. style III.9–26 gives a range of metaphorical extensions.
[4] Cf. above, Chapter IV 5.
[5] See D. A. Russell, *Plutarch*, 100 ff.; and B. Bucher-Isler, *Norm und Individualität in der Biographien Plutarchs*, Bern (1972).

3

The tendency of Greek thought to proceed by defining pairs of opposites is well known: day and night, right and left, male and female set a pattern of dichotomy on which much thinking about many subjects was inevitably grounded. It is no surprise that our earliest account of differences in stylistic tone should be of this kind. The *agōn* between Aeschylus and Euripides in the *Frogs* is of course comic in purpose:[6] both parties are meant to appear ridiculous. But the intended contrast is fairly plain, and the vocabulary seems to have influenced later and more serious criticism very considerably. Both writers compose, of course, within the limits of tragedy, the nature of which is to be grandiloquent. If Euripides fails to maintain this grandeur, the failure is relative: even the traits which Aristophanes holds up to ridicule—'Aether my pasture' and the like—are in the grand manner. Now the special qualities attributed to Aeschylus are plain enough: resounding magniloquence, based largely on compound words 'bolted together', and powerful emotional effects, mostly related to the fears and excitements experienced in war or danger. As his subjects are larger than life, so are his words: 'great words', as he is made to say, are the necessary outcome of 'great attitudes and thoughts'. This tells us nothing of the pathos of Aeschylus, the speculative power, the occasional realistic humour; but it created a stereotype which later authors—notably Dio Chrysostom in his account of the three tragedians' Philoctetes plays,[7] but also 'Longinus'—accept without question. In the *Frogs*, it is Euripides, not Aeschylus, who makes claims for his art. He has found tragedy in an unhealthy state, and has put her on a diet to slim her down. He gives tragedy a new adornment in the shape of 'monodies', and a strictly economical and intelligible plot. Dio Chrysostom's account of Euripides' *Philoctetes* makes the same point: Aeschylus did not bother to motivate the presence of his chorus of Lemnians, while Euripides painstakingly makes them apologise for their long neglect of the crippled hero, in order to make the situation seem probable. A certain degree of realism is regu-

[6] Cf. above, Chapter II 2 (*ALC* 8 ff.).
[7] *Oration* 52 (*ALC* 504 ff.). Cf. above, p. 63.

larly thought of as a Euripidean characteristic. But the strictly
stylistic qualities, as Aristophanes sees them, are not so clear.
We hear of precision (the key word is *saphēs*, 'clear', 'distinct'),
elegance (the key adjective is *leptos*), ingenuity, sharp arguments, and words suited to the real world. In brief, Euripides
deliberately avoids the grand words on which Aeschylus depends, and the grand conceptions that go with them; instead,
he gives his plays a stricter intellectual discipline, and the
appropriate language of argument. In terms of the effect on the
hearer, Aeschylus 'amazes' (*ekplēttei*),[8] and stirs his audience to
martial enthusiasm by his heroic images. This is 'Longinus' '
picture too. Euripides, on the other hand, stimulates the mind
by forcing us to think about the mythical situation and see it in
terms of real life. Aristophanes' critique of course is not a purely
literary one: he also sees the contrast between the two poets as
a manifestation of the conflict of old and new, between accepted patriotic values and questioning revaluation, which was
a leading feature of the public consciousness of his age.

4

What is essentially Aristophanes' dichotomy appears, though
in various forms, as the most widely accepted classification of
what may be called literary tones throughout antiquity.
Grandeur, *ekplēxis*, natural ability, emotion stand on one side;
realism, persuasion, art and *ēthos* on the other. It is worth while
looking at some of the guises in which this antinomy appears.

Dionysius of Halicarnassus uses a simple variety of it to begin
his classification of forms of word-arrangement (*sunthesis*), a
formal feature with which content has little or nothing to do:

Under pleasurableness (*hēdonē*) I class: freshness (*hōra*), charm
(*charis*), euphony (*eustomia*), sweetness (*glukutēs*), persuasiveness
(*pithanon*) and the like. Under 'beauty' (*kalon*) I class: magnificence
(*megaloprepeia*), weight (*baros*), solemnity (*semnologia*), dignity (*axiōma*),
the patina of age (*pinos*).[9]

Here, the two basic qualities are called *hēdonē* and *kalon*: a

---

[8] *ekplēttein* and *ekplēxis*, 'astonishment', are important terms: 'Longinus' 15.2,
with my note *ad loc.*

[9] *De compositione verborum* 11.37 (*ALC* 331).

slightly unexpected pair, until we recall that they are commonly opposed to each other in an ethical sense, as 'pleasure' and 'honour'. Under *hēdonē* come two sets of qualities. One is represented by *pithanon*, 'persuasiveness'. This includes the notion of plausible argument, the appeal to the rational; but it includes also an element of ingratiation. The other terms—*hōra*, *charis* and so on—have to do with the euphony and elegance of discourse, not with its intellectual content. On the other side, we have the qualities which can be seen as varieties of *kalon*. It is at once noticeable that they do not include anything which rouses fear, though in Aristophanes—and later in 'Longinus'— this is an integral element of most forms of grandeur. This omission does not seem to be due simply to the fact that Dionysius' subject is *sunthesis*, for he later[10] discusses Homer's ingenuity in adapting sound to sense in passages of pathos, fear or heroism. Moreover, when he comes to identify the main types of *sunthesis*, these prove to be three in number— 'rough', 'smooth' (*glaphura*) and 'mixed'—and the 'rough' is meant to express emotion, and is exemplified by the work of Aeschylus and Thucydides. What we have in the list we are considering is essentially a contrast between the dignified and the charming; this is an antinomy which has obvious social overtones. It matters little that it is applied to *sunthesis* and not to *lexis* in general.

The differences between this and Aristophanes are worth noting. In the *Frogs*, Dionysus takes pleasure (*hēdetai*) in Aeschylus, whom he chooses to take back to earth, and yet Aeschylus' power lies in grandeur and *ekplēxis*, for he shocks and stimulates by an assault on our primitive passions and fears. Euripides, as we saw, stands for ingenuity, realism, neatness of workmanship; he stimulates us to exercise our analytical powers. In Dionysius' antithesis, neither of the two terms is quite the same. 'Pleasure' is actually opposed to grandeur— though this may be only a verbal point of no significance—and seems to stand for something inoffensive, likeable rather than admirable, and eliciting a response of painless acceptance; grandeur rouses respect rather than fear. Neither disturbs, and neither excites.

[10] 16.97 ff.

The antinomy, in one form or another, had a long life, and outlasted many changes of taste and circumstance. One version of it is the basis of the treatise of Demetrius, whose four *charaktēres*, though he proves them to be independent of one another, naturally group themselves into two pairs: the grand (*megaloprepēs*) and the forceful (*deinos*) stand opposed to the elegant (*glaphuros*) and the plain (*ischnos*). Another, and simpler, application is to be found in the musical writer Aristides Quintilianus, for whom the opposing tones are quite simply identified with 'male' and 'female'; even the use of a feminine noun (*limnē*) for the ocean can be said to add 'charm' to a passage of Homer.[11]

5

This dichotomy represents the simplest possible answer to the question what differences of *lexis* there are. It must always be 'grand' or 'not grand'. But it does not tell us 'what constitutes a good style'. This question first comes to the front in Aristotle, though it must have been discussed from the earliest days of prose literature, since, while poetry has other features beside *lexis*—metre and accompanying music—which contribute to its excellence, prose has only words and their arrangement. It is noticeable that Aristotle regards the problem raised by some predecessors (perhaps Theodectes) of how to make style 'agreeable' or 'grand' (*hēdus, megaloprepēs*) as of no importance: these are 'moral virtues', not properly qualities of *lexis* in itself.[12] If it is important that *lexis* should give an impression corresponding to these qualities, that will follow from its possession of its own essential virtues. These are correctness, clarity, a certain measure of dignity (*onkos*), and finally propriety (*prepon*), that is to say a capacity to adapt itself to the required emotion, character and subject-matter. This theory of *aretai* ('virtues') is both intelligent and coherent. It applies to poetry also, with certain modifications: poetical language avoids 'meanness' in all circumstances,[13] not merely in accordance with the demands of the particular situation, and also admits more foreign words and metaphors. The theory of 'virtues' has thus nothing

---

[11] 2.8–9 (*ALC* 552 ff.).
[12] *Rhetoric* 1414^a 20.   [13] *Poetics* 1458^a 18.

to do with the distinction of what we are calling 'tones' of discourse, which Aristotle clearly dismisses as secondary and ir-
relevant to his problem in the *Rhetoric*. The demand for *onkos*
should of course not be confused with a demand for 'grandeur'
(*megaloprepeia*); it is simply a requirement for that degree of fullness and dignity which distinguishes public utterance from
private. The requirements of correctness—*Hellēnismos*, in
Roman writers *Latinitas*—and distinctness (*saphēneia*) are basic.
Aristotle is much impressed by the difference between the
written style, meant to be used in a cool hour, and the style of
impromptu speech, meant only to be heard.[14] When we write
to be read, we no longer have expressiveness of voice or gesture
to help us in making our meaning clear. Punctuation and word-
division hardly existed in Greek at this time; and Aristotle is
commending a kind of *akribeia* ('exactness') which makes the
written word unambiguous, even in these conditions. Isocrates
had gone far to achieve this, largely by the careful syntactical
control of his periods.

Aristotle's doctrine of *aretai* was developed to some extent by
Theophrastus, who replaced *onkos* by *kataskeuē*,[15] and probably
also took the step of characterising this as 'pleasing', thereby
beginning the process of conflation between 'virtues' and
'tones' which is noticeable in many later theories. The Stoics,
we are told, added *suntomia*, 'conciseness', to the essential virtues; but basically the Peripatetic scheme was taken for
granted throughout antiquity. Pollio's famous remark that
Livy had 'Patavinitas' is a parody of it;[16] it means simply that
the historian's *Latinitas* was an inferior, rustic imitation; he did
not possess the sure grasp of grammar and syntax that marks
the correct, urban speaker.[17]

[14] Cf. above, Chapter III 1.

[15] This is a more external feature: 'ornament', 'presentation', rather than
'size'. Cf. Cicero *Orator* 79.

[16] Quintilian 1.5.56; K. Latte, *CP* 35 (1940) 56 f. (= *Kleine Schriften* 896 f.).

[17] It is noteworthy that Aristotle uses *asteios* (urban, urbane, witty) for the
quality that makes clever expression successful: *Rhetoric* 3.10 (*ALC* 150, with
Miss Hubbard's note). The town was thought to be the milieu in which the
best speech was found; we may contrast later Roman archaising tastes which
admired the conservative language of house-bound women (Cic. *De oratore*
3.45).

In Dionysius we find an elaborate form of the doctrine of 'virtues', which he uses rather mechanically to describe the qualities of the classical orators and historians.[18] 'Purity', 'clarity' and 'brevity' are 'necessary' virtues, together with the preference for literal over metaphorical expression and the capacity to 'round off and turn' the thought—that is to say, to compose coherent periods. But there is also a range of 'additional' virtues (*epithetoi aretai*): vividness (*enargeia*), characterisation (*ēthopoiia*), decorum (*prepon*), persuasiveness (*pithanotēs*), charm (*charis*), sense of timing (*kairos*), elevation (*hupsos*), grandeur (*megaloprepeia*) and forcefulness (*deinotēs*). Not all of these need be present in any one author, however great. Some, as will be obvious, are qualities which define a certain character or tone of writing; they are, as Aristotle would put it, 'ethically' differentiated. The sharp distinction between *charaktēr* and *aretē* is now thoroughly blurred.

6

It is in the context of this blurring that we should consider the classification of stylistic tones into three, not two or four,[19] main categories which is the best known form of stylistic theory in the Roman times. This 'tripartite scheme' is found again and again in Cicero, Dionysius and Quintilian.[20] It was traditionally illustrated out of Homer, the fount of all wisdom, who was naturally imagined to have known this also.[21] The grand style and the plain were described, it was believed, in the account of the oratory of Odysseus and Menelaus in the third book of the *Iliad*: Odysseus' words 'came like the snows of winter', while

---

[18] *Lysias* 13.

[19] Four not only in Demetrius, but in [Plutarch] *Life of Homer* 73, Macrobius *Saturnalia* 5.1.7, Proclus in Photius cod. 239 (see Appendix, p. 201).

[20] See especially Cicero *Brutus* 40; Dionysius *Demosthenes* 1 ff. and 8 (*ALC* 307 ff.); Quintilian 12.10.58 ff. (*ALC* 413).

[21] See, e.g., Cicero *Brutus* 40 (*ALC* 222); Quintilian 12.10.64 (*ALC* 414); Gellius 6.14.7; [Plutarch] *Life of Homer* 172; Radermacher, *Artium scriptores*, 6 ff. The passages of Homer are *Il.* 3.212 ff. and 1.249. Libanius (*Decl.* 3 and 4) invented stylistically contrasting speeches by Menelaus and Odysseus claiming Helen back from the Trojans.

the laconic Menelaus 'spoke little, but never missed the point'.
With them, wherever this illustration is found, appears also the
figure of Nestor, whose words, as we learn from another
passage of the epic, are 'sweeter than honey'. The division of
stylistic tones thus portrayed now includes Isocratean smoothness and sweetness as a third characteristic kind, side by side
with stormy power and laconic simplicity. Whether this scheme
was an invention of Theophrastus has been much debated. [22] It
probably does date from about his time. It can be seen as a
formulation of distinctions close to those of Aristotle, since the
plain style may be thought of as a reproduction of natural
language, the Odyssean storms as the emotive style of the courts
and assemblies (*lexis agonistikē*) and Nestor's smoothness as
language meant for reading (*anagnōsis*). Moreover, the system
is taken for granted in what is generally believed to be the
earliest of the late Hellenistic treatises to survive, the *Rhetorica
ad Herennium*.[23] Once accepted, such a scheme offered a tempting way of classifying writers in any genre. Thucydides,
Herodotus and Xenophon stood for the 'three styles' in history;[24] Demosthenes, Isocrates and Lysias in oratory; Hesiod
demonstrates the 'middle style', and Antimachus the forcible,
in epic.[25] This kind of labelling, whether based strictly on the
tripartite scheme or on some version of the doctrine of *aretai*,
was obviously superficial and unsatisfactory; Horace was quite
right to make fun of it as applied to the early Roman poets.[26]

It is natural to ask what the relationships of the three styles to
one another was supposed to be. Can they coexist in a single
author? And is one better than the others?

Cicero certainly thought that an orator should be master of

[22] For the many problems in this; see Hendrickson, *AJP* 25 (1904), 248–
290; Grube, *AFP* 73 (1952) ff.; Austin on Quint., loc. cit. We should not think
of the identification of the mean or middle style with sweetness or smoothness,
or the accompanying illustration of Nestor, as Theophrastan; but *some* notion
of an 'intermediate' between two recognised extremes was probably a part of
his theory.

[23] Book IV contains invented specimens of the three styles and the
corresponding perversions.

[24] Marcellinus, *Life of Thucydides*, 35 ff. (Appendix, p. 197).

[25] Quintilian 10.1.52 f. (*ALC* 388).

[26] *Epist.* 2.1.55–9.

all. He associated the grand style with the orator's function of
exciting emotion, the smooth with his giving pleasure, the plain
with his conveying information.[27] Moreover, he claimed to have
composed three speeches which might serve as models of the
three kinds: *pro Caecina* in the plain style, especially in the
narratio; *pro lege Manilia*, with its large panegyric element, in the
middle style; and *pro Rabirio*, which deals with a highly emotive
political subject, in the grand.[28] Indeed, the highest kind of
orator—who, for Cicero, was the one best capable of rousing
emotion—actually needed the skills of the other two styles in
order to make his own manner acceptable.

It is easy to see how this kind of description and characterisation of styles could be used for the purposes of literary controversy, that is to say for advocating a taste for certain kinds of
writing and disparaging others. Cicero's formula was put forward, to a certain extent, in self-defence against the criticisms
of purists.[29] 'Longinus' too clearly uses this whole range of
ideas in a polemical way. Of course, *hupsos* as he sees it is not
just a matter of *lexis*; indeed, choice of thought is a very much
more important part of it. But it is none the less a specific 'tone':
serious, moving, eloquent in one of several ways, and sharply
opposed to any kind of triviality. 'Longinus', it is important to
note, does not in fact use the 'tripartite' scheme, though he must
surely have known of it.[30] Instead, he treats certain manifesta-
tions of the 'middle style'—'panegyric' writing, amplification
and abundance—as contributing to *hupsos*, others as detracting
from it. *Hupsos*, we recall, occurred in Dionysius' list of *epithetoi
aretai*. In 'Longinus', it is both an *aretē* and a *charaktēr*; further
evidence of the blurring of the two concepts.

7

From this point of view, Longinian *hupsos* would fit quite well

---

[27] *Orator* 97 ff., 100 ff. (*ALC* 244 f.).
[28] So one might suggest as short specimens: *Pro Caecina* 20–1, *Pro Rabirio*
11–13, *Pro lege Manilia* 69–70.
[29] Cf. above, Chapter III 5.
[30] It is perhaps implied in 3.4.

among the multifarious *ideai*[31] of the later rhetoricians, for
these too are based both on *aretai* and on *charaktēres*. But
'Longinus' ' uniqueness must not be forgotten. He alone of the
stylistic theorists identifies the quality he is discussing with the
essence of the higher kind of literature and regards the ex-
ponents of other qualities as practising an inferior art. Moreover, he has a clear conviction that a certain kind of moral
excellence is necessary to achieve his end, and that this must
come—or is most likely to come—from the personal qualities
of the writer. Still, so far as the logic of his system goes, he is of
much the same school as the rhetors we have now to consider.
'Aristides' and Hermogenes are the chief of these.[32]

Their *ideai*—like Demetrius' *charaktēres*—involve thoughts
and ways of putting them—*ennoiai* or *gnōmai* and *schēmata* or
methodoi[33]—as well as features of language. This is connected
with the fact that both writers import into the discussion a distinction between the various kinds of prose writing with which
they were familiar. In 'Aristides' this takes the form of a
separation between 'oratorical' language (*politikos* or *agonistikos*
logos) and 'simple' language (*aphelēs* or *haplous logos*); the latter
is represented especially by Xenophon's *Cyropaedia* and by
various Socratic works. 'Aristides' hardly has a system; but the
qualities he assigns to *politikos logos* fall into two groups. One
comprises the qualities of grand and powerful oratory, the
other those of the lighter, more 'Attic' kind. *Aphelēs logos* has a
less overt structure, less scope for elaboration and force, more
emphasis on character, a readiness to accept humble examples
and a more personal tone. Something like this broad distinction of genres was common doctrine in later rhetoric; we find it,
for example, in the rhetor Menander.[34] In Hermogenes,
though his terminology fluctuates, the *panegurikos logos* comes to
be opposed to the *politikos*, the exemplar of it is Plato, and it can

[31] Isocrates (13,16) had already used the term *idea* in a stylistic context. In
'Aristides' *idea* and *aretē* are linked.
[32] 'Aristides': text in Spengel 2.459 ff. and W. Schmid (1926); Hermogenes: Spengel 2.265 ff., and H. Rabe (1913) 213 ff. See Hagedorn, and also
J. Sykutris, *Gnomon* (1930) 528 ff. (in R. Stark, *Rhetorica*, 440 ff.).
[33] *Methodoi* are in fact often simply 'figures of thought'.
[34] Cf. Menander 400.8 Spengel, with Russell and Wilson's note.

be held to include not only philosophy and history, but poetry as well.[35]

It is worth while dwelling on Hermogenes for two reasons. The first is that he does make some attempt to justify his method. The other is that we can see him at work as a practising critic and teacher, thanks to the fullness of his exposition and the wealth of examples.

Hermogenes' object[36] is to give a rationale for the practice of *mimēsis*, a set of principles that will, he hopes, make it something better than a matter of an irrational knack. He therefore isolates from Demosthenes a number of characteristics, which he calls *ideai*. Demosthenes, we are told, mastered all these, held them in balance, and used them as required, whereas in all other writers one or more of the *ideai* predominates, colouring the whole style. Demosthenes' *deinotēs* thus consists in his control of the whole gamut; he is the universal master for the orator, as Homer is for the poet.

Hermogenes' *ideai* fall into five main groups. The first is 'clarity' (*saphēneia*), which has 'purity' (*katharotēs*) and 'distinctness' (*eukrineia*) as members. The second, 'dignity, size and grandeur' (*axiōma kai onkos kai megethos*), embraces 'solemnity' (*semnotēs*), 'brilliance' (*lamprotēs*), 'abundance' (*peribolē*), and the ill-distinguished triad of 'roughness', 'culminating effort', and 'vehemence' (*trachutēs, akmē, sphrodrotēs*). Third comes a section of features contributing to 'carefulness and beauty' (*epimeleia kai kallos*), mainly points of sentence-structure and ornamentation by means of vocabulary and figures. *Gorgotēs*, the fourth main head, may be rendered 'tautness'; it involves rapidity and tension, and is opposed to slackness and flabbiness of writing. Finally there is *ēthos*, a general term for all the qualities associated with Attic delicacy and charm: 'simplicity' (*apheleia*), 'sweetness' (*glukutēs*), 'tartness' (*drimutēs*), fairness and sincerity (*epieikeia, alētheia*)—these last being qualities of thought rather than of language. Even this does not exhaust the complexity of this rambling system, which was naturally capable of modification whenever the author wanted to make a new point, or attack the interpretation of a rival.

[35] Cf. above, Chapter VIII 1.
[36] 213 ff. Rabe (=*ALC* 560).

To illustrate Hermogenes' ingenuity, I take a single and relatively uncomplicated example. This is the discussion of 'brilliance' (*lamprotēs*), one of the qualities contributing to grandeur and dignity.[37] It is indeed an essential factor, needed to counteract the harsh or dry effect (*austēros* is Hermogenes' word) that would result from unmitigated solemnity, roughness and vehemence, such as sharp debate demands. So it is a kind of 'brightness' (*phaidrotēs*), but not the kind that depends on ornament or sweetness, nor yet that of the smooth, careful manner that is to be found in less elevated parts of Demosthenes. *Lamprotēs* is always dignified. It displays the speaker's confidence in the impressiveness of what he is saying, his own success, and the pleasure of the audience in what he tells it. An example is Demosthenes' proud boast:

Not with stones or bricks did I fortify the city, nor is this, of all my achievements, the one of which I am most proud. If you want to see my fortifications, you will find arms, cities and places, harbours and ships, horses in great number—and the men to fight for all these things.[38]

So far as subject matter is concerned, *De corona*, with its confident pride, is an obvious source for *lamprotēs*.[39] It provides also an illustration of the *methodoi* which this *idea* requires. One should state what has to be said without hesitation or doubt. The famous Marathon oath[40]—eloquently and much more perceptively annotated by 'Longinus'—is, for Hermogenes, an example of brilliant *methodos*, because it makes the prestige of the matter even greater than it would have been if expressed as a simple analogy. In other words:

No, you did not do wrong—by those of your ancestors who risked their lives at Marathon, you did not do wrong,

is more 'brilliant' than, for example:

You did not do wrong in running a risk for the freedom of Greece; for this is what those who risked their lives at Marathon did.

[37] 264 ff. Rabe.   [38] *De corona* 299.
[39] E.g. 96, 98, 188.   [40] 208: 'Longinus' 16 (*ALC* 480).

Sometimes, however, Demosthenes wishes to vary the 'brilliant' effect with something else. For example:

Such was the beginning and first foundation of the affair of Thebes, whereas previously the cities had been brought into a state of hatred, dislike and mistrust by these men. This decree made the danger that hung over our city pass away like a cloud.[41]

In this, the omission of the words from 'whereas' to 'these men' would (we are told) have given uninterrupted 'brilliance'. Demosthenes wanted to avoid excess and the consequent satiety.

Hermogenes' prescription turns then to vocabulary; in this 'brilliance' does not differ from 'solemnity'. Its sentence-structure, however, is distinctive: there should be long cola, and a certain amount of complexity of syntax—genitive absolutes, indirect speech, and the like. Very straightforward narrative in simple statements is 'pure and simple' but not 'brilliant'.[42] Finally, the rhythms: these should be in general grand and solemn, though occasional trochaic patterns may be allowed.

Hermogenes' range of examples is limited, and his anxiety to define distinct qualities leads him often into unconvincing special pleading. But the ingenuity and sensitivity are evident. To read *De corona* with Hermogenes would have been a strenuous business. He comes as near as any ancient author ever does to giving articulate expression to his sense of stylistic nuance and colour.

8

In doing all this, Hermogenes, like Demetrius and 'Longinus', makes considerable use of the doctrine of 'figures' and 'tropes', a conspicuous and notorious element in most ancient criticism of individual texts.[43] In his model passages of *De*

---

[41] 188.

[42] Hermogenes' example (268, 3 Rabe) is Demosthenes 20 (*Leptines*) 11.

[43] Basic texts: *Ad Herennium* 4, Cic. *De oratore* 3. 148–71, Quintilian 8–9, Rutilius Lupus (ed. E. Brooks, 1970), and especially 'Longinus' 16–29; later Greek treatises in Spengel, *Rhetores Graeci* (note recent editions of Tryphon by

corona (299 and 188), Hermogenes isolates two phenomena
which he regards as 'figures' (*schēmata*) of diction. In one—
'Not with stones did I fortify the city'—we have *anairesis*,
'negation'. In the other—'This was the beginning of the
Theban affair'—he sees *apostasis*, 'detached phrasing'. These
are uncommon technicalities; they serve to remind us of the
length to which this labelling of ornamental abnormalities
was taken.

Both the theory of 'figures' and that of 'tropes' date from the
Hellenistic period. The ornaments themselves are of course as
old as literature; almost all could be found in Homer, while
early Greek prose, such as that of Gorgias, conscientiously exploited the sound-effects of alliteration and rhyme. There is
also some pre-Hellenistic theory. Aristotle discussed metaphor
—later to be regarded as the most important 'trope'—from a
characteristically intellectualist point of view. He believed that
the capacity to invent metaphors was an index to the writer's
understanding of the world, because it showed that he could
discern likenesses between dissimilar things. And he was interested in the logical difference between metaphorical expressions
in which the genus stands for the species, those in which the
reverse happens, and those which form a kind of proportion. It
is these last—'old age is the evening of life'—that later writers
normally mean by 'metaphor', as distinct from metonymy or
synecdoche. There is no doubt that it was Stoic grammatical
theory that classified and elaborated the doctrine of tropes: the
basic eight—onomatopoeia, catachresis, metaphor, metalepsis,
synecdoche, metonymy, antonomasia, antiphrasis—occur in
almost all later texts, and may be regarded as forming a coherent
set.[44]

M. L. West [*CQ* n.s. 15 (1965)] and Tiberius by G. Ballaira, 1968). General
discussions: Volkmann 415–505, Martin 261–315, Schenkeveld 131–4, K.
Barwick, *Probleme der stoischen Sprachlehre und Rhetorik*, 88–111, B. Vickers,
Classical Rhetoric in English Poetry, 83–150, W. G. Rutherford, *A Chapter in the
History of Annotation*, and my note on 'Longinus' loc. cit.
[44] So Barwick, op. cit. See ps.-Plu *Hom.* 16 ff. (7. 345 ff. Bernardakis). A
note of his definitions may help. 'Onomatopoeia' is the imitation of sense by
sound (*doupos*, 'crash'; *rhokthei*, 'surged'). 'Catachresis' is the use of a word for
something which does not have a name of its own: *kuneē* means originally a
cap of dog's skin (*kuōn*, 'dog'), and it is a catachresis when Homer uses it for

The distinction between the 'tropes' and the 'figures' is probably also Stoic. It is that a 'trope' is a deviation from nature (*phusis*) in the use of an individual word, while a 'figure' is a similar deviation in the arrangement of words or the cast of thought. Naturally, these distinctions were hard to maintain in practice; and the ancient treatises on these subjects, like their mediaeval and Renaissance successors, present an extraordinary and frustrating confusion of terminology. Nevertheless, the basic assumption of the theory, namely that there is in fact a 'natural' use of a word and a 'natural' way of putting things, is clearly important. It implies a sense of a norm in language which makes little allowance for historical differences and for the conventions of different kinds of speech. The theoretical difficulties were indeed not altogether neglected: witness the discussion in Alexander[45] of the question whether or not there was in fact a distinction between 'natural' and 'figured' thought. But in general, grammarians and rhetors confined themselves to identifying and labelling, without thinking too much either of the theoretical basis of their procedures, or of the critical value of what they were doing.

The doctrine of the figures—both 'of speech' and 'of thought' —was, like that of the tropes, a Hellenistic product. The definitive systematisations were made in the first centuries B.C. by two men: Gorgias,[46] who taught Cicero's son at Athens in 44 B.C.

---

a goatskin cap. 'Metaphor' is a transfer from the thing properly signified by a word to something which is analogous to it: the 'head' of a mountain, an island 'garlanded' by sea. 'Metalepsis' is the use of a synonym for one sense of a word in another sense which it can bear. *Oxus*, 'sharp-ended', is a natural epithet of islands. But it also means 'quick', and in this sense *thoos* is its synonym. Homer uses *thoos* of islands by metalepsis. 'Synecdoche' is the use of 'part for whole'; 'metonymy' is, for example, the use of 'Demeter' for corn or 'Hephaestus' for fire. 'Antonomasia' is exemplified by saying 'Pelides' for Achilles or 'Tritogeneia' for Athena. 'Antiphrasis' apparently is a sort of irony: Achilles 'was not pleased' means he 'was very much distressed'. 'Plutarch' adds also 'emphasis', the use of a word which suggests something which is not made explicit: 'we *went down into* the Horse' implies that the Horse was a vast thing. This trope is not so commonly identified; and there are of course others; a common list numbers fourteen (see Rutherford, op. cit.).

[45] Appendix, p. 176.
[46] Cic. *Ad. fam.* 16.21.6; Sen. *Contr.* 1.4.7.

and later declaimed at Rome in the hearing of the elder Seneca; and Caecilius of Caleacte, better known as the opponent attacked in *On sublimity*. Part at least of Gorgias' treatise survives in the Latin adaptation of Rutilius Lupus, and a good deal of Caecilius' can be reconstructed from later authors.[47]

'Longinus' no doubt himself used Caecilius when he tried to enumerate the 'figures' which could contribute to *hupsos*. His discussion (16–29) is much the most valuable and intelligent that we have. He alone makes a serious effort to explain how the identification of these abnormalities can contribute to our understanding of the writer's intentions and qualities. He discusses rhetorical questions, asyndeton, combinations of anaphora and asyndeton, polysyndeton, hyperbaton, polyptoton, plural for singular, present for past, apostrophe, and periphrasis; later on, under the general heading of diction, he deals with the important trope of metaphor. But he makes no attempt to be exhaustive. The essence of his discussion is to show that none of these ornaments by itself has the desired effect; everything depends on its appropriateness to its context, and on a reciprocal alliance between the formal structure and the underlying thought. This principle is set out right at the beginning in the analysis (16) of the famous 'Marathon Oath' in Demosthenes (*De corona* 208). This was a much discussed passage, and we can compare the treatment of it in various authors.[48] The rhetor Tiberius may well reproduce what Caecilius said: he regards it not as a simple *paradeigma* ('example') but as the same underlying thought figuratively expressed as an imaginary oath (*horkos*), with a view to brilliance and cogency (*lampron . . . axiopiston*). 'Longinus' goes much further. He dubs the figure 'apostrophe', because it involves turning aside to address the Athenians. He sees that it is admirably suited to the situation, and to the need to answer Aeschines. The 'oath' made the heroes of Marathon and Salamis appear divine. It also made the hearers 'think big'. It

---

[47] See E. Ofenloch, *Caecilii fragmenta*, 32 ff.

[48] *De corona* 208 ff. (with H. Wankel's commentary); Tiberius 3.69, 3.71 Spengel; Quint. 9.2.62; [Aristid.] *Rhet.* 4.14 ff. Schmid; Caecilius fr. 60 Ofenloch.

gave the bare statement an emotional form. And the reference to the victories of Marathon and Salamis ennobled the defeat by Philip. So the passage fulfilled a number of purposes, much more than any other rhetor saw: it demonstrated the rightness of the Athenians' actions, it offered a *paradeigma*, it proved the case and it comprised both an encomium of the men of old and an exhortation to the present generation. To make his point clear, 'Longinus' adduces a piece of scholarly erudition: 'some people', he says, say that the 'seed' (*sperma*) of this passage was an oath spoken by an old soldier in a comedy of Eupolis: 'By Marathon, by my own battle, no one shall grieve my heart and go away rejoicing.' Here, he says, the situation was different, for the Athenians were still successful, and needed no comfort. Moreover, instead of making the men into gods by whom one could swear a solemn oath, Eupolis 'wandered off into the inanimate', making the 'battle' the object. These critical judgments are, of course, of no great value as regards Eupolis. 'Longinus' takes no note of his paratragic manner, or of the comic purposes, whatever they were, which determined his choice of expression. And the contrast of 'inanimate' and 'animate' is forced and mechanical. But they do quite success-fully underline the basic principle of interpretation: it is 'the where and the how, the occasion and the purpose' that deter-mine the success or otherwise of the figurative turn. In this instance, as so often, we come back to 'Longinus' for the best in ancient criticism, a recognisable power to transcend its pedantry and limitations.

CHAPTER TEN

Classification of Literature

I

THE idea that works of literature all belong to definable classes is commonly thought central to any understanding of ancient literature. Scholars and critics, from the Renaissance to the present day, have generally acted on the assumption that there was present in the minds of all ancient writers what Horace calls *lex operis*, 'the law of the work', and that they either followed its prescriptions or infringed them deliberately and of set purpose. This attitude has undoubtedly strong justification in the practice of the ancient writers. Early Greek lyric poetry, for example, was clearly composed in accordance with rigid conventions of content, metre and music, which were determined by the occasions for which the songs were made up. It is so in most pre-literary societies throughout the world. This differentiation of lyric by occasion, the structural elaboration of Attic tragedy and comedy in their earliest known phases, and later the rhetorical precepts that seem to govern so much prose writing, all lend support to the view that the critic's primary task should be to establish categories and assign the individual works to them.

In other words, the key to understanding the literature is to be found in the study of its genres. It is idle to protest against this word. Time has hallowed the Gallicism. But it has no advantage in precision over native synonyms. Indeed, it suffers from a disadvantage of its own: its exotic look makes us hope for the exactness of a term of art; and we are of course disappointed, for it is used to denote classes formed on various principles. Historically, 'genre-theory' is very much more a Renaissance inheritance than an ancient one; when we come to look for it in the critics of antiquity, as of course we must, it appears a much more patchy and incomplete thing than is commonly supposed. Moreover, the gap between theory and practice, as in other areas which we have been considering, is uncomfortably wide.

In this chapter, I shall consider some of the classifications which our texts present, and try to show on what principles and for what purposes they were made. Rules and categories which are not made explicit in this way, but can be inferred from the practice of poets and prose-writers, fall outside our subject; but they cannot altogether be left out of mind.[1]

2

The most general principle of classification is that which states the differentia of poetry. We have seen that, with the exception of Aristotle, the ancient critics took a rather naïve view of this. Verse remained an essential characteristic. It might be possible occasionally to call a prose-writer a poet—Plato for the fire of his language, the historian Ctesias as a 'craftsman of vividness'[2]—but this was little but an instructive hyperbole. Verse apart, the main characteristic of the poet was his 'licence' (*exousia*), the liberties of language and fancy granted him, it could be said, in compensation for the restriction of form.[3] 'Longinus', who illustrates the difference between 'rhetorical' and 'poetical' *phantasia* with considerable intelligence, clearly regards the poetical kind as inferior, because less involved with reality.[4] It is perhaps grandeur of language rather than imaginative reach of subject that was regarded as the special realm of the poet's art. He rode his chariot, the prose-writer followed on foot: *pezos logos*, *pedestris oratio* are the standard expressions for prose. The analogy contrasts neatly with Valéry's comparison with walking and dancing, for it says nothing of the inherent value, the element of play, and the

---

[1] On these, and on the whole problem of the relation between practice and theory, see L. E. Rossi, *BICS* 18 (1971), 69–94.

[2] Cicero *Orator* 67; Demetrius 215 (*ALC* 209).

[3] Quintilian 10.1.29.

[4] 'Longinus' 15.

symbolic character that, to most of us, characterise what the poet does. Moreover, the ancient grammarians and rhetors normally regarded poetry as paraphrasable; its content could be expressed in other words. Not that the poets necessarily thought this; we have the explicit testimony of Horace to the contrary[5] and it is difficult to read his contemporary Virgil without being sure that he could have had no such illusion.

3

The first theoretical distinction of 'kinds' of poetry seems to be that propounded by Plato.[6] As we have seen,[7] he set out an exhaustive division into 'mimetic', 'narrative' and 'mixed'. This is a division based not on occasion, nor on content, but on the presence or absence of mimicry. In drama, the whole thing is mimicry of persons; in the dithyramb, everything is narrative; in epic, there is something of both. In terms of later thinking, this is a little odd. For Aristotle and his successors, the distinction between narrative and dramatic is identical with that between epic and drama. That the epic poet reports his characters' words does not make him an actor. Yet Plato evidently thought it did. He did of course need this for the general drift of his argument, which was to find Homer no less guilty than the dramatists of the evils of *mimēsis*. This gives him motive enough; but the argument must have seemed plausible also. Perhaps we have here a salutary reminder of the extent to which theory may be suggested and shaped by what actually happens. For Plato, epic was a performance. The recitation was highly dramatic, the poet or rhapsode really did become each character in turn. By Aristotle's time, the situation was different; the epic was for reading only, tragedy primarily for performance, but also for private reading.

4

The subject of Aristotle's *Poetics* is '*poiētikē* and its kinds (*eidē*)'.

[5] *Satires* 1.4, 56–62; cf. above, Chapter II 4.
[6] *Rep.* 392D (*ALC* 61).
[7] See above, Chapter VII 4.

The kinds, it appears, are tragedy, comedy, epic and dithy-ramb—the last standing for a range of lyric forms which Aristotle is not concerned to differentiate. The first three of these differ from one another in 'media', 'objects' or 'mode'; and these criteria would serve to define any other 'kind' which came into prominence. As a preface to a treatment of drama, these distinctions are satisfactory enough, and they prepare the way for the thesis that drama is a higher form than epic. But they do not enable Aristotle to give an adequate account of lyric poetry, or of the epigram, or indeed of any form of non-dramatic verse other than epic narrative.

The definition of tragedy[8] follows from the general considerations advanced in the early chapters. It is presumably a model of how an *eidos* should be defined. It makes four points: tragedy is (i) a *mimēsis* of a certain kind of action, namely an 'elevated' and 'complete' one; (ii) expressed in speech enhanced by rhythm, harmony or song, the nature of the enhancement being different in different parts of the play; (iii) a dramatic, not a narrative, performance; (iv) productive of a certain emotional effect, namely the *katharsis* of emotions of the group to which pity and fear belong. The second of these requirements prompts reflection. It is of course true of Greek tragedy that it is a mixed entertainment: choral song and dance, lyrical monody and spoken verse all go to make up the play. But it is not the mere fact of the presence of these kinds of enhancement that makes a tragedy what it is, it is the particular nature and order of them; prologue, parodos, epeisodion, stasimon and so on must follow a certain pattern. These elements, and the pattern they make, are quite different from the elements and pattern of comedy. Now Aristotle deals with these 'quantitative' features, as he calls them, only in chapter 12 of the *Poetics*, and there are well-founded doubts of the genuineness of that chapter.[9] The *Poetics* looks below the surface; Aristotle is not content with enumerating the terms of art used by playwrights themselves, he wants to uncover what he regards as the real structure of a play, and deduce its definition from his general principles. *Poiētikē* is not merely a set of rules for

---

[8] 1450[a].

[9] See Lucas *ad loc.*; Taplin, loc. cit. above, Chapter II, n. 30.

the practitioner. There is a close analogy between this procedure and what both Plato and Aristotle clearly thought about
the common precepts of rhetoric. Here too, the ordinary
teachers enumerated the parts of a speech in order, from prologue to epilogue, and gave instruction on how to compose
them. But all this, for Plato[10] and for Aristotle, is 'preliminary to
the art', not the art itself. We do not possess Aristotle's book on
comedy; but the analogy of the account of tragedy suggests that
we should have missed in it an account, for example, of the
formal features of the comic parabasis, though we can see from
Aristophanes that the poets themselves had clear rules about
this. Let me generalise the point I am trying to make: the genre-
rules which poets observed are not recorded by the philosophical critics, because they regarded them as superficial and
not going to the heart of the matter. If we want to know about
them, we have to infer them from the poems themselves.

5

This tendency to classify on very general principles rather than
to record actual practice persisted in later criticism. This is not
surprising, since literary theory remained, for the most part,
firmly in the tradition of Plato and Aristotle. The compilation
called *Tractatus Coislinianus* is a good example.[11] The writer
divides poetry into 'mimetic' and 'non-mimetic', but he uses
these words in a sense somewhat different both from Aristotle
and from Plato. 'Mimetic' poetry consists of 'narrative'
(*apangeltikon*) and 'dramatic', and the latter has the obvious
subdivisions of comedy, tragedy, mime and satyr-play. The
'non-mimetic' branch is meant evidently to find room for the
didactic poetry that Aristotle deliberately excluded. It is thus
subdivided into 'historical' and 'educative': 'historical' here
covers all knowledge, whether humane or scientific, which
ministers to our curiosity: 'educative', with its subdivisions
'directive' and 'theoretical', presumably covers gnomic and

---

[10] Plato *Phaedrus* 266D ff. (*ALC* 75).
[11] Text in Kaibel, *Comicorum Graecorum Fragmenta* i. See Grube 144 ff.
Appendix, p. 204.

philosophical poetry.[12] This classification, again, is imperfect. It leaves no place for lyric, except for such as is gnomic or educational in content.

This is a classification by content, with no mention of style or metre. In that respect it is unusual. Horace's *Ars* is perhaps more typical of post-Aristotelian thinking. For Horace, the key is *decorum* (*prepon*) : there must be a relation of appropriateness between form and content, and both terms are needed to characterise the 'genre'. Thus hexameter epic, votive elegy, encomiastic lyric and so on are easily distinguished; no one who does not understand this deserves the name of poet. Horace works out one example in detail: the satyr play. This is distinguished from tragedy by subject, for the heroes and divinities in it act ridiculously; and from comedy by the fact that its characters are not drawn from daily life, but from the world of myth and legend. But this is not all: the language and versification of the satyr-play are essentially those of tragedy, not of comedy. It is not clear that Horace sees this quite as we do, when we observe the style and metre of the *Ichneutai* or the *Cyclops*; but he sees plainly enough that the special character of the genre demands a stylistic level which is distinct from both the major genres to which it is related.

6

We must now turn from theorists to grammarians. There can be little doubt that the forms of early lyric were regulated by the conventions attaching to occasions and ceremonies. Much of it was, in a broad sense, religious. When Alexandrian scholars came to classify the poems they had collected, they did so on the basis of what they knew of these often obsolete and unrecorded conventions. Pindar was edited under nine heads: hymns, paeans, dithyrambs, prosodia, partheneia, hyporchemata, encomia, *thrēnoi* (dirges), epinicia.[13] Only the last survive; but the whole range was known and studied in

---

[12] So Kaibel; the manuscript tradition makes these a subdivision of the 'historical' branch, which cannot be right (*pace* Grube, loc. cit.).

[13] See, e.g., Pfeiffer, *History of Classical Scholarship* i, 182 ff.

Hellenistic and Roman times.[14] A very late source gives us a summary of an important scholarly work on these 'kinds', the critical classification by the grammarian Proclus, derived from late Alexandrian scholarship, presumably from Didymus.[15]

For Proclus, prose and poetry have the same virtues though in different degree, and the same 'three styles', though in poetry these look rather different: the 'big' style (*hadron*) is the one that best produces amazement (*ekplēxis*) and poetical beauty; the 'slender' style (*ischnon*) 'pursues metaphorical and ornamental composition, but is composed of relaxed elements, so that it is in general best fitted for lamentation'. Between these two styles lies a 'middle' style, but this is not the same as the 'florid' kind (*anthēron*),[16] since this is found in combination with all the other three, and especially in descriptions of places like meadows and groves.[17]

This stylistic theory, whatever its origin, reveals an attempt to adapt rhetorical principles to the conditions of poetry. It is unfortunate that its details are not disclosed; Proclus evidently discussed the 'judgment of poetry', and in this connection examined the difference between *ēthos* and *pathos*. We are however told more about his actual classification. 'Narrative' poetry was conveyed in hexameters, iambics, elegy or lyric: in other words, a classification by metre sufficed here. 'Imitative' poetry, on the other hand, fell into the three classes of tragedy, comedy and satyr-play, as in the Hellenistic tradition we know from Horace.

It is the division of lyric poetry that seems, at first sight, to bring us nearer to the poems themselves. Yet here too there is

[14] See Horace *Odes* 4.2. (Appendix, p. 192).

[15] Photius *Bibliotheca*, cod. 239 (ed. R. Henry, *Photius*, vol. 5 (1967), 155 ff. The date of this 'Proclus' has been disputed; it is sometimes held that he is the same as the fifth-century Neoplatonist, but there are good reasons for thinking him much earlier. Dependence on Didymus (for whom see Pfeiffer, op. cit., 274 ff.) seems certain. Extract in Appendix, p. 201.

[16] This view appears to be directed against that stated in an even later source for the same material ('Heliodorus', *Scholia in Dionysii Thracis artem* 449 Hilgard), which identifies *anthēron* with *meson* ('middle'). Henry (on Photius, loc. cit.) seems to me wrong in renouncing the use of 'Heliodorus', who may in some respects preserve a truer account of the original doctrine.

[17] Note Horace *Ars poetica* 16 f.; *lucus et ara Dianae et properantis aquae per amoenos ambitus agros* (*ALC* 280).

an *a priori* basis of classification: lyric poems are addressed to gods, to men, or to both, or else relate to certain circumstances. Somewhat obscurely, the author says that this last class 'are not kinds of lyric poetry, but were attempted by the poets themselves'. This presumably means that 'hymn', 'paean', 'dithyramb', 'epithalamium', 'partheneion' and the like are names of actual *eidē*: 'georgics', 'gnomological poems', 'apostolics' and the like are descriptions invented by poets, or applied to poems of a certain type.[18] The whole classification then involves three main elements: (i) a distinction between poems 'to gods' and 'to men'; (ii) a list of titles derived from early custom and religion; (iii) a supplementary list covering, in the main, elegiac, gnomic and didactic poetry.

7

We come next to classifications of prose. We have had occasion to consider the division of oratory into epideictic, deliberative, and forensic. This could be represented as an exclusive, *a priori* division—the subject-matter of the three kinds related respectively to present, future and past—but it was also a practical one, differentiating the activities of entertainer, politician and litigant. There is only one complication: the ambiguity in the term 'epideictic', which sometimes covers not merely 'praise and blame' but all kinds of display speech, even those which mimic the deliberative or forensic.[19]

For the relationship between oratory and other kinds of literature we may turn to Cicero.[20] The orator, he says, is to be distinguished from four other kinds of writer. These are the philosopher, the sophist, the historian and the poet. By 'philosopher', he means primarily the writers of dialogues and popular treatises. They write *ornate*, but also in a quiet,

---

[18] Note the full list (159, 8 Henry; 166, 32 Henry): *pragmatika, emporika, apostolika, gnōmologika, geōrgika, epistaltika*. The first two of these ('poems of action' and 'of trade') are mysterious: *pragmatica* are narratives of actions; *emporika* are about travel; *apostolika* (cf. also 'Heliodorus', 450.11) are letters making requests or giving advice; *gnōmologika* are poems of moral precepts; *geōrgika* are on farming; *epistaltika* are again letters.

[19] Cf. above Chapter II 6, with n. 26.

[20] *Orator* 61–8.

unprovocative manner, suitable to the grave conversation of the learned. Their writing is better called *sermo* than *oratio*. The 'sophist' is, in a broad sense, the epideictic orator, and differs in degree rather than in kind from the orator whom Cicero is trying to delineate; his characteristic is to give delight, rather than to effect persuasion, and as a main object rather than incidentally. He seeks elegance more than plausibility, weaves myth into his discourse, and adorns his style with metaphor and figures, especially those of balance and antithesis. It is interesting that Cicero stresses the resemblance of history to the work of these 'sophists': the historian's narrative is 'ornate', his speeches 'smooth and fluent'; in both respects he resembles the sophist, not the practical orator.[21]

8

Finally, note must be taken of the way in which some rhetors of the imperial period classified, or rather listed, the various kinds of epideictic speeches practised in their day. Very largely, these second- and third-century writers—Menander and 'pseudo-Dionysius'[22]—adapted the terminology of the grammarians who had studied lyric poetry. They spoke of a 'monody' when they meant an emotional expression of grief, an 'epithalamium' for a marriage speech, and so on. This was natural; the oratory for which they were prescribing was thought of as a substitute for, or rival to, poetry. But not all their terminology came from this source. The 'consolation' (*paramuthētikos*) for example was never a poetical form. In particular, they drew an important distinction between formal and informal addresses, calling the latter 'talks' (*laliai*, in Latin perhaps *sermones*) and prescribing for them not only radical departures from standard rhetorical structure but a non-periodic style, based to a certain extent on Xenophon and the lighter parts of Plato. They called this style *sungraphikos*, meaning that it was appropriate to a written treatise rather than to a speech.

[21] Hermogenes, *De ideis* 403 ff. Rabe, regards Plato as the exemplar of the pure panegyric, but reckons the historians as falling under the same general head. His point of view is not very different from Cicero's.

[22] Translations of both of these texts in Russell and Wilson ed. of Menander Rhetor (1981).

When we recall that Plato[23] took formality and ornament to be the marks of a *sungramma*, it is an interesting question how the word came in the end to have almost the opposite associations. The answer lies as much in the difference of context as in the historical development. Plato was contrasting the natural language of conversation with the formality of something meant to last. He was not thinking of oratory at all; the *Phaedo* is a representation of educated people talking seriously about serious subjects in the language of the heart. The late rhetors took as their standard the structured, periodic manner of literary oratory and they set against it other types of classical prose of which they were aware, whose characteristics they wished to imitate and develop for their own purposes. They were high-class entertainers, appealing to a public who regarded appreciation of such things as an indication of standing and prestige. They therefore combined a high level of verbal skill and virtuosity in orations and 'essays' with an unswerving concern never to shock or offend by an unwelcome or disturbing idea. Novelty was admissible only in form or detail.

Now the prescriptions of these teachers are very minute. They lay down both topics and order (*diairesis, divisio*). It is this care for detail which has led scholars to regard them as the best sources we have for the conventions which governed, for example, poems of welcome or leave-taking, of marriage or bereavement, throughout antiquity.[24] People sometimes use the word genre of such species as these, but it is important to be aware that this is a different sense from that in which we speak of epic or tragedy or even pastoral as a genre. It is entirely a matter of content; the 'genre' becomes a complex of topics, not a form. Now it may well be that much can be learned from these rhetors about the poets; this is because they, or their predecessors, studied the poets from a rhetorical point of view, in the way that we saw in Quintilian, pseudo-Dionysius and Servius,[25] and applied to their own work the hints they thought most useful. Moreover, the very point that makes the

---

[23] *Phaedo* 102D 3.

[24] See esp. F. Cairns, *Generic Composition in Greek and Roman Poetry*, Edinburgh 1972.

[25] Above, Chapter VIII 4–6.

prescriptions seem most precise and meaningful, the orderly
progression of topics, comes straight from the preliminary exercises
(*progumnasmata*) practised in rhetorical schools since Hellenistic
times.[26] This is something we have not hitherto had to consider,
since it has in itself no bearing on the judgment of literature,
however great its influence may have been on the actual practice of writers. The young student was taught to set out a fable,
an anecdote, a commonplace or an encomium according to
certain rules, mostly derived from common sense, but sometimes also from classical models. If the student grew up to be a
poet—an Ovid, for example—he might go on performing these
exercises in verse, though if he was a good poet they would play
only a minor rôle in his processes of composition. In Menander
and 'Dionysius', however, the *progumnasmata* are naturally the
main stuff of the prescriptions. *Encomium* is the most important.
Its main heads—origin, upbringing, achievements and virtues,
comparison with others—were laid down in the early days of
rhetoric, and never changed much.[27] It is the application of
these rules to the various private and public occasions that the
epideictic orator might be called upon to celebrate that produces the firm structure of these so-called Menandrean 'genres'.
It follows that their value as evidence either of poetic practice
or of 'genre theory' is limited and uncertain.[28]

---

[26] See D. L. Clark, *Rhetoric in Greek and Roman Education* (1957), 177–212.
[27] Inescapable evidence in Agathon's speech in Plato's *Symposium*, 194E ff.
[28] In general, cf. Russell and Wilson, op. cit., xxix–xxxiv.

CHAPTER ELEVEN

Literary History

I

THERE can be little doubt that the historical study of literature in antiquity was very rudimentary by modern standards. The 'consciousness of definitely distinguishable periods', which Ernst Curtius regarded as essential to 'a historical sense', is totally absent.[1] Ancient writers seldom go beyond the distinction into 'old' and 'new': 'Periclean', 'Alexandrian', 'Augustan' —if they mean more than merely chronological limits—are modern terms. Only isolated observations can be found about the relations between literary and political or social developments, and these seem to be confined to two topics: the association of oratory with republican liberty;[2] and the widely-held view that affluence led to corruption, in literature as in other things. Nevertheless, the Greco-Roman critics were not without historical preoccupations. For one thing, they were undoubtedly concerned with two essential preliminaries to literary history: problems of authenticity, and biographical facts about authors.

The scholarly investigation of dates and authenticity is something which was very well understood even in classical Greek times. The records of Athenian dramatic festivals, inscribed on stone from earlier documents in the fourth century, and studied by Aristotle, gave a firm foundation for the chronological study of Attic drama.[3] In the third century, the

[1] *Latin Literature and the European Middle Ages* (E.tr.), 252.
[2] Cic. *Brutus* 46; Tac. *Dialogus* 36–40; 'Longinus' 44.
[3] A. Pickard-Cambridge, *Dramatic Festivals of Athens* (1953), 68 ff.; Pfeiffer 81. Cf. above, Chapter II 8.

Alexandrian scholars who carried on the tradition of the Peripatos devoted much care and trouble not only to tragedy but to other poetic genres and also to oratory. All this raised difficult questions. The authorship of books in antiquity was often unsure. [4] Styles and techniques were stable and often lacking in individuality. Internal evidence often failed. Literary property was not very closely guarded, at least in classical times. It was apparently quite easy for collections of rolls associated with a writer—belonging to his library, for example—to be believed to be his own work. The intractable problems of authenticity that remain even in the scanty remains of ancient literature are a reminder of this situation.

We do of course possess a good deal of evidence about the scholarly techniques which were used in antiquity to deal with such things. One example must suffice: Dionysius' treatise on the orator Dinarchus. [5] This is one of the latest and most sophisticated of Dionysius' works. It is based on a good deal of learning. We find him using an archon list, and knowing the titles and contents of a large number of speeches. He begins by reconstructing the essential biographical facts. Dinarchus, on his own showing, returned from exile 'as an old man'. This, says Dionysius, means that he was about seventy. We must therefore regard as probably spurious any speeches which appear to have been written either before Dinarchus was 26 or 27, the age when an orator may be expected to begin to practise, or again during the period of his exile. Such argumentation is neither better nor worse than that on which much of our conventional literary history is built; and Dionysius makes it clear that he knows that he is working in probabilities, not in certainties. Next follows an analysis of Dinarchus' character, in fairly general terms; and the last extant part of the treatise is devoted to a critical list of genuine and spurious speeches. Dionysius never argues the case for authenticity. Despite his scepticism about received opinions and his flat distrust in the titles (*epigraphai*) of books, he evidently assumes that the burden of proof lies on those who wish to reject the traditional authorship.

[4] Cf. K. J. Dover, *The Lysianic Corpus* (1968), 23 ff., 153 ff.
[5] Recent separate edition and commentary by G. Marenghi, Milan, n.d.; see also K. J. Dover, op. cit., 19 ff.

By contrast, he does present the arguments for his rejections. In the majority of cases, the reason given is that the speech is known to have been delivered in one of the 'unlikely' periods. Failing this, Dionysius falls back on stylistic criteria, with occasional recourse to other historical considerations.

Now the purpose of all this is certainly not solely historical. Dinarchus, in Dionysius' view, is not a great orator. He belongs neither to the group of inventors (*heuretai*)—Lysias, Isocrates, Isaeus—to whom are attributed the innovations that made Attic oratory possible—nor to the 'perfectors' (*teleiōtai*)— Demosthenes, Aeschines, Hyperides—who brought the promise to fulfilment. He is an imitator. Having no special manner of his own, he dips now into one, now into another. All such imitators lack 'natural grace', and a taste attuned to the masters will at once discern this lack. Now it has been shown[6] that Dionysius' interests developed in the course of his studies of the orators, and that the historical rôle of Isaeus as Demosthenes' teacher led him to devote more attention to that orator than he would have done if he had been thinking simply of his value as an object of imitation. This is true; nevertheless, in the *Dinarchus* these historical inquiries are clearly undertaken for a rhetorical purpose, namely to point out the difference between mere imitation and the natural acquisition of rhetorical excellences (6). We thus have a further example of the dominance of rhetorical considerations: literary history is here simply the servant of rhetorical instruction. It is natural to compare the famous passage in 'Longinus' 16, where as we have noted, the author points out that the 'seed' (*sperma*) of Demosthenes' 'oath by the men of Marathon' is said to be certain lines of the comic poet Eupolis; he adduces this neither to show Demosthenes as unoriginal, nor as objective *Quellenforschung*, but to demonstrate the superiority of the fruit to the seed, and point out where its rhetorical virtue lies.

2

Dionysius' *Dinarchus* began, as we saw, with a 'life' (*bios*). This was nothing new: biographical interest in literary figures goes

[6] S. F. Bonner, *Dionysius of Halicarnassus*, 57.

back to early times.[7] The archaic Greek poets were to some extent persons of legend. Hesiod defeats Homer at the funeral games of Amphidamas. Sappho leaps from the rock. Ibycus' murder is avenged by cranes. The eagle drops the tortoise on Aeschylus' head. Such legends may be based on poems, or they may be folk-tales given a new name and habitation. They tell us that the poet is famous, not that his life helps to explain his poems. That needs one further step: the acceptance of the proposition that people of a particular kind write poetry of a particular kind. This is well formulated by Aristophanes' Agathon:

> A poet ought to have
> Manners related to the play he's writing.
> For instance: if he writes a feminine piece
> His person also needs its feminine side . . .
> A masculine piece needs masculinity.
> And where we're lacking, imitation then
> Supplies the want . . .
> Consider how the famous Ibycus,
> Alcaeus and Anacreon of Teos,
> Who gave a delicate flavour to their songs,
> Wore turbans and, in true Ionic fashion,
> As men, were broken . . .
>   For of necessity
> One's poetry is like one's nature.[8]

Ribaldry apart, this represents a common unreflecting view. It is a moralising view, not only in the sense that it relates *mores* to writing, but because it almost always involves moral judgments. There is an obvious link between this passage of Aristophanes and Seneca's formulation of the principle *talis oratio qualis vita,*[9] and his portrayal of the effeminate Maecenas, whose style demonstrated that 'he was the man whose attendants, when he

---

[7] On literary biography see F. Leo, *Die griechisch-römische Biographie*, 11 ff.; A. Momigliano, *The Development of Greek Biography* (1971), esp. 69 ff.

[8] *Thesmophoriazusae* 149 ff.,— 'Broken' (*dieklônto*) is to be taken in a sexual sense: compare Dion. Hal. *Comp. Verb.* p. 83, 16 ff. U-R, where Hegesias is said to have written like 'women or broken men'. Cf. also Petronius 5.

[9] *Epist.* 114.1 (cf. above, Chapter IV 5), with Abrams, *The Mirror and the Lamp*, 226 ff.

went about in public, consisted of two eunuchs—and they were better examples of manhood than he'.

This simple principle plays a large and conspicuous part in most ancient criticism. In conjunction with the rhetorical habit of studying and judging persuasive effectiveness, it formed what we may treat as the consensus critical attitudes of later antiquity. We see it everywhere. It is implied, for instance, in the common and traditional apologia of the frivolous or indecent poet: *carmen lascivum, vita pudica mea.* An Ovid or a Martial has to make a special claim to be thought an exception.[10]

Surviving lives of ancient authors—which are numerous, mostly late, but often based on early material, especially Peripatetic researches of the fourth and third centuries B.C.— are full of this approach.[11] Very often, it is the poetry that is made to cast light on the man, and not vice versa. Alcman's nationality is debated on the evidence of what he says.[12] Euripides' hatred of women and love of the sea are inferred from his plays.[13] Virgil's homosexual relationship with an Alexis is made up out of the second Eclogue.[14] Afranius introduces homosexual affairs into his poetry, 'displaying his own morals'.[15] Most of this is fiction. By contrast, we hear very little of aspects of the matter that are central to any modern literary biography: precise associations of poems with private occasions, or the development either of character or of technique. This is not surprising; it is in general true that the Greeks and Romans thought of a man's *bios* more statically and less dynamically than we do, and inclined always to view his actions and his words as revelations of an underlying, comparatively unchanging nature.

Talis oratio qualis vita is not only applicable to individuals; it

[10] Cf. Catullus 16.5; Ov. *Tristia* 2.354; Martial 1.4.8; Apuleius *Apol.* 11.
[11] The most convenient collection of Greek texts is still A. Westermann, *Biographi Graeci minores* (1845). Lives are however often printed in editions of the authors to whom they refer (and often accompany their work in mediaeval manuscripts). See in general M. R. Lefkowitz *CQ* 28 (1978) 450 ff., and (on Euripides' life) *GRBS* 20 (1979) 187 ff.
[12] D. L. Page, *Poetae melici Graeci*, 10.
[13] *Vita Euripidis* 5 (p. 137 Westerman).
[14] Donatus *Life of Virgil* 44: see Appendix, p. 186.
[15] Quint. 10.1.100.

can be generalised. Nations have their peculiar *mores* and there-fore styles: the exuberance of the 'Asianists' is associated with ethnic characteristics—or at least with the prejudice that Orientals are wild and uncontrolled in expression.[16] More im-portant, generations have characteristics also: the archaism of Sallust became a fashion among his followers.[17] But the most influential universalisation is one which we find already in Aristotle's *Poetics*. When Aristotle has explained that poetry derives from our natural inclinations to imitation and to rhythm and harmony, he continues:

Poetry was split according to the various characters of the poets: the more dignified (*semnoteroi*) represented noble actions and those of like persons, the viler sort (*eutelesteroi*) represented those of inferior per-sons, first composing invectives, as the other group composed hymns and encomia.[18]

There follows a piece of historical speculation. Aristotle ap-parently posits two parallel developments. One includes hymns and encomia, Homeric epic and tragedy. The other includes invectives, Homer's *Margites* and comedy. The basis of this is the correspondence between character and production. This is history written on *a priori* principles, in much the same vein as most ancient theorising about the origin and development of civilisation.

3

This passage of the *Poetics* in fact introduces a second historical principle: that of development. It goes on thus:

Tragedy, after starting from an impromptu origin . . . gradually grew, as people developed what was to be seen in it, and, after under-going many changes, finally stopped changing because it had reached its natural stature (*esche tēn hautēs phusin*).[19]

Vahlen observed that Aristotle, a few lines above, had left

[16] Cicero *Brutus* 51. See, most recently, T. Gelzer in *Entretiens Hardt* 25, 29 ff.
[17] Sen. *Epist.* 114.8.
[18] 1448[b] 24 ff. Cf. above Chapter VI 7.
[19] 1449[a] 9.

open the question whether or not tragedy 'is now adequate in its formative constituents', either in itself or in relation to its audiences, whereas the statement that it has achieved its 'natural stature' entirely excludes the possibility of future development in the 'formative constituents'. But this is not a very fair inference. What Aristotle puts off is a *discussion* of the question. The answer seems clear: tragedy could *not* develop further: the *phusis* of a thing, we read in the *Politics*, is said to be what it is like at the completion of the process of its coming-to-be (*genesis*).[20] In tragedy, subject, metre and scale are now all fixed. It has reached its adult state, the end result of innovations and additions by a succession of *heuretai*, gifted individuals, some of whom can actually be named. Future changes in technique do not matter. If extensive enough, they presumably lead to something other than tragedy. Aristotle thus postulates an analogy between the development of a genre and the life-history of a living animal. This analogy applies to growth but not to decline. If we ask under what conditions Aristotle thought an art or art-form might degenerate, we should have to turn to the *Politics* for an answer, and it would be in terms of moral decline and growing luxury. The seeds of decay lie in morals and society, not in the art-form itself. Desire for novelty, an obvious mechanism of change, is a moral matter; it does not affect the properly regulated mind, which wants goodness and truth, not novelty.

That Aristotle had a genuine historical interest, and was not merely concerned to work out the probable consequences of his very general hypotheses, is obvious from his other historical researches and is shown by a curious feature of this discussion itself. His account of the 'growth' of tragedy actually conflicts with the idea that literary kinds depend on the moral characteristics of the composer. For from this latter point of view Aristotle ought not to have derived tragedy 'from the satyric', whatever precisely that may mean. Not surprisingly, his Hellenistic successors reversed the order, and treated the satyr-play, as Horace does, as a later innovation, made necessary by

[20] 1252[b] 32. The model of plant-growth is evidently in Aristotle's mind: cf. H. Lloyd-Jones, *Ant. Cl.* 33 (1964) 372 (= *Aeschylus* [Wege der Forschung 465] 121 ff.).

the need to titillate a jaded audience.[21] They were less appreciative of fact than their master, and more wedded to theory.

4

Aristotle appears as potential historian again when we turn to
rhetoric. He put forward two theories which bear on its history.
One relates to language: Gorgias and the early orators imitated
the grandiloquence of poets; they were wrong to do so, because
the diction of prose is distinct from that of poetry.[22] This is presumably the germ of the common later view—in Strabo and in
Plutarch for example—that poetry preceded composition in
prose; 'prose' is called 'speech on foot' (*pezē lexis, pedestris oratio*)
in Greek and Latin, because it came down from the chariot and
walked on its own feet.[23] The other theory concerns the origins
of oratory and of rhetorical teaching.[24] Oratory too was a
technē advancing by successive discoveries. It all began, as we
have seen, in Sicily, in the fifth century, though the centre of
activity soon moved to democratic Athens. The essential point
here is the link between oratory and political history. It has an
obvious plausibility; and we find it again and again in later
texts, in various guises. For Cicero, peace and ease are the
conditions of eloquence: *pacis est comes otique socia.*[25] It does not
arise in nascent societies, in conditions of war or poverty, or
under tyranny. To the writers of the empire, the change from
libertas to *dominatio* was one of the causes of decline; it had
brought a withdrawal of the orator from the courts to the
schools, from great causes to unreal and frivolous pedantry.
'Longinus', who views all literature on essentially rhetorical
lines, considers this political change as one possible explanation
for the 'universal dearth' of which he complains, but he rejects
it in favour of a moral one, based not on changes in the political
structure but on luxury, emotional breakdown, and warring

---

[21] *Ars poetica* 220 ff. (*ALC* 285).
[22] *Rhetoric* 3. 1404^a (*ALC* 136).
[23] Cf. above, Chapter X 2.
[24] Cf. above, Chapter VIII 2 (and *ALC* 219, 223).
[25] *Brutus* 45.

desires.[26] The younger Seneca flirts with a cyclical hypothesis. Velleius—who earned Sainte-Beuve's approval for including a couple of paragraphs on literature in the first book of a general, universal history—does not even consider the political hypothesis as an explanation of the concentration of works of genius in short periods to which he draws attention.[27] For him, the possible mechanisms of change are purely psychological: emulation, whether friendly or envious (an idea as old as Hesiod);[28] the principle that 'what cannot go forward, must go back'; and our natural tendency to look for fields where easy laurels can be won. 'Frequent and inconstant change is the greatest hindrance to perfection.'

Most first-century discussions of this sort of thing are, we should remember, accounts of decline. They are in the tradition of Plato's and Aristotle's political theory rather than in that of the literary theory of the *Poetics*. But we do also possess some explanations of progress, notably Dionysius' preface to his book on the classical orators,[29] which proclaimed a renaissance of good taste under the benevolent aegis of the enlightened Roman governing class. Both advance and decline, however, are thought of in a way that does not involve objective descriptions of qualitative differences. It is usually taken for granted that the effeminate is inferior to the virile, the modern to the ancient. When anyone advances the contrary of this last proposition— as Aper does in the most interesting of all these works, Tacitus' *Dialogus*[30]—this again is an evaluative discussion, not a narrative. It does however happen that advocates of one side or the other have occasion to indicate the author with whom the decisive change came: Demetrius of Phalerum in Greek oratory, Cassius Severus in Latin.[31] We should note here the underlying notion of an *inclinatio* realised by an individual; it is one more item in the slender stock of literary-historical themes.

---

[26] 44.
[27] Velleius 1.16–17. See Appendix, p. 206.
[28] *Works and days* 11 ff.: 'So there is not just one kind of strife but two upon earth: one to be praised when you notice it, one blameworthy.'
[29] *ALC* 305; cf. above Chapter IV 1.
[30] 16 ff. (*ALC* 441).
[31] Cicero *Brutus* 26: Tac. *Dialogus* 19 (*ALC* 219, 443).

5

For the stock is indeed slender. The critique of classical authors contained in the extant treatises on 'imitation' by Dionysius and Quintilian is often thought to constitute a sort of literary history. But it is nothing of the sort. The arrangement, though often chronological within genres, is not designed to demonstrate historical links, but rather to make comparisons of style and purpose. Only occasional touches suggest a historical interest. In Quintilian, this appears most clearly in the statement that Menander admired and followed Euripides. Though working in different genres, they were pupil and master.[32]

On the other hand, parts of Philostratus' *Lives of the Sophists* do have a claim to be literary history. The introduction discusses the origins of extempore speaking, and the characteristics of the 'old' and the 'new' sophists.[33] But, like other literary biographies, most of the work is anecdotal: the sophists' teachers are named, but very little use is made of this in explaining their stylistic characteristics. Though it is obvious enough that this whole second-century movement was very much a matter of local schools and their influence, we should know hardly anything of this from Philostratus.

In summary: neither rhetors nor biographers are much interested in the transmission of literary characteristics, or in the relation between literary events and those in the world outside. This weakness on the historical side marks one of the great differences between literary scholarship and understanding in antiquity and the corresponding activities of our own day.

[32] Quintilian 10.1,69 (*ALC* 390).
[33] See the opening chapters of Book I (accessible in English in the Loeb ed. of W. C. Wright).

CHAPTER TWELVE

Epilogue

ONE function of an epilogue, according to rhetorical theory, is to recapitulate. It is the only function I shall try to fulfil here.

I have tried to sketch, first, the history of what may conveniently, if inaccurately, be called literary criticism in the classical world. I began with the early Greek poets and ended with the pagan philosophers, rhetors and grammarians of late antiquity. Many areas of this history are dark; only occasionally can we see the interaction of criticism and practice in the tastes and styles of particular epochs. Nor is there very much development. The basic questions were almost all asked by the time of Aristotle; and Aristotle's own sophisticated and provocative analysis had less effect in later times than the simpler attitudes of rhetoric and naïve poetics which he endeavoured to reject. Apart from the more or less fanciful speculation of the Neoplatonists, no new ideas appeared. We have to wait for the impact of Christian thinking before the traditional rôle of the 'styles' could be re-assessed, or fresh thought given to the ancient problem of the relation between poetical fiction and the world which it 'represents'. Nevertheless the historical circumstances in which ancient 'criticism' moved are full of interest, not least, perhaps, because so much of it is grounded on the practices of education. For the rhetorical criticism of antiquity is very largely the work of teachers. Dionysius, 'Longinus', Quintilian, even Aristotle and Plato, envisage young audiences whose tastes are to be formed and skills developed. There is here a resemblance, perhaps uncomfortable, to the state of affairs in our own day. True, we no longer teach rhetoric but only encourage 'creativity'. We no longer make the ancient classics of our literatures the foundation of study, or trust to a thorough soaking in them to bring up a man in the way he should go—though we did just this less than a century ago. But the justification of the study of literature, when one has to be made, still commonly lies outside the verbal art itself, in moral goals of integrity, emotional maturity, or recommended social attitudes. Our predecessors, the rhetors and grammarians of antiquity, trod, if not the same path, one that pointed in the same direction. And so, given the constancy in their educational aims, it is no wonder that the semblance of a coherent system can be constructed out of their writings. At least, there is a set of interlocking problems, which can be put in some kind of order. This is the second thing I have tried to do.

(i) I began with the poet. Whence come his powers? Are they entirely derived from human skill, or entirely dependent on something beyond ordinary rational principles? Or is some consensus of impulse and effort needed? And, if so, what comes from without, and what from within? Closely linked with these questions is the problem of the poet's function. Is it entertainment or instruction—or, again, can we have it both ways?

(ii) These questions, which were prominent in the thinking of Democritus and Plato, 'Longinus' and the Stoics, imply a further and more searching set of issues, relating to the nature of poetry itself. These centred, in all ancient speculation, on the notion of *mimēsis*. Was it right to consider poetry an 'imitation' of reality, in the way that painting and sculpture were fairly obviously 'imitations' of objects in the sensible world? Or has 'imitation', when applied to poetry, to be used in a new way, or even in more ways than one? Practically the whole of ancient literary theory—that is to say the search for principles which might form a framework for critical judgment, and set 'literature' in an understandable place among other human activities —turned on the significance and aptness of this notion of *mimēsis*.

(iii) From the theoretical point of view, as Aristotle for example understood it, and rightly understood it, verbal communication for the sake of persuasion was not 'imitative' at all. Rhetoric and poetics were two distinct branches of knowledge. There was an overlap of medium—words—but no overlap of purpose. The only part of rhetoric which was of significance for the understanding of poetry, on this view, was the study of style—diction, word-arrangement and figures. But we do not, of course, find this attitude at all in Aristotle's successors, or in the mass of comment on poetry that survives from Hellenistic and Roman times. We cannot understand Dionysius or 'Longinus' without both thinking of the rhetorical study of style and of 'invention' and being prepared to read the poets as though they too, like the orators, aimed to 'persuade'. I have therefore attempted a brief outline of these topics also. It is a fact of ancient history that much 'criticism' was derived from instruction given to budding orators, originally for wholly practical purposes. What was this instruction like? And in what ways did its existence affect the ways in which people read literature of all kinds?

(iv) And finally, what would that last phrase, 'literature of all kinds', have conveyed to our witnesses? In other words, what sort of map of literature can be reconstructed? Here, the answers I have suggested will perhaps seem too negative. Differentiation by genre, undeniable in ancient practice, is less clear in theory than has often been thought. And the historical dimension, the differentiation of literature by chronological periods, was something very imperfectly understood.

I end on a personal note. Some twenty years ago, when I embarked on a fairly serious study of 'Longinus', I felt that this was something likely to help me, and also those whom I was trying to teach, to understand the qualities of ancient literature better. It filled gaps, supplied the context that Plato and Virgil took for granted. I still feel this is largely true. Despite ineptitudes—his lack of understanding of *urbanitas*, his pedantic application of the rules of *decorum*—'Longinus' has important things to say. He was right, it seems to me, in associating the 'decline' which preoccupies him with a lack of capacity to feel and convey genuine emotion. It is a distinctive mark of the Greek literature of the empire that, though elegant, powerful in description and much concerned with the external world, it has little human interest. 'Longinus' put his finger on this, whatever we may think of his conventionally moralistic explanation. And his combination of rhetorical and moral thinking in the interpretation of orators and poets still provides a model—best shown in his famous treatment of the Marathon oath commonplace—for close reading of ancient literature within its tradition. What he says—and the same goes for the less attractive Dionysius and Demetrius—is often true, and always worth thinking about. It never amounts to the whole truth. But what criticism could claim that?

Appendix

THE translations which follow are intended to illustrate the foregoing narrative and discussion by providing a few additional pieces of evidence, not in *ALC*.

The arrangement of authors is alphabetical, not chronological.

AGATHARCHIDES

Criticism of Hegesias

See Chapter III 1. The extract given here is taken from Photius *Bibliotheca*, cod. 250, 445^b ff. (ed. R. Henry, vii, 147 ff.). It is not always clear how much is Agatharchides, and how much is Photius' own words; but the main lines of the criticism are clear enough. My translation diverges from Henry's in several places.

The quotations from Hegesias are edited in F. Jacoby, *Fr. Gr. Hist.* 142F6–17, 25–6.

Many orators and poets have not known how a man who has not experienced the dangers should report extreme disasters. There is no clear way of doing this except by giving an adequate reason for describing the situation.

Alexander and Philip sacked and rased to the ground the two

cities of Olynthus and Thebes.[1] The horror of the unexpected event
made many of the Greeks desperately concerned about their whole
situation and afforded many orators grounds for representing it
in a manner suitable to the disaster. Some therefore spoke of it
allegorically and in what is thought to be elaborate language, others
more weightily, not avoiding common words and literal expressions
in the terrible circumstances. We shall show examples of both of
these, so that you may compare the two styles and judge which is
better and which is worse.

Hegesias, who often mentions the destruction of the cities, is a
cheap writer (*euteles*). One who is unwilling to express himself in a
manner appropriate to the situation, but forces himself to display ingenuity over a serious matter, no doubt achieves his own aim to some
extent, but does not set his sights on the importance of the underlying
facts. Hegesias can be detected committing this fault in his speeches.
For example: 'We left a city and took a name.' Now consider. This
causes no emotional impact; it makes us concentrate on the special
emphasis of the words and makes us wonder what he means. When
one produces intellectual uncertainty, one instantly loses emotional
force. Why? Because sympathy comes from clearly understanding
what is said; a writer who fails to achieve clarity also loses vigour
(*energeia*: a variant reading gives *enargeia*, 'vividness').

He writes of the Thebans in similar vein. 'Disaster has made
speechless the place that spoke so loud.' And again of the Olynthians:
'I left a city of ten thousand people, and when I turned back I saw
it no more.' Well, what were you looking for? These words, bearing
such special emphasis, have distracted the mind from the subject. A
writer who aims at pity must give up wit, and set out the facts to
which the emotion is related, if he is not merely to produce an elegant
verbal effect but to get right into the cause of the disaster.

But let us look at another example. 'Alexander, imagine Epamin-
ondas can see the ruins of his city, and stands beside you and pleads
on its behalf with me.' A childish demand, a harsh metaphor—and a
total failure to express the grimness of the event. Again: 'The city
collided with a king's madness and became more pitiful than a
tragedy.' The sophist has evidently provided for anything rather than
what he ought, and the consequence is that he fails to touch the point
at issue. It is grievous to observe the language of mockery in such a
grievous situation.

Again: 'Why speak of the sufferings of the Olynthians and the
Thebans, the death of whole cities?'

---

[1] Philip sacked Olynthus in 348 B.C., Alexander sacked Thebes in 335.

Another example of the same kind borders on both silliness and undignified flattery:

'When you rased Thebes to the ground, Alexander, it was as if Zeus cast the moon out of its place in heaven. For I leave the sun to Athens. These two cities were the eyes of Greece. I fear now for the other. For one eye, the city of Thebes, has been cut out.'

It seems to me that in this passage the sophist is ridiculing the misfortunes of the city, not lamenting them, and seeing how he can chop up his speech small, in the most rapid manner, not how he can bring the disaster under our eyes by vivid description.

Another similar instance: 'Neighbouring cities wept for the city, seeing that what was there before was there no longer.' If anyone had uttered periods like this to the Thebans and Olynthians as an expression of sympathy at the time of the capture of the cities, I fear they would have laughed at the writer and thought him, in a way, wretcheder than they were themselves.

Let us look at another type of example, in (?) the same sophist: 'it is dreadful that the land that bore the Sown Men should be unsown.' This is not how Demosthenes (whose idea Hegesias has here ruined) had put it. Demosthenes says that it is shocking that Attica, the first land to bear cultivated crops for men, should be grazed by sheep.[2] Hegesias—in saying that the land that bore the Sown Men was unsown—takes his antithesis from words, not from facts. The consequence is appalling frigidity, like that of Hermesianax[3] in his encomium of Athens: 'Born out of the head (*kephalē*) of Zeus, it is natural she should have the sum (*kephalaion*) of happiness.'

[Other similar examples from Hegesias follow.]

Agatharchides then produces orators who spoke on the same theme with clarity and appropriate decency. Stratocles: 'The citadel of the Thebans is ploughed and sown—the Thebans, who fought at your side against Philip!'[4] This passage both gives a clear account of what happened to the city and calls to mind the Athenians' friendship with that unhappy people; juxtaposition of terror with friendly feeling adds weight to expression of pity.

He also cites Aeschines: 'A city, our neighbour, has vanished from the midst of Greece.'[5] This excellently conveys the speed of the de-

---

[2] In a lost speech, apparently.

[3] *Fr. Gr. Hist.* 691 T2.

[4] Son of Euthydemus; a prominent orator of the later fourth century. These extracts probably come from his speech on the Harpalus affair: cf. Dinarchus 1.24.

[5] *Against Ctesiphon* 133. Curiously, this text does not reproduce the feature

struction by the metaphor, and also brings the dangers vividly to mind by showing that the sufferers are the neighbours of the audience.

Demosthenes made Alexander the subject. 'He dug up the city from its foundations, leaving not even the ash in the hearths, and distributed the children and wives of the one-time leaders of Greece among the tents of the barbarians.'[6] Demosthenes here takes the extreme consequences of each action, and expresses them bitterly, clearly and concisely; but he has not forgotten the vividness that makes facts clear.

Demosthenes again on the Olynthians: 'Olynthus and Methone and Apollonia—and two and thirty cities in the Thracian area—all of which he destroyed so savagely that a visitor could not easily tell if they had ever been inhabited at all.'[7] Demosthenes here underlined the number of the cities and then added the misfortunes of the inhabitants, so that the particular compassion aroused by the paradoxical fact might move the sympathy of the hearers all the more.

'ALEXANDER NUMENIU'

The theory of figures

This Alexander, 'the son of Numenius', lived in the time of Hadrian. He was an important and influential rhetor. The following extract comes from a version (of uncertain provenance and authenticity) of his treatise on figures. See Th. Schwab, 'Alexandros Numeniu', Würzburg 1916. Text from Spengel, *Rhetores Graeci*, 3.11.18–3.13.20. See Chapter I n. 29, IX 8.

Before proceeding first to consider Figures (*schēmata*) of Thought, let us briefly answer those who entirely deny their existence. There are some who say that there is nothing special about a Figure of Thought,

---

of the passage which was most admired for its pathos—the repetition 'Thebes, Thebes . . .'.

[6] Again in a lost speech.

[7] Cf. *Philippics* 3.26.

for no unfigured discourse (*logos*) can easily be found. This, they say, is inevitable, since discourse depends on the configuration (*diatupōsis*) of the mind (*psuchē*), and indeed was invented to express the mind's forms, experience and movements in general. Now the mind is in constant motion, and takes on many figurations (*schēmatismoi*), e.g. when it defines, reproves, takes counsel, or does or experiences any one of the things which happen to it. Thus discourse, inasmuch as it is a copy (*mimēma*) of the mind, will necessarily have some figure (*schēma*) or other.

In reply to this, we can say:

(i) If there were no distinction between natural thought (*kata phusin dianoēma*) and thought that is figured (*eschēmatismenon*), orators would be no different from laymen (*idiōtai*, i.e. ordinary people) nor from one another; the simpler unadorned writers would be no different from the more vivid and elaborate. Now it is clear that the orator does differ from the layman in the way he fashions his figures, as orators differ one from another in the frequency and appropriateness of their use of figures.

(ii) Although the mind is inevitably always in a certain configuration, it has some 'natural' and some 'unnatural' movements. This applies both to its stable, rational condition and to its emotional states, which are the source of emotional discourse. Similarly, discourse may have a natural or habitual configuration, and this (we say) does not amount to a 'figure', and also a consciously formed (*peplasmenos*) configuration, which does amount to what we call 'figured' discourse.

(iii) Even if one were to grant that every discourse has its own figure by nature, nevertheless, oratorical and literary discourse (*politikos kai sungraphikos logos*) does not possess this naturally, but by imitation of the other kind. Evidence of this may be seen in the following example. There is a way of speaking which naturally expresses a certain distraction of the mind: 'Which way shall I go—this or that?'[1] This expression does not have a figure, we say: and why? Because it is expressed naturally and the speaker is really at a loss. There is another expression, produced in imitation of this, also involving doubt: 'In the other Greeks—should we say their cowardice or their ignorance or both? . . .'[2] Now this does contain a figure. The speaker is not really at a loss, but pretends to be so, and imitates a bewildered speaker by avoiding straightforward expression. We can

[1] Euripides *Hecuba* 163.
[2] *De corona* 20.

therefore answer those who deny the existence of Figures of Thought by saying that, even if every discourse has its own figure by nature, there is nothing to prevent discourse from being contrived and feigned in imitation of this.[3]

What is feigned in this way is thus called 'figure' in a special sense, and it is this that we are now discussing, not all discourse which possesses any kind of configuration. A further sign that there are figures 'by nature' and figures 'by art' is that every figure—in the sense in which we are using the word—may be reduced to its natural condition. This is very clear in some cases—e.g. irony, allegory and hyperbole—but difficult to see in others, e.g. various kinds of rhetorical questions and figures of doubt.

The same reply may be made also to those who deny the existence of Figures of Diction, on the ground that every verbal composition (*sunthesis*) has its own figure (*schēma*) and nothing recondite or artificial (*kata plasin*). But rhetorical *plasis*, we may say, is different from that of laymen, and one orator speaks better than other. Again, there are indeed particular natural figures of verbal composition, and also figures derived from these by imitation through the art of the orator. And finally, figures of diction may be reduced to their natural condition with varying degrees of difficulty.

ANONYMOUS

Why did Plato compose dialogues?

This extract is from chapters 14–15 of an anonymous 'Introduction to Plato', of late Neoplatonic origin (ed. L. G. Westerink, Amsterdam 1962). See Chapter IV 8.

A further question deserving investigation is why Plato used the dialogue form (*charaktēr*). But before discussing this let us explain what dialogue is.

It is a *logos* without metre, consisting of questions and answers by

[3] Text and sense uncertain; I read *ouden an kōluoi* for *oudeis an eipoi* in 12, 32.

various characters, with the appropriate characterisation (*ētho-poiia*) . . .

It is worth inquiring why, when Plato elsewhere is hostile to variety[1] . . . he has nevertheless himself used the literary form of the dialogue, made up as it is of various characters. It may be suggested that the variety of character in comedy and tragedy is not the same as in Plato. In comedy and tragedy, the characters are good and bad and remain the same, whereas in Plato, although both good and bad characters are to be found, we see the bad changed by the good, instructed and purified and generally withdrawn from their material life. 'Variety' then is different in Plato and in the other authors; so he is not guilty of self-contradiction.

We have therefore now to explain the reason why he employed this form of writing.

Our answer is that it is because the dialogue is a sort of universe (*kosmos*). For, just as, in a dialogue, there are different persons each speaking as is appropriate, so in the universe as a whole there are different natural things uttering their different voices; for each speaks according to its proper nature. Plato therefore did this in imitation of the works of the divine craftsman, namely the universe.

An alternative reason is that the universe is a dialogue. For just as, in the universe, there are superior and inferior natures, and the soul agrees now with the one and now with the other, so in the dialogue there are characters who refute and others who are refuted, and our soul, like a judge, surrenders itself first to the one and then to the other.

Or again, it may be because, as Plato himself says, a speech is analogous to a living animal, and the finest speech will therefore be analogous to the finest animal—and that is the universe. Now the dialogue, as we have seen, is analogous to this; it is therefore the finest kind of speech.

A fourth argument is the following. Our soul enjoys imitation, and the dialogue is an imitation of different persons. He therefore does this to charm our soul. That the soul does take pleasure in imitation is shown by the fact that, as children, we like stories.

A further argument of the same kind is that he adopted this form of writing so as not to present us with bare facts, stripped of persons. For example, in discussing friendship, he desired not to speak of friendship itself but of friendship existing in certain individuals, and similarly with ambition. Seeing others refuted or commended, as it were, our soul is compelled to assent to the refutation or admire those

---

[1] I.e. in his discussion of music and drama in *Republic* II–III.

who are commended. This is like the souls in Hades who see others
punished for their sins and become better out of fear of the penalties
that they endure.

A sixth argument is that he adopted the dialogue form because he
was representing dialectic. A dialogue consists of persons asking and
answering questions, just as dialectic arises from question and answer.
He therefore used this form of writing in order to compel the soul, as
dialectic does, to bring to birth the thought it has within it; he does
not believe the soul to be an uninscribed tablet.

Seventhly: he wants to make us attend to what is said by making the
speakers different, and prevent us from nodding off because one
person is instructing us all the time. (This happened to Aeschines the
orator, on a public appearance . . . standing on the platform and
speaking, with no conversation, question or answer, he failed to keep
the jury awake, and they drifted off into sleep; the orator observed
this, and said 'Have a good dream about the case!') Those who
take part in a conversation are aroused by asking and answering
questions.

CALLIMACHUS

See above, Chapter III 1. These two short extracts give the
essence of 'Callimachean' poetic ideals. See M. E. Hubbard,
Propertius, pp. 78 ff.

(a) The mighty river and the limpid spring

Malice spoke softly in Apollo's ear: 'I do not admire the poet whose
song is not as great as the sea's.'

Apollo kicked Malice with his foot, and said: 'Great is the stream
of the river of Assyria, but it drags down on its waters all the filth and
rubbish of the land. Yet the Bees[1] do not bear water to Deo from every
source, but only from the little trickle that springs pure and undefiled
from a holy fountain, the fine flower of waters.

                                                    (*Hymn* 2, 105–12)

[1] Melissai, priests of Deo (=Demeter).

(b) Apollo's advice to the poet

When I first set my tablet on my knees, Lycian Apollo said to me: 'Poet, rear your sacrificial victim as fat as you can, but please keep your Muse thin.[2] And I give you one other instruction: tread the paths the waggons do not go by; do not drive your chariot in the tracks of others, nor on the broad road, but by untrodden paths, even if you drive a narrower way.'

I did as he said. I sing among those who like the clear note of the cicada, not the noise of donkeys. Let others bray like long-ear; I would rather be the little winged one, at any cost—to sing and drink the dew that drops from heaven, and strip off old age, that lies upon me heavy as the three-pointed island lies on dread Enceladus.[3]

(Aetia fr. 1.21–36)

DIO CHRYSOSTOM

On the licence of poets, and especially of Homer

See Chapter VIII 8. This extract (*Or.* 12.66 ff.) comes from a speech (delivered at the Olympic games in 97 or 101 A.D.) on the ways in which men acquire a knowledge of God. See in general M. Pohlenz, *Die Stoa* ii, 119; K. Reinhardt, *Poseidonios*, 408 f. The sculptor Phidias is imagined explaining how much easier the poet's craft is than his own. Man has a rich inheritance of words, and poets are especially blessed.

The art of the poets is particularly free from constraint and criticism, especially that of Homer, who has the greatest liberty of any. Homer did not choose a single type of speech, but took the whole Hellenic language, formerly divided into the languages of the Dorians, Ionians and Athenians, and mixed it all together, as painters do colours, only more freely still. Nor did he confine himself to his own time, but his

---

[2] Cf. Virgil *Ecl.* 6.1 ff.

[3] For this comparison, cf. Eur. *Hercules Furens* 637 ff., where old age is 'heavier than the rocks of Etna'.

love of words led him to pick up obsolete ones from his predecessors, like old coins from a treasure that no one owned. He took up many words from the barbarians too, sparing nothing so long as it seemed to offer a pleasing or vigorous effect. He took metaphors not only from neighbouring fields, near to the original concept, but from more remote areas also, so as to bewitch, amaze and charm his hearers. Nor indeed did he leave these words as they were, but lengthened, contracted and otherwise distorted them. Finally, he declared himself to be a maker (*poiētēs*) not only of metres but of words, producing them entirely out of his own head. Sometimes he would simply assign names to things, sometimes he would give new names over and above the proper ones (*kuria*), adding a clearer and yet more obvious mark (*sphragis*) to existing ones, as it were. No noise defeated him; he could imitate the sound of rivers, forests, winds, fire and sea, of bronze and stone and every living creature or tool—birds and beasts, flutes and pipes. He invented *kanachē* and *bombos*, *ktupos* and *doupos* and *arabos* [i.e. clash, boom, clatter, crash, rattle]; he spoke of murmuring rivers, screaming arrows, clamorous waves, angry winds and all sorts of strange things like that, thoroughly confusing and disturbing the mind. Consequently, he had no lack of words both frightening and pleasing, smooth and rough, and indeed possessing countless other differences in sound and in sense. With this poetic skill he was able to implant any emotion in the mind that he wished. . . . It is easy for poets to embrace many shapes and forms of all kinds in their poetry, assigning movement and rest to them as they judge appropriate at any given moment, and also actions and words, change and development in time.[1] For the poet is carried away by a single idea and impulse of his mind and draws up a quantity of words, like water bubbling up from a spring,[2] before his fantasy and idea fail and disappear. Our art, by contrast, is laborious and slow, proceeding step by step and with effort, working as it does in solid, stony material. The hardest thing of all is that the sculptor has to keep the same image in his mind all the time, until he has finished the work, often for many years. It may indeed be true, as they say, that eyes are more reliable than ears; but they are much harder to convince and need a much clearer impression. For sight contributes to the objects it sees, whereas hearing can be deceived and excited by sending in its direction imitations endowed with the magic of metre and sound. Moreover, the limits of our art in respect of number and size are fixed by necessity, but poets

---

[1] I translate Emperius' *allagēs*, though without confidence. The tradition has *apatēs*, 'deceit'.

[2] Cf. above Chapter V 2.

can make things as big as they like. It was easy for Homer to say of
Strife that 'she had her head in heaven, and yet walked upon the
earth'.[3] But I have to be satisfied to fill the space allocated to me by the
Eleans or the Athenians.

'DIONYSIUS'

Principles of criticism applicable to declamations

These two extracts from the 'Art of Rhetoric' falsely ascribed to
Dionysius of Halicarnassus come from the sections discussed in
Chapter I 4. See also *Entretiens Hardt* 25 (1979) 113–34.

(*a*) *Art of Rhetoric* 11 (*On the examination of speeches*), 1 (374, 6–376, 7
Usener-Radermacher).

The greatest danger, both for young and old, is concerned with the
judgment of speeches (*logoi*). We are always praising and blaming at
random, our opinions unsupported by knowledge. Consequently, not
only are the same objects both praised and blamed at different times
by different people, but at different times by the same people. Those
who are ignorant of arithmetic never say the same either to one another or to outsiders concerning the same question; their ignorance
is demonstrated by their disagreement. Most of us are in this state as
regards speeches. Our opinions are never stable; we praise what we
formerly found fault with, and find fault with what we formerly
praised. For we are beguiled by the repute of those who express their
views and have regard to their prestige, rather than using our own
judgment. We need a rule, a standard, a well-defined touchstone, by
considering which we can incline our judgment one way or the other.
I will put my view to you. In my opinion, there are four points on
which appreciation and judgment should rest. These are: character
(*ēthos*), thought (*gnōmē*), art (*technē*), diction (*lexis*). We must therefore
always consider, in relation to everything that we read aloud or hear
or get to know in any way, what benefit or disadvantage it gives in
these four respects. There are no standards apart from these.

[3] *Il.* 4.443.

It is important to understand what I mean. *Ethos*, I say, is of two kinds: general and particular. I will explain how I define the difference. 'General' *ēthos* is that which is based on philosophy. What is this? It is that which encourages us to virtue and dissuades us from vice. By 'particular' *ēthos*, I mean the rhetorical kind. And what is this? It consists in speaking on the subject in hand in a manner suitable and appropriate to the speaker, the hearer, the subject, and the opponent. Here is the test for all the books (*biblia*), ancient and modern. And what do I mean by that? The books are full of characters of justice and injustice, temperance and intemperance, courage and cowardice, wisdom and folly, good temper and anger. One can leave out the names, abstract the characters, and philosophise about life, imitating some while avoiding the others. For example, take the character of Alexander [i.e. Paris] in Homer: he despoils a host's household and carries off another man's wife. One may detest his character and avoid his misfortune—his native city was destroyed, his house was overthrown and he was grievously punished both by the gods and by men.

(*b*) *Art of Rhetoric* 10 (*On mistakes in declamations*), 1 (359, 3 ff. Usener-Radermacher).

The following are mistakes in declamations. Some compose their speeches with no attention to characters, because they think the case is one of fact and character is an incidental. Others are no good at the combination of characteristics. If the character is simple and evident to anyone, they see it and fall upon it and make use of it; but if it is double or triple or more complicated still, they make no study of divisions of characters or trouble themselves with their combination. Consequently, they do not contest the case at all in terms of character; this aspect is confined to what are called *epiphonēmata*, a few accidental characteristic remarks. They are actually commended for this naked expression of character, whereas the whole case ought really to rest on character, and characters ought to be woven into the facts, like the soul in the body. Again: they do not present the one 'great' character —that which comes from philosophy—on which all the individual characters, with their appropriateness to individual persons, depend. They are thus inferior in their use of character, because, even when they attempt characters, they fail to preserve grandeur (*megaloprepes*), which is something that must be maintained throughout. For, just as Reason must prevail in the soul and Passion and Desire be subservient to it, so that our exercise of passion is accompanied by reason and our indulgence in desires is not altogether unreasonable, so in a speech the one great character, derived from philosophy, should play the part of Reason in the speech as a whole, while the other elements —anger, pity, wit, bitterness, envy—should be added in dependence on reason and in such combinations with one another as are necessary.

DONATUS

Life of Virgil

This 'Life' is largely based on Suetonius; I give an extensive extract from it both for its own interest and as a specimen of ancient literary biography (see Chapter XI). Text in C. G. Hardie, *Vitae Vergilianae antiquae* (1954).

P. Vergilius Maro of Mantua was of humble parentage, especially on the side of his father, who is said by some to have been a potter, but by most to have been the hired servant of one Magus, a *viator*,[1] and subsequently, thanks to his industry, this man's son-in-law; it is said too that he notably increased the substance of his property by buying woods and keeping bees.

The poet was born in the first consulship of Cn. Pompeius Magnus and M. Licinius Crassus [i.e. 70 B.C.], on the Ides of October, in a village called Andes not far from Mantua. During her pregnancy, his mother dreamt that she gave birth to a branch of bay, which grew as soon as it touched the ground and soon developed into what seemed a mature tree, laden with fruit and flowers of various kinds. The next day, when she was travelling with her husband to a country place in the neighbourhood, she turned off the road and was delivered of her child in the adjoining ditch. They say that the baby did not cry when it was born, and had such a gentle expression that even at that moment it gave a sure hope of a happy geniture. Another portent followed: a poplar wand, planted by local custom on the spot where the child was born, grew so quickly that it equalled poplars planted long before. It was called Virgil's tree, and was held sacred by the

[1] A subordinate official, employed in summoning persons before magistrates.

religious observances of pregnant women, who both made and paid
their vows there.

He spent his early life at Cremona, until he assumed the man's toga,
which was on his seventeenth birthday, under the same consuls as he
was born, now serving their second consulship; and it chanced that
the poet Lucretius died that same day.

Virgil then moved from Cremona to Milan, and thence soon after
to Rome.

He was tall of stature, of swarthy complexion, with the look of a
countryman, and uncertain health, for he suffered much from the
stomach, the throat and headaches, and often spat blood. He took
little food or wine. His sexual appetite inclined to boys, of whom he
particularly loved Cebes and Alexander, whom he calls Alexis in the
second eclogue of the Bucolics, and who was a present to him from
Asinius Pollio. Both were men of learning, and Cebes was also a poet.
It is commonly said that he also consorted with Plotia Hieria. Asconius
Pedianus however affirms that the lady herself used to say, when she
was old, that Virgil had often been invited by Varius to share her, but
had pertinaciously refused. Certainly, in the rest of his life, he was so
pure of speech and mind that at Naples he was commonly called
Parthenias, 'the Virginal'. Whenever he was seen in public at Rome,
where he very rarely went, he escaped those who followed and
pointed at him by taking refuge in the nearest house.

He could not bring himself to accept the property of an exile which
Augustus offered him.

He possessed nearly 10,000,000 sesterces, thanks to the generosity
of his friends, and had a house at Rome on the Esquiline next to the
Gardens of Maecenas; but he spent most time in retirement in
Campania and Sicily.

He was a grown man when he lost his parents (his father was blind)
and his two brothers, Silo dying as a boy, Flaccus in early manhood;
it is Flaccus' death he mourns under the name Daphnis.

Among his other studies, he gave special attention to medicine and
especially to mathematics. He pleaded one case before a jury, but
only one; Melissus reports that he spoke very hesitantly and almost
like one untrained.

His first poetical attempt, as a boy, was a distich on the schoolmaster Ballista, who was stoned to death for his infamous brigandage:

> Beneath this mound of stones Ballista lies;
> Go, traveller, safely, night or day, by road.

Next the *Catalepton*, *Priapea*, epigrams and *Dirae*, also *Ciris* and *Culex*, when he was twenty-six . . . He also wrote *Aetna*, the authorship of which is questioned. Later, after beginning a poem on Roman history, he found the subject troublesome and moved over to the *Bucolics*, principally in order to praise Asinius Pollio, Alfenus Varus and Cornelius Gallus, because they had saved him from loss in the distribution of the lands beyond the Po which were divided among the veterans after the victory of Philippi by order of the triumvirs. Next he wrote the *Georgics* in honour of Maecenas, who had given him help, before he was at all well known, against the violent conduct of a veteran, by whom he was almost killed in a quarrel arising out of a rural law-suit.

Last, he began the *Aeneid*, a poem of varied and complex plot, equivalent as it were to both Homeric epics, concerned equally with names and things both Greek and Latin, and intended—this indeed was his main object—to embrace the origins both of Rome and of Augustus.

When he was writing the *Georgics*, it is said that each day he composed a large number of lines in his head in the morning and dictated them, and then spent the rest of the day working over them and reducing them to very few; he well said that he gave birth to the poetry like a mother bear, and then licked it into shape.

The *Aeneid* was first composed in prose and arranged into its twelve books; he then proceeded to put it into verse bit by bit as he pleased, not taking things at all in order. To prevent anything holding up the force of his impulse, he left some parts unfinished and propped up some with trivial lines which he used jokingly to refer to as his 'scaffolding', put there to hold the work up till the solid columns arrived.

He completed the *Bucolics* in three years, the *Georgics* in seven, and the *Aeneid* in eleven. He published the *Bucolics* with such acclaim that they were often recited by singers on the stage. He read the *Georgics* aloud, over a period of four days, to Augustus, on his return after the victory at Actium, when he was staying at Atella to restore his throat. Maecenas took turns at the reading, when Virgil himself was hindered by a weakness of the voice. His pronunciation however was pleasing and wonderfully seductive. Seneca reports that the poet Julius Montanus used to say that he would have stolen some lines from Virgil, if he could also have stolen his voice, expression and dramatic delivery: lines that sounded well when Virgil read them were empty and dumb without him . . . He later recited to Augustus, when the work was complete, Books II, IV and VI [of the *Aeneid*]; Octavia, who was present at the recitation, was greatly moved and is

said to have fainted and to have been revived only with difficulty at
the lines about her son: 'Thou shalt be Marcellus . . .' He read aloud
to larger audiences also, but not often, and generally passages about
which he was in doubt, so as to test people's opinion of them. His
freedman and scribe Eros used to say, in his old age, that Virgil once
completed two half-lines extempore in the course of a recitation.
Having got as far as

'Misenus Aeolid'

he added:

'than whom no better
to trumpet men'

and then, on a second occasion, inspired with similar heat, added also:

'and kindle Mars with music.'[2]

Both supplements he ordered Eros to write in the book immedi-
ately. . . .

   Virgil never lacked detractors. This is no wonder, for neither did
Homer. When the *Bucolics* came out a certain Numitorius wrote
Antibucolics, two eclogues of inept parody, the first beginning:

Why, Tityrus, if you've a good warm cloak,
go to the beech for shelter?

and the second:

'Tell me, Damoetas: "cuium pecus"; can it be Latin?
'No, but they speak like that down Aegon's way
in the country.'

Another objector, when Virgil read out:

'naked plough and naked sow,'

added

'you'll catch a feverish cold.'

There is also a book against the Aeneid by Carvilius Pictor, called
Aeneidomastix, 'Scourge of the *Aeneid*'.
   M. Vipsanius said that Virgil was put up by Maecenas as an inventor of a new *cacozēlia*, not the bombastic kind or the thin kind,
but made up of ordinary words and so not noticed . . . Asconius
Pedianus in his book 'against Virgil's detractors', made a few objections himself, mostly relating to fact (*historia*) and based on his taking

[2] *Aen.* 6. 164–5.

so much from Homer. He reports however that Virgil defended himself against this charge by saying: 'And why don't they try the same thefts? They would soon understand that it's easier to pinch Hercules' club than a line from Homer' . . .

FRONTO

An archaist's advice

In this letter to his pupil, the future emperor Marcus Aurelius (*Ad M. Caesarem* 4.3.2) Fronto makes it clear that he regards an archaising vocabulary as the most important element in a good style. See Chapter IV 7.

Consequently, very few of the old writers committed themselves to the effort, trouble and risk involved in seeking words carefully. Of the orators, the only one in all history to have done so is M. Porcius Cato, with his constant follower Sallust; of the poets, we have especially Plautus, and very especially Q. Ennius, whom L. Caelius, Naevius, Lucretius and also Accius, Caecilius and Laberius all carefully imitated. Apart from these, one can find writers elegant in part, that is in parts of their work; such are Novius and Pomponius and all that tribe, in rustic, humorous and farcical words; Atta in women's language; Sisenna in erotic vocabulary; and Lucilius in terms appropriate to various arts and businesses.

You may perhaps have been asking where I place M. Tullius, who is reputed the head and fountain of Roman eloquence. I am of opinion that he consistently spoke in the most beautiful words, and had a grandeur in adorning what he had to say surpassing all other orators. But I also think that he was a long way from the scrupulous search for words—either out of greatness of mind, or out of indolence, or out of confidence that he would find in his hand without any search what others could scarcely secure for all their labours. Having read all his writings very carefully, I think I have assured myself that he had a most copious and abundant control of most kinds of words— literal, metaphorical, simple, compound, splendid (*honesta*) (a brilliant feature of all his work) and very often elegant (*amoena*). At

the same time, you will very rarely find in any of his speeches unexpected or unlooked for words, which are only discovered as a result
of study, effort, watchfulness and much learning in old poems. By
unexpected and unlooked for, I mean a word which surprises the
expectations and ideas of the hearer or reader, yet, if you take it away
and ask the reader to think of a word himself, he will be unable to find
one, or at least one so well suited to the meaning. I therefore commend
you very much for devoting care and effort to digging out words, and
making them suitable to the meaning. However, as I said to begin
with, there is a great danger in this—a danger of placing the word
unsuitably or with a want of clearness or appropriateness, as the half-
learned do. It is much better to use common and ordinary words
than recondite and obscure ones, if the meaning is not adequately
represented.

'HERACLITUS'

Allegory in defence of Homer

I give here the greater part of the opening chapters of the book
of 'Homeric Problems' whose author is known as Heraclitus.
Date uncertain: common opinion says first century A.D. Text
and French translation: F. Buffière (1962). See above Chapter
VI 9, p. 95.

Great and grievous is the case brought from heaven against Homer for
his irreverence towards the divine. If everything he wrote is not an
allegory, everything is an impiety. Sacrilegious tales full of blas-
phemous folly run riot throughout both epics. If we are to believe that
it is all said according to poetical tradition, with no philosophical
basis and no concealed allegory, Homer is a Salmoneus or a Tantalus
'with tongue unchastened, worst disease of all'.[1]
    It therefore surprises me very much that a religious way of life,
devoted to temples and shrines and annual festivals of the gods,

[1] Euripides *Orestes* 10.

should have so affectionately embraced the impiety of Homer, singing his wicked words from memory. From the earliest stage of life, our infant children in their first moments of learning are suckled on him; we are wrapped in his poems, one might also say, as babies, and nourish our minds on their milk. As the child grows and comes to manhood Homer is at his side, Homer shares his mature years, and the man is never weary of him even in old age. When we leave him, we feel the thirst again. The end of Homer is the end of life for us.

All this, in my view, makes it obvious that there is no stain of wicked tales in the epics. The *Iliad*, and later the *Odyssey*, with one consent utter a voice which is pure and free of any pollution in proclaiming their piety:

> I would not fight the gods of heaven, not I;
> great fools are we who burn to vie with Zeus.[2]

How splendidly is Zeus in heaven sanctified in the poem, moving the world with his imperceptible nod! And see how when Poseidon moves, then all of a sudden 'great mountains and forests tremble'.[3] One might say the same of Hera:

> She moved on her throne, and made great Olympus shake.[4]

[Other examples follow]

Should there be persons who do not recognise Homer's allegory and have not penetrated into the recesses of his wisdom, but have made rash judgments of truth without testing them, and seize on what appear to be mythical fictions because they do not understand the philosophical intention—well, let them go their way, while we, who have been made pure within the holy precincts, pursue the solemn truth of the poems in the proper manner.

Away too with the flatterer Plato, false accuser of Homer, who sent him away from his private Republic, an honoured exile, garlanded with wool and with his head soaked in expensive perfume! Nor do we take thought for Epicurus, who cultivates his undignified pleasure in his own Garden, abominating the whole of poetry as a fatal trap of fable. I feel inclined to sigh deeply and say

> Ah me! How mortal men do blame the gods![5]

The most distressing feature of it all is that both these thinkers owe the origin of their own doctrines to Homer, and are thus ungratefully impious towards the very person from whom they have had the greatest benefit to their own learning! . . .

---

[2] *Iliad* 6.129, 15.104.   [3] *Iliad* 13.18.   [4] *Iliad* 8.199.   [5] *Odyssey* 1.32.

We must now make a few brief technical remarks about allegory. The actual name, which is very aptly chosen, reveals what the thing is. 'Allegory' is the name given to the trope which says one thing but signifies something else (*alla . . . agoreuōn*).

Thus Archilochus, caught in the Thracian troubles, compares war to a storm at sea:

> Glaucus, look, the sea is stirring, and the waves disturb
> > the deep,
> and a cloud stands over Gyrae, towering high, the sign of
> > storm;
> unexpected terror hits us . . .[6]

Again, we often find the Mytilenean lyricist [Alcaeus] allegorising. For example, he compares the disturbances of tyranny in a similar manner to a stormy sea . . .[7]

It would be tedious to review all the allegories in poets and prose-writers. It must suffice to show the general nature of the phenomena by a few examples. Not even Homer's allegories are always in doubt or a subject of inquiry: he gives us a perfectly clear example of this trope of style in the passage in which Odysseus speaks of the evils of war and battle:

> the bronze lays much straw on the ground,
> but poor indeed is the harvest, when Zeus turns the scale.[8]

The words denote farming, but the thing intended is battle; only he has intensified(?) the meaning by the contrast between two opposing things. And so, since the trope of allegory is so common in all other writing, and is known to Homer also, why should we not find the remedy for what appear to be bad statements in Homer about the gods in a defence of this kind?

HORACE

Odes 4.2 is an important statement of Horace's own ideals. See Chapter IV 3.

---

[6] Archilochus fr. 105 West.
[7] The passage quoted next is a famous one: Alcaeus fr. z2 Lobel-Page. Cf. Horace *Odes* 1.14, Quintil. 8.6.44.
[8] *Iliad* 19.222–4.

The inimitable Pindar

He who would rival Pindar, Iulus, relies on wings waxed by Daedalus' skill, and will give his name to a glassy sea.

As a river runs down from the mountain, when rains have swollen it above its known banks, so Pindar seethes and rushes measureless with deep voice, deserving Apollo's bay, whether he rolls down new words in bold dithyrambs and moves in measures that know no law,

or sings of gods and of kings, the children of gods, by whose hands fell to a just death the Centaurs and the dread Chimaera's flame,

or speaks of those escorted home by the victory-palm of Elis, great as gods, boxer or horse, and gives them a gift worth more than a hundred statues,

or again laments a young man snatched from his weeping bride, and raises to the stars valour and mind and character of gold, grudging them to black Death.

Whenever, Antonius, the swan of Dirce wings his way to the high ranges of the clouds, a strong wind raises him; while I, in the manner and fashion of the Matine bee that gathers sweet thyme with much toil round the wood and banks of watery Tivoli, I, tiny creature, mould my laborious songs.

MACROBIUS

These extracts from Macrobius' *Saturnalia* (ed. J. Willis, 1963) have been abridged somewhat. They are intended to illustrate (*a*) the study of Virgil's rhetorical technique, (*b*) the criteria by which his *imitatio* of Homer was judged, (*c*) the view taken of his style. See above, Chapter VII 9, VIII 4. Macrobius, who wrote in the early fifth century, used earlier sources, and thus gives us some idea, however confused, of the course of Virgilian criticism.

(*a*) *Saturnalia* 4.2

Let us now see by what tone of speech emotion is expressed. And first let us ask what advice the art of rhetoric has to give about this.

Emotional (*pathētika*) speech must be directed either at indignation or at pity, which are called in Greek *deinōsis* and *oiktos*. The former is necessary for the accuser, the latter for the defendant. The former requires an abrupt beginning, for it does not suit angry people to start softly. And so Juno[1] in Virgil . . .

> O hated race, and Phrygian destiny
> to ours opposed. . .

Nor is it only the beginning that must be of this kind; if possible, the whole speech must appear emotional, short sentences and frequent changes of figure making it appear as it were storm-tossed on the waves of anger. So the one Virgilian speech may serve as an example. The initial exclamation (*ekphōnēsis*) 'O hated race . . . ' is followed by short questions

> and could they fall upon Sigeum's plain?
> Captured, be captured? Did burning Troy cremate them?

And then a hyperbole:

> Through battle-lines and fire they found a way.

Then irony:

> My power, I fancy, has grown tired, or else
> I've had my fill of hate and now I rest.

Then she complains of the futility of her efforts:

> Through seas I dared pursue, and face
> the fugitives the ocean over . . .

A second hyperbole:

> Spent on the Trojans strength of sea and sky.

And various complaints:

> What good was Syrtis, Scylla, vast Charybdis, to me?

To increase the emotion she uses an argument *a minore*:

> Mars had the power to ruin the dread race of the Lapithae.

Mars was a lesser person, and so she continues:

> But I, Jove's mighty wife . . .

---

[1] The passages cited (some of Macrobius' examples are omitted) are all from the speech in *Aeneid* 7. 293 ff.

Having explained the causes, how violently she then proceeds!

> And yet I turned myself to everything!

She does not say 'I cannot ruin Aeneas' but:

> I am beaten by Aeneas.

Next she strengthens her resolve to do harm, and shows herself content to hinder, though he despairs of being able to accomplish her aim. This is typical of angry people.

> If I cannot bend heaven, then I will stir the power of Hell.
> It is not mine to bar him from his kingdom;
> So be it: drag it out, delay the issue,
> exterminate the nations of both kings,
> that's possible.

And finally, as angry persons often do, she curses her opponent:

> Your dowry, maid, shall be Rutulian blood and Trojan.

And she follows this with an appropriate argument from analogy drawn from previous events:

> Not only Hecuba,
> pregnant with torches, bore a wedding flame.

You see how often he changes the style and varies it with frequent figures, because anger, that 'brief madness', cannot continue a single tone of speech long.

(*b*) In *Saturnalia* 5.11, Macrobius lists a large number of 'parallels' between Homer and Virgil. I select the following (see also Gellius 9.9 and 17.10 in *ALC* 548 ff.).

(i) *Aen.* 1.430 f., *Il.* 2.87 f.

Virgil describes the bees as workers, Homer as wanderers; the one expresses their scattering and the various directions of their flight, the other the duties of their natural skill.

(ii) *Aen.* 1.198 ff., *Od.* 12.208 ff.

Ulysses reminds his companions of one trouble only; Aeneas, in order to make them hope for relief from present trouble encourages them by talk of the upshot of two events. Homer's

> 'I am sure you will remember this'

is obscure; Virgil's

'we shall enjoy remembering even this hereafter'

is clearer. Moreover, what your poet added is a stronger comfort. He encouraged his men not only by the example of escape, but by hope of future felicity, promising them, as a result of this effort, not only a peaceful home but a kingdom.

(iii) *Aen.* 3.626, *Il.* 13.389 and 16.482.

Your poet has expressed the difficulty of cutting down a huge tree; Homer's tree is cut down without any trouble.

(iv) *Aen.* 4.365, *Il.* 16.33 (cf. Gell. 12.1.20)

Virgil did not confine himself, as his model did, to the topic of birth, but also attacked his subject's upbringing as harsh and bestial, for he added on his own:

And Hyrcanian tigers gave you suck,

because the nature of the nurse and the quality of the milk plays a large part in fixing character.

(v) *Aen.* 9.675, *Il.* 12.131

The Greek soldiers Polypoetes and Leonteus stand before the gates and await without moving the approach of their enemy Asius, like trees rooted there. That is as far as the Greek description goes. Virgil's description makes Bitias and Pandarus open the gate of their own accord, offering the enemy what he wanted, the chance to seize the camp, and thus putting themselves in the enemy's power. He calls the two heroes 'towers', but also describes them as glittering with the brilliance of their helmets. He does not, like Homer, pass quickly over the comparison with trees, but describes the trees more richly and beautifully.

(c) Styles (*Saturnalia* 5.1.7 ff.)

'There are four types of style,' said Eusebius, 'the copious, in which Cicero is the leader, the concise, where Sallust is king, the dry, which is ascribed to Fronto, and the rich and florid, exemplified by the luxuriance of Pliny and now of our friend Symmachus, who is as good as any of the ancients. In Virgil however you will find all these styles . . .

[Examples: *Aen.* 3.11 (concise); 2.324–7, 241–2, 361–3 (copious); 9.46–9 (dry); 11.768–84 (florid); *Georgics* 1.84–93 (mixture of all four). Virgil also contains instances of the grave and mature style (*Aen.* 12.19) and of the ardent and vigorous style (*Aen.* 10.599)].

'It seems to me that Virgil . . . followed no master but nature herself, in thus weaving this harmony of dissonants, to use a musical metaphor. For if you look closely at the world itself, you will find much similarity between that work of God and this work of the poet. Just as Maro's eloquence is adequate to all characters—now brief, now copious, now dry, now florid, sometimes gentle, sometimes in flood—so the earth herself is in places rich with crops and meadows, in places rough with woods and rocks, dry in deserts, well-watered with springs, or exposed to the vast sea. Forgive me—do not think me extravagant in comparing Virgil with Nature. It seems to me an inadequate account of his greatness to say that he had simply combined in one the style of the Ten Orators who flourished at Athens in Attica.'

Evangelus looked amused at this. 'You do well,' he said, 'to compare the poet from the Mantuan countryside with the creator god. I don't suppose he ever read a word of the Greek orators you have mentioned.'

MARCELLINUS

Stylistic aims and models of Thucydides

The Life of Thucydides from which this extract is taken is attributed to Marcellinus, probably to be identified with a fifth-century scholiast on Hermogenes. The author defends Thucydides against the strictures of Dionysius. I give §§35–42; text in OCT Thucydides, vol. i. See above, Chapter IX 6.

In his arrangement (*oikonomia*) Thucydides was an imitator (*zēlōtēs*) of Homer, and in his natural grandeur and elevation of style, of Pindar. His obscurity is deliberate; he did not wish to be accessible to all or to cheapen himself by being easily understood by all and sundry; he wished rather to be judged and admired by the wisest. For he who is praised by the best and achieves well-judged renown wins honour recorded for all time, honour which is in no danger of being wiped out by later judgment. He also imitated, as Antyllus says, the parisoses and verbal antitheses of Gorgias of Leontini, which were well thought of in Greece at that time; and also the precision of vocabulary of Prodicus of Ceos. But, as I said, he particularly imitated Homer in his choice of words, exactness of word-arrangement, and the strength, beauty and rapidity of his expression. Earlier prose-writers and historians put no life into their writings but used bare narrative throughout, not assigning speeches to their characters nor composing orations; Herodotus did indeed attempt this, but with no great effect, for he gave short speeches only, more as dramatisations (*prosōpopoiiai*) than as orations. It was Thucydides who invented public orations and composed them in complete form, with headings and a division (*diairesis*), which is the mark of the complete speech.

Of the three types of style (*charaktēres phrastikoi*)—the elevated (*hupsēlos*) the slender (*ischnos*) and the middle—he pursued only the elevated, as being suitable to his own nature and appropriate to the scale of the great war. Where deeds are great, the words that relate to them should be great also.

To remind you of the other styles, let me say that Herodotus used the middle style—neither elevated nor slender—and Xenophon the slender.

It is because of his elevation that Thucydides often used poetical expressions and some metaphors. Indeed some have gone so far as to declare that the manner of his writing throughout the work is poetical, not rhetorical. That it is not poetry is obvious from the fact that it is not in metre. If anyone then says that not all prose is rhetorical—for instance Plato's works and medical books—we reply that history is divided by headings and is thus brought into the category of rhetoric. History in general belongs to the deliberative branch—though some say it is panegyric, because it praises heroes of war—but Thucydides comes into all three classes: deliberative oratory because of his speeches (with the exception of the speeches of the Plataeans and Thebans in Book III); panegyric because of the funeral speech; forensic because of the Plataean and Theban speeches which we excluded above. (In this case, the Lacedaemonians who are present are the judges, the Plataean is judged in relation to the question put to him, and defends himself at length on the questions asked, while the Theban opposes him, inciting the Lacedaemonian to anger: the arrangement, method and figure (*taxis, methodos, schēma*) are all signs of the forensic form.)

PROCLUS

The three kinds of poetry

On the Republic 1.177 Kroll: trans. A. J. Festugière, *Proclus: Commentaire sur la République* (1970), 1.197. See above, Chapter IV 8, VII 5.

Very well. Let us now turn to the discussion of poetry, and consider what kinds of poetry there are according to Plato, what poetry he was considering when he expounded the criticisms of it in the Tenth Book of the *Republic* and, finally, how, even here, Homer is shown to be exempt from the criticisms which apply to most poets. To make this clear also, let us begin our lesson with the following observation.

We affirm that there are, to speak in general terms, three lives in the soul.

(i) The best and most perfect is that in which the soul is linked with the gods and lives the life most closely akin to them and united with them in extreme similarity, belonging not to herself but to them, rising above her own intellect, and awaking in herself the ineffable symbol (*sunthēma*) of the unitary existence of the gods, joining like with like, her light to the light yonder, the most unitary element of her own substance and life to the One that surpasses all substance and life.

(ii) The life second to this in honour and power, the midmost life, set in the midst of the soul, is that in which the soul turns to herself, descending from the divinely inspired life, but makes intellect and knowledge the principles of her activity; she unrolls multitudes of arguments, contemplates all kinds of changes of the forms, brings together that which thinks and that which is thought, and makes an image of the intelligible substance by comprehending the nature of Intelligibles in one single unity.

The third life is that which moves among the lower powers and is active with them, employing also visions (*phantasiai*) and sensations, and entirely filling itself with inferior realities.

These being the three types of life seen in souls, let us consider the division of poetry on a similar principle. Poetry also descends from above with the manifold lives of the soul and is diversified into first, middle and last kinds of activity. For in poetry also there is one type which is the highest and is full of divine goods, setting the soul amid the principles that are the causes of existing things, and bringing together that which fills and that which is filled in an ineffable unity, laying out the former for illumination immaterially and nontactually, and at the same time summoning the latter to share its light,

> as channels mingle of unquenchable fire
> the work performing

as the Oracle says[1] . . .

This madness, in a word, is better than sanity and is limited only by the measure of God; and just as other kinds of madness bring men to other gods, so this one fills the inspired soul with due measure; and therefore it adorns its last activities with metre and rhythm. And so, just as we say that prophetic madness exists in relation to truth and the madness of love in relation to beauty, so we say that poetic madness is defined by reference to divine measure or proportion.

The poetry which is inferior to the first inspired kind, and is seen to have a middle place in the soul, has its being by reference to the actual intelligent and scientific disposition of the soul. It knows the substance of real things, contemplates noble and good deeds and words, and brings everything to metrical and rhythmical expression. Many of the works of good poets may be seen to be of this kind. Wise men admire them. They are full of admonition and good advice, and laden with intelligent moderation; they enable those who have a good natural endowment to share wisdom and other virtue, and they afford means of recalling to mind the periods of the soul and the eternal principles and various powers contained in these.

Third comes the poetry which is mixed with opinions and imaginings, composed by means of imitation, and wholly 'mimetic', in fact as well as in common parlance. Sometimes this makes use merely of copying (*eikasia*), sometimes it puts forward an apparent but not real resemblance, raising small events to grand proportions, amazing its hearers by words and expressions of this kind, changing the disposition of the soul by changes of harmony and diversity of rhythm, and displaying the nature of things to the mass of mankind not as they are but as they may appear. It is a shadow—drawing of reality, not exact knowledge. The goal it sets itself is the beguilement (*psuchagōgia*) of the hearers, and it looks especially to the element of the soul which is emotional and given to joy and sorrow. As we explained, part of this kind of poetry is of the nature of copying (*eikastikon*)—this aims at

---

[1] *Oracles chaldaïques*, ed. E. des Places (1971), fr. 66. There is an ambiguity in the line, which the translation tries to preserve.

correctness of imitation—and part, as we said, of the nature of
fantasy (*phantastikon*), providing only an apparent imitation.

PROCLUS THE GRAMMARIAN

See above, Chapter X 6, with notes 15 and 16. It is uncertain
whether this author is the same as the famous fifth-century
philosopher, from whom the last extract was taken. This is not
in itself impossible, but the more probable (and more usual)
view is that we have here an earlier writer, perhaps of the
second century A.D. In any case, the writer draws on sources of
the Hellenistic age, and specifically on Didymus. Text in
Photius *Bibliotheca*, cod. 239 (ed. R. Henry, v. 155).

Read: extracts from the book entitled Short Manual of Literature
(*Chrestomatheia grammatikē*) by Proclus. The work is divided into
four parts.

In the first, he states that the virtues of prose and poetry are the
same, but differ in degree. Style (*plasma*) is either full-bodied (*hadron*),
slender (*ischnon*) or intermediate (*meson*).

The full-bodied is the richest in startling effects (*ekplēktikōtaton*),
elaboration and poetical beauty. The slender certainly pursues metaphorical and elaborate arrangement, but is made up of more loosely
connected elements, so that it is in general best suited to lamentation.
The intermediate style is, as its name implies, midway between the
other two. There is no 'florid' (*anthēron*) style as such; this goes with,
and is combined with, the two just mentioned, and is appropriate to
topographical passages and description of meadows and groves.

Those who fail in attempting these styles (*ideai*) fall from the full-
bodied into the stiff and awkward, from the slender into the low, and
from the intermediate into the flabby and loose.

He also gives indications on the judgment of poetry, in the course
of which he explains the difference between character (*ēthos*) and
emotion (*pathos*).

He divides poetry into narrative and mimetic; the narrative branch
is expressed in hexameters, iambics, elegy or lyric; the mimetic in
tragedy, satyr-plays and comedy.

QUINTILIAN

Emotion and imagination (6.2.26–32)
See Chapter VII 7.

So far as my understanding goes, the most important factor in producing emotional effects is to be moved by emotion oneself. The
imitation of grief, anger or indignation may actually prove ridiculous
if we fail to adjust our minds to it, and not merely our words and facial
expression. Why is it that persons who grieve for a recent sorrow often
appear to utter words of the highest eloquence, while anger sometimes
makes even the untaught into orators? It is because of the psychological force and feeling in them. So, when we want to produce
lifelike effects, we need to resemble in our feelings those who really
experience them. The speech must come from the state of mind which
we want to induce in the juryman. Is he going to feel grief, if he hears
that I, who am speaking for this very purpose, do not feel any myself?
Is he going to be angry, if the would-be exciter of his wrath feels
nothing of what he demands himself? Will he accord tears to a dry-
eyed advocate? Impossible. Nothing burns but fire, nothing wets but
water, nothing imparts a colour which it does not possess itself.

So, first of all, the feelings which we wish to prevail with the juryman
must prevail with us. We must be emotionally moved before we try
to produce such emotions in others. Now how can we do this? Emotions are not in our power. I will try to explain this also.

The most effective producer of emotion will be the person who has
formed successfully what the Greeks call *phantasiai*—let us call them
visions—by means of which images of absent things are so brought
before our minds that we seem actually to see them with our eyes and
have them before us.

Some people use the word *euphantasiōtos*, 'imaginative', to describe
the person who is best at inventing events, words and actions realistic-
ally. Now we can easily achieve this if we so wish. All we have to do is
to transfer one of our mental weaknesses to useful ends. When we are
mentally idle, indulging in vain hopes, or as it were day-dreaming,
the visions of which I am speaking pursue us—we imagine ourselves
travelling, sailing, fighting battles, addressing multitudes, disposing
of wealth we do not possess—and actually doing these things, not
merely thinking about them. I am complaining about a man's
murder: am I not to have before my eye all the circumstances which
one may believe to have been present at the time? Will not the
assassin leap out suddenly? Will not the victim feel terror as he is penned

in, cry out, plead, try to run away? Shall I not see the blow struck and the body fall? Will not the blood, the pallor, the groans, the last breath of the dying man, stick in my mind? The result will be *enargeia*: Cicero calls it *inlustratio*[1] or *evidentia*; it shows rather than explains in words, and emotional effects follow as if we were present ourselves.

SERVIUS

The literary character of Aeneid 4

Commentary on *Aeneid* 4.1 (p. 458 Thilo-Hagen). Cf. Macrobius *Saturnalia* 5.17.4. See Chapter I 3.

Apollonius wrote an *Argonautica* and introduced Medea in love in Book III. The whole of the present book was transferred from this. It consists almost entirely of affection (*adfectio*: possibly 'state of mind', Greek *diathesis*), though it has strong emotion (*pathos*) at the end, where Aeneas' departure produces sorrow. It is certainly made up entirely of deliberations (*consilia*) and intrigue (*subtilitates*), for the style is almost comic—and no wonder, when the subject is love.

THEOPHRASTUS

Audience-orientation and subject-orientation

Fr. 65 Wimmer. See Chapter I 2.

Since there are, according to the distinction drawn by the philosopher Theophrastus, two orientations (*scheseis*) of discourse, one

---

[1] This is not in Cicero's works as we have them.

towards the hearers (to whom it signifies something) and one towards the facts concerning which the speaker proposes to persuade the audience, poetry and rhetoric are concerned with the orientation towards the hearers, because it is their business to select the more dignified words, as opposed to the common and vulgar ones, and weave them together harmoniously . . . The philosopher on the other hand is primarily concerned with the orientation of discourse towards facts, refuting falsehood and demonstrating the truth.

'TRACTATUS COISLINIANUS'

Comedy and its rules and methods

First edited in the last century from a Paris manuscript—'Coislinianus'—this short summary of part of a treatise on poetry has been much discussed. Cramer, Bernays and others have argued that it represents much of Aristotle's treatment of comedy; but parts of it seem rather to be an unintelligent adaptation of the definition of tragedy in *Poetics*. The translation follows G. Kaibel's text (*Comicorum Graecorum Fragmenta* i.50 ff.). See Chapter II 8, X 5.

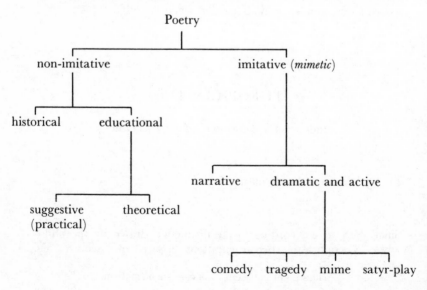

Tragedy removes emotions of fear from the soul by means of pity and fear; it aims at a due measure of fear; and grief is its mother.

Comedy is an imitation of a ridiculous action which has no complete magnitude; with each part in a separate form, and involving actors, not employing narrative, effecting by means of pleasure and laughter a *katharsis* of such feelings. Laughter is its mother.

Laughter is produced:

(a) from language:

    (i) by homonyms;
    (ii) by synonyms;
    (iii) by repetitiveness;
    (iv) by plays on words;
    (v) by hypocoristic uses;
    (vi) by exallage;[1]
    (vii) by figure of speech

(b) from situations:

    (i) from similarity (either with what is better or what is worse);
    (ii) from deceit;
    (iii) from impossibility;
    (iv) from inconsequential possibility;
    (v) from the unexpected;
    (vi) from low characters;
    (vii) from vulgar dancing;
    (viii) when someone who has power passes over great prizes and receives a poor reward;
    (ix) when the words are unconnected and have no sequence of thought.

Comedy differs from invective, since invective sets forth the evils attached to its object without disguise, whereas comedy needs what is called 'emphasis'.

The jester seeks to expose faults of mind and body.

There should be a due measure of fear in tragedy and of the ridiculous in comedy.

The material of comedy: plot, character, intellectual content, diction, song, spectacle. A comic plot is one which consists of ridiculous actions. Comic characters are the buffoon, the 'humorist' (*eirōn*) and

---

[1] Probably 'variation in the form of words'.

the boaster (*alazōn*). Intellectual content has two divisions: thought (*gnōmē*) and proof (*pistis*). [Proofs are of five kinds: oaths, agreements, evidence of witnesses, tests, laws.]

The diction of comedy is common and everyday. The comic poet must give his characters his own native dialect, and to strangers their native tongue.

Songs belong to music, and the independent principles should be learned from that art.

Spectacle contributes much (?beguilement) to plays.

Plot, diction and song are seen in all comedies, intellectual content, character and spectacle in a few.

The four parts of comedy: prologue, choral song, episode, exodos. The prologue is the part of a comedy up to the entrance of the chorus. The choral song is what is sung by the chorus, if it is long enough. An episode is the part between two choral songs. The exodos is what is said by the chorus at the end.

Old Comedy has a preponderance of the ridiculous; New Comedy abandons this and inclines to seriousness. Middle Comedy is a combination of the two.

VELLEIUS PATERCULUS

A historian reflects on the course of literature

1.16–18. Text: Stegmann von Pritzwald (1933). See Chapter XI 4.

This part of my work has already exceeded its intended scale, and I realise that, in this headlong rush, which like a wheel or rushing stream never lets me stand still, it is more likely that I shall have to leave out essential details than include superfluous ones. Nevertheless, I cannot resist setting down in writing a question which I have often turned over in my mind and never brought to a clear solution. Who can marvel enough at the fact that the most outstanding talents in any profession come together in similar forms and within the same narrow confines of time? Animals of various species, when they are shut up in a cage or other enclosure, nevertheless separate themselves from one another, and each species forms its own group. Similarly, minds capable of particular kinds of distinguished work separate themselves off from others, similar abilities finding similar times in which to develop. A single period of not many years brought glory to tragedy through the inspiration of Aeschylus, Sophocles and Euripides. A single age did the same for Old Comedy under Cratinus, Aristophanes and Eupolis. Menander and his contemporaries—though by no means equals!—Philemon and Diphilus, invented New Comedy and left it in inimitable perfection, all within a few years. The philosophical geniuses deriving from the teaching of Socrates, whom I enumerated above, flourished but a short space after the death of Plato and Aristotle. What distinction was there in the orators before Isocrates, or again after his pupils and those who learned from them? The chronological limits are so narrow that everyone worth mentioning could have been seen by all the rest.

This is as true in Roman history as in Greek. If we discount the rude beginnings, memorable for the fact that they mark the first invention of the genre, Roman tragedy is confined to Accius and his circle. The delicate humour of Latin wit shone almost simultaneously in Caecilius, Terence, and Afranius. As for the historians, counting Livy among the ancients, and excluding Cato and a few obscure primitives, a space of eighty years held them all. Our wealth in poetry went no further back, and no further forward. Oratory, forensic effectiveness and the perfection of prose—again excluding Cato, and begging pardon of Crassus and Scipio, Laelius, the Gracchi, Fannius and Servius Galba—burst on the world so completely under its great monarch Cicero, that there are very few before his time in whom one can take pleasure, and none that one can admire who was not either seen by Cicero himself or saw Cicero. Anyone who studies the chronology will discover that the same holds of scholars, sculptors, painters, and engravers: the acme of every art is confined within the narrowest temporal limits. I often ask myself what is the cause of this limitation of like talents in particular periods, this concentration on particular studies and their rewards; but I find no cause that I can regard as certain, though perhaps some probable ones, of which the following are the most important. Talent is nourished by emulation; jealousy and admiration both kindle the desire to imitate. It is natural that a pursuit earnestly followed should rise to great heights. But it is difficult to stay in a perfect state, and it is natural for things to fall back when progress is no longer possible. Just as we are first moved to pursue those we think better than ourselves, so, when we have come to despair of the possibility of surpassing or equalling them, our enthusiasm wanes as our hope does. We cease to pursue the unattainable. We abandon exhausted material and look for new. Passing over fields where we

cannot excel, we seek something where we can shine. Thus frequent
and rapid change becomes the greatest hindrance to perfect work.

It is not only the chronological limitations, but the geographical
ones, that excite wonder. The single city of Athens, over a period of
many years, flourished in literature and art more than the whole of the
rest of Greece. Physically, that nation spreads over many cities; its
intellectual strength, one might well judge, is confined within the
walls of Athens alone. No less surprising is the fact that there is not a
single Argive, Theban or Spartan orator judged of any authority while
he lived or worth remembering when he died. These cities indeed were
barren in other branches of literature also, except that Pindar's one
voice is the glory of Thebes. The Spartan claim to Alcman is false.

Bibliography

Texts

(a) Collections and anthologies

ALC   *Ancient Literary Criticism*, the principal
                        texts in new translations, ed. D. A. Russell
                        and M. Winterbottom, Oxford 1972
Benson and Prosser   *Readings in Classical Rhetoric*, ed. T. W.
                        Benson and M. H. Prosser, Boston 1969
Preminger   *Classical and Medieval Literary Criticism*, ed.
                        A. Preminger, O. B. Hardison and K.
                        Kerrans, New York 1974 (translations of
                        some central texts)
Lanata   *Poetica pre-Platonica*, ed. G. Lanata,
                        Florence 1963 (texts with Italian trans.
                        and comm.)
Radermacher, *AS*   *Artium Scriptores*, ed. L. Radermacher,
                        1951 (texts of pre-Aristotelian rhetoric)
Spengel   *Rhetores Graeci*, ed. L. Spengel, 3 vols,
                        Leipzig 1856 (texts of the main authors;
                        partly replaced by later editions, but still
                        the most convenient collection for refer-
                        ence)
Walz   *Rhetores Graeci*, ed. C. Walz, 9 vols, 1832–6
                        (still the fullest collection of rhetorical
                        texts, partly replaced by more modern
                        editions)
Halm   *Rhetores Latini minores*, ed. R. Halm, 1863

(b) Individual authors (a brief selection of texts and translations)

Aristides
  Quintilianus   ed. R. P. Winnington-Ingram, 1963
Aristotle, *Poetics*   ed. I. Bywater, Oxford 1909 (with trans-
                        lation); ed. R. Kassel, Oxford 1965
                        (with comm. by D. W. Lucas, Oxford
                        1968); trans. M. E. Hubbard (in *ALC*).
Aristotle, *Rhetoric*   ed. R. Kassel, Berlin 1976
                        ed. with comm., E. M. Cope 1877
                        Trans. J. H. Freese (Loeb)
[Aristotle] Rhetorica
  ad Alexandrum   ed. M. Fuhrmann, 1966
                        trans. E. S. Forster (Oxford Aristotle vol.
                        11, 1924)
Caecilius   *Fragmenta*, ed. E. Ofenloch 1907
Cicero   *De Oratore*   ed. K. F. Kumaniecki, 1969
                        ed. A. S. Wilkins (with commentary)
                        trans. E. W. Sutton and H. Rackham
                        (Loeb)
         Brutus   ed. H. Malcovati
                        ed. O. Jahn—W. Kroll—B. Kytzler (with
                        commentary) 1962
                        ed. A. E. Douglas (with commentary)
                        1966
         Orator   ed. J. E. Sandys (with commentary) 1885
                        ed. W. Kroll (with commentary) 1913
  See also Barwick.
[Cicero]   *Rhetorica ad Herennium*, ed. H. Caplan
                        (Loeb)
Cornutus   *Theologia Graeca*, ed. C. Lang, 1881
'Cornutus'   *Cornuti Artis Rhetoricae epitome*, ed. J.
                        Graeven, 1891 (= 'Anonymus Segueri-
                        anus')
Dionysius of
  Halicarnassus   *Opuscula*, ed. H. Usener—L. Rader-
                        macher, 2 vols., 1899, 1904 (vol. 2 includes
                        the pseudo-Dionysian treatises, grouped
                        together as 'The Art of Rhetoric')

On Literary Composition, ed. W. Rhys Roberts, Cambridge 1910
Three Literary Letters, ed. W. Rhys Roberts, Cambridge 1901
Critical Essays, vol. I, ed. S. Usher (Loeb), 1974 (contains 'Ancient Orators' 'Demosthenes', and 'Thucydides')
Dinarco, ed. G. Marenghi 1970
On Thucydides trans. with comm., W. K. Pritchett, 1975

See also Bonner, Schenkeveld

Demetrius　　　　*On style*, ed. W. Rhys Roberts (1902); L. Radermacher (text only) 1897; trans. H. A. Moxon (Everyman's Library); G. M. A. Grube (with comm.) 1961; D. C. Innes (part only) in *ALC*

See also Schenkeveld

Dio Chrysostom　　ed. H. von Arnim (1893–6) G. de Budé (1919); J. W. Cohoon and H. K. Crosby (Loeb)

Gellius, A.　　　ed. P. K. Marshall, Oxford 1968
'Heraclitus'　　*Homerica Problemata*, ed. F. Buffière (1962)
Hermogenes　　ed. H. Rabe (1913)
Horace　　　Apart from the standard editions (esp. A. Kiessling—R. Heinze, with appendixes by E. Burck; 1955–7), see C. O. Brink, *Ars Poetica*, 1971; and *Prolegomena to the Literary Epistles*, 1963
'Longinus'　　'On the Sublime', ed. (with trans. and notes) W. Rhys Roberts (1899, 1907); (with comm.) D. A. Russell (1964, 1968; trans. in *ALC*)
Menander Rhetor　'On Epideictic Oratory', ed. (with trans. and comm.) D. A. Russell and N. G. Wilson (1981)
Philodemus　　C. Jensen, *Philodemus über die Gedichte: fünftes Buch* (1923)
Philostratus　　*Lives of the Sophists*, ed. W. C. Wright (Loeb)

	Life of Apollonius of Tyana, ed. F. C. Conybeare (Loeb): trans. G. W. Bowersock (Penguin)
Plato	ed. J. Burnet (O.C.T.)
	Republic, trans. H. D. P. Lee (Penguin)
	Laws, trans. T. J. Saunders (Penguin)
See also Vicaire	
Plutarch	*Moralia* is completely translated in the Loeb series: vol. 1 includes 'On listening to poets', vol. 10 'Comparison on Aristophanes and Menander' and vol. 11 'On the malignity of Herodotus'
Quintilian	ed. M. Winterbottom (Oxford 1970). Trans. H. E. Butler (Loeb; not wholly reliable)
	Separate editions of Book x (W. Peterson) and xii (R. G. Austin) have useful commentaries
Suetonius	*De grammaticis, de rhetoribus*, ed. A. Rostagni, 1944

Books and articles

[Any of the following may be referred to in the footnotes by the author's name or by an abbreviated title.]

Abrams, M. H. *The Mirror and the Lamp*, Oxford 1953

Arbusow, L. *Colores Rhetorici*, ed. 2, Göttingen 1963

Arrighetti, G. *Satiro: Vita di Euripide*, Pisa 1964

Atkins, J. W. H. *Literary Criticism in Antiquity* (2 vols), Cambridge & London, 1934, 1952

Auerbach, E. *Literary Language and its Public in Late Latin Antiquity and the Middle Ages* (E.tr.) London 1965

Avenarius, G. *Lukians Schrift zur Geschichtschreibung*, Meisenheim-an-Glan 1956

Axelson, B. *Unpoetische Wörter*, Lund 1945

Baldwin, C. S. *Ancient Rhetoric and Poetic*, New York 1924 (reprint 1959).

Bardon, H. *La Littérature latine inconnue* (2 vols), Paris 1952, 1956

Barwick, K. *Das rednerische Bildungsideal Ciceros*, 1963

Blume, H.-D. *Untersuchungen zur Sprache und Stil der Schrift Peri Hupsous*, Göttingen 1963

Bompaire, J. *Lucien écrivain*, Paris 1958

Bonner, S. F. *Dionysius of Halicarnassus*, Cambridge 1939
  Roman Declamation, Liverpool 1949
  Roman Education, London 1977

Bornecque, H. *Les Déclamations et les déclamateurs d'après Sénèque le père*, Lille 1902

Buchheit, V. *Untersuchungen zur Theorie des Genos Epideiktikon*, Munich 1960

Buffière, F. *Les Mythes d'Homère et la pensée grecque*, Paris 1956

Büher, W. *Beiträge zur Erklärung der Schrift vom Erhabenen*, Göttingen 1964

Cairns, F. *Generic Composition in Greek and Roman Poetry*, Edinburgh 1972

Causeret, C. *Etude sur la langue de la rhétorique et de la critique littéraire dans Cicéron*, Paris 1886

Clark, A. M. *Studies in Literary Modes*, Edinburgh 1946

Clark, D. L. *Rhetoric in Greco-Roman Education*, New York 1957

Clarke, M. L. *Rhetoric at Rome*, London 1953

Cousin, J. *Etudes sur la poésie latine*, Paris 1945
  Etudes sur Quintilien, Paris 1936

Cupaiuolo, F. *Tra Poesia e Poetica*, Naples 1966

Curtius, G. R. *European Literature and the Latin Middle Ages*, (E.tr.) London 1952

D'Anna, G. *Le idee letterarie di Suetonio*, Florence 1954

Douglas, A. E. 'A Ciceronian contribution to rhetorical theory', *Eranos* 55 (1957) 18–26

Eisenhut, W. *Einführung in die antike Rhetorik*, Darmstadt 1974

Ernesti, J. C. G. *Lexicon Technologiae Graecorum Rhetoricae*, 1795 (repr. 1962)
  Lexicon Technologiae Latinorum Rhetoricae, 1797 (repr. 1962)

Flashar, H. *Der Dialog Ion als Zeugnis platonischen Philosophie*, Berlin 1958

Fletcher, A. *Allegory, the Theory of a Symbolic Mode*, Cornell 1964

Fraser, P. M. *Ptolemaic Alexandria*, Oxford 1972

Fuhrmann, M. *Einführung in die antike Dichtungstheorie*, Darmstadt 1973

Grube, G. M. A. *The Greek and Roman Critics*, Toronto 1965
Gudeman, A. *Grundriss der Geschichte der klassischen Philologie*, ed. 2, Leipzig 1909
Guthrie, W. K. C. *A History of Greek Philosophy*, Cambridge 1962–78
Hagedorn, D. *Zur Ideenlehre des Hermogenes* (Hypomnemata 8), Göttingen 1964
Harriott, R. *Poetry and Criticism before Plato*, London 1969
Harvey, A. E. 'The classification of Greek lyric poets', *CQ* 6 (1955) 157–75
Hellwig, A. *Untersuchungen zur Theorie der Rhetorik bei Platon und Aristoteles* (*Hypomnemata* 38) Göttingen 1973
Henn, T. R. *Longinus in English Criticism*, Cambridge 1934
Herrick, M. T. *The Poetics of Aristotle in England* (Cornell Studies in English), 1930
   Comic Theory in the XVIth Century (Illinois Studies in Language and Literature) 1950
Kennedy, G. A. *The Art of Persuasion in Greece*, Princeton 1963
   The Art of Rhetoric in the Roman World, Princeton 1972
   Quintilian, New York 1969
Koster, S. *Antike Epostheorien*, Wiesbaden 1970
Kostas, G. S. *Studies in Byzantine Rhetoric*, Thessaloniki 1973
Kroll, W. *Studien zum Verständnis der römischen Literatur*, Stuttgart 1924, 1964
La Rue Van Hook. *The Metaphorical Terminology of Greek Rhetoric and Literary Criticism*, Chicago 1905
Labarbe, J. *L'Homère de Platon*, Paris 1949
Lausberg, H. *Handbuch der literarischen Rhetorik*, Munich 1960
   Elemente der lit. Rhet., ed. 2, Munich 1963
Lebek, W.-D. 'Zur rhetorischen Theorie des Archaismus', *Hermes* 97 (1969) 57–78
Leeman, A. D. *Orationis Ratio*, Amsterdam 1963
Lewis, C. S. *The Allegory of Love*, Oxford 1936
Lodge, D., ed. *20th-century Literary Criticism: a reader*, London 1972
Long, A. A. *Hellenistic Philosophy*, London 1974
Lossau, M. *Untersuchungen zur antiken Demosthenesexegese* (*Palingenesia* II), 1964

McCall, M. H. *Ancient Rhetorical Theories of Simile and Comparison*, Harvard 1969

Maehler, H. *Die Auffassung des Dichterberufs im frühen Griechentum (Hypomnemata 3)*, Göttingen 1963

Martin, J. *Antike Rhetorik: Technik und Methode*, Munich 1974

Monk, S. H. *The Sublime*, Ann Arbor paperbacks ed., 1960

Mühmelt, M. *Griechische Grammatik in der Vergilerklärung (Zetemata 37)*, Munich 1965

Nettleship, H. *Lectures and Essays, Second Series*, Oxford 1895

Neumeister, C. *Grundsätze der forensischen Rhetorik*, Munich 1964

Nicev, A. *L'énigme de la catharsis tragique dans Aristote*, Sofia 1970

Norden, E. *Antike Kunstprosa*, ed. 5, Stuttgart 1958

North, H. 'The use of poetry in the training of the ancient orator', *Traditio* 8 (1952) 1 ff.

Olson, E. (ed.) *Aristotle's Poetics and English Literature*, Chicago 1965

Pfeiffer, R. *History of Classical Scholarship, from the beginnings to the end of the Hellenistic Age*, Oxford 1968

Podlecki, A. J. 'The Peripatetics as literary critics', *Phoenix* 23 (1969) 114–37

Pohlenz, M. *Kleine Schriften*, Hildesheim 1965

Pollitt, J. J. *The Ancient View of Greek Art*, Yale 1974

Rees, B. R. 'Pathos in the *Poetics* of Aristotle', *Greece and Rome* 19 (1972) 1 ff.

Richards, I. A. *Principles of Literary Criticism*, ed. 2, 1926

Russell, D. A. 'Rhetoric and criticism', *Greece and Rome*, 14 (1967) 130–44

'Ancient theories of literature and taste', in *Literature and Western Civilization*, ed. D. Daiches, vol. 1, 'The Classical World,' 1972

'De Imitatione', in *Creative Imitation and Latin Literature*, ed. D. West—A. Woodman, Cambridge 1979

'The pseudo-Dionysian *Exetasis* and *Mistakes*', in *Entretiens Hardt* 25 (1978), 113–34, Geneva 1979

'Longinus revisited', *Mnemosyne* (1981)

Schenkeveld, D. M. *Studies in Demetrius on Style*, Amsterdam 1964

'Theories of evaluation in the rhetorical treatises of Dionysius of Halicarnassus', *Museum Philologicum Londinense* 1, 93–107

'Strabo on Homer', *Mnemosyne* 29 (1976) 52–64

Schlunk, R. R. *The Homeric Scholia and the Aeneid*, Ann Arbor 1974

Schütrümpf, E. *Die Bedeutung des Wortes* Ethos *in der Poetik des Aristoteles* (*Zetemeta* 49), Munich 1970

Sheppard, Anne D. R. *Studies on the 5th and 6th Essays of Proclus' Commentary on the Republic* (*Hypomnemata* 61), Göttingen 1980

Stark, R. ed. *Rhetorika*, Hildesheim 1968

Stanford, W. B. *Greek Metaphor*, Oxford 1936

Stinton, T. C. W. *Hamartia in Aristotle and Greek tragedy*, CQ 25 (1975) 221–54

Süss, W. *Ethos: Studien zur älteren griechischen Rhetorik*, Leipzig 1910

Verdenius, W. J. *Mimesis*, Leiden 1962

Vicaire, P. *Platon: critique littéraire*, Paris 1960

Vickers, B. *Classical Rhetoric in English Poetry*, London 1970

Volkmann, R. *Die Rhetorik der Griechen und Römer*, ed. 2, Leipzig 1885

Wehrli, F. *Theoria und Humanitas*, Zürich 1972

Wellek, R.-Warren, A. *Theory of Literature*, Peregrine Books ed., London 1963

Wilkinson, L. P. *Golden Latin Artistry*, Cambridge 1963

Wimsatt, W. K. *The Verbal Icon*, Kentucky 1954

Index

This selective index concentrates on proper names and technical terms on which some substantial observation is made in the text.